THE GROWTH AND DEVELOPMENT OF MUTUAL FUNDS IN INDIA

THE GROWTH AND DEVELOPMENT OF MUTUAL FUNDS IN INDIA

Soheli Ghose

KALPAZ

ISBN: 978-93-5128-184-9

Price: ₹ 850/-

First Published 2016

Published by

Kalpaz Publications
C-30, Satyawati Nagar,
Delhi - 110052
E-mail: kalpaz@hotmail.com Ph.: 9212142040

Printed at : G. Print Process, Delhi

Cataloging in Publication Data--DK
Courtesy: D.K. Agencies (P) Ltd. <docinfo@dkagencies.com>

Ghose, Soheli, author.
The growth and development of mutual funds in India / Soheli Ghose.
pages cm
Includes bibliographical references.
ISBN 9789351281849

1. Mutual funds--India. I. Title.

HG5734.5.G46 2016 DDC 332.63270954 23

Contents

Preface

According to the Association of Indian Mutual Fund Industry, "A Mutual Fund is a trust that pools the savings of a number of investors who share a common financial goal. The money thus collected is then invested in capital market instruments such as shares, debentures and other securities. The income earned through these investments and the capital appreciation realised is shared by the unit holders in the proportion to the number of units owned by them. Thus, a mutual fund is the most suitable investment for the common man as it offers an opportunity to invest in a diversified professionally managed basket of securities at a relatively low cost." Of all investing institutions, Mutual Funds have grown at the fastest rate due to their operational flexibility and because they provide better returns to the investors and also serve as a sophisticated market clearing agent. Middle class, salaried employees, generally choose mutual fund investments, as they don't have the time or expertise to invest in company stocks directly. An individual investor, without spending considerable time and money small investors can enjoy the facility of diversification reducing and spreading the risk factor of investors. Mutual funds are considered as one of the best available investments as compared to others they are very cost-efficient and also easy to invest in, thus by pooling money together in a mutual fund, investors can purchase stocks or bonds with much lower trading costs than if they tried to do it on their own.

In the past decade, Indian Mutual Fund industry has seen enormous quantitative growth. 2006 and 2007 are considered as the golden period for Indian Mutual Funds with many new schemes being launched and most of the schemes registering very high returns. Mutual fund industry has changed in past few years with more multinational companies coming into the country, bringing in their professional expertise in managing funds worldwide. The financial crisis has shown its implications on the industry as a whole. Presently, the Indian Mutual Fund industry is going through a fluctuating phase as the financial markets are stabilising gradually.

The book would help to know in details about mutual fund industry right from its inception stage, growth and future prospects. It would also help in understanding different schemes of mutual funds, their growth and evolution and the returns associated with those schemes. Some very pertinent questions have been dealt with to give the readers a wholesome understanding of the investment process. Suggestions for investing in the appropriate manner have been discussed in details. Ultimately this would help in understanding the functioning and benefits of mutual funds to investors. It will help all the stakeholders of the mutual fund industry in India to make better informed decisions.

Soheli Ghose

Acknowledgement

I do not know how to express my deep sense of gratitude to Dr Dipti Kumar Chakravorty, Professor of Commerce, University of Calcutta, who, amidst all his pre-occupation, found time to help with his profound knowledge, advice, comments, suggestions and constant support during various stages of this study, without which it would have been impossible for me to complete this work.

I am indebted equally to all the faculty members of the Department of Commerce, University of Calcutta, for their kind help and suggestions at different stages of work. I am also grateful to my colleagues for their constant advice for pursuing my research work. I would like to remember the sacred memories of my late father Mr Shakti Prasad Ghose and my late grandmother Mrs Sudha Das who were a constant source of encouragement for my higher studies. I also convey my most heartfelt regards to my mother Mrs Prativa Ghose who is my strongest support and biggest inspiration.

Soheli Ghose

1

Mutual Funds and Their Growth in India: Meaning and Concept of Mutual Funds

According to the Association of Indian Mutual Fund Industry, "A Mutual Fund is a trust that pools the savings of a number of investors who share a common financial goal. The money thus collected is then invested in capital market instruments such as shares, debentures and other securities. The income earned through these investments and the capital appreciation realised is shared by the unit holders in the proportion to the number of units owned by them. Thus, a mutual fund is the most suitable investment for the common man as it offers an opportunity to invest in a diversified professionally managed basket of securities at a relatively low cost." Mutual funds act as a financial intermediary in activities of fund mobilisation and investment. The essence of a mutual fund is the diversified portfolio of investment, which diversifies the risk by spreading out the investor's money across available or different types of investments. Thus, Indian Mutual Funds are playing a very crucial developmental role in allocating resources in the emerging market economy. Of all investing institutions, Mutual funds have grown at the fastest rate due to their operational flexibility and because they provide better returns to the investors and serve as a sophisticated market-clearing agent. When one invests in a mutual fund, buys the units or portions of the mutual fund and thus on investing becomes a shareholder or unit holder of the fund.

Thus, mutual fund is a trust that pools money from a group of investors (sharing common financial goals) and invest the money thus collected into asset classes that match the stated investment objectives of the scheme. A mutual fund can not deviate from its stated objectives at any point of time. Mutual funds have a fund manager who is responsible for investing the gathered money into specific securities (stocks or bonds). Every mutual fund is managed by a manager, who using his investment management skills and necessary research works invests the gathered money into specific securities ensuring much better return than what an investor can manage on his own. The capital appreciation and other incomes earned from these investments are passed on to the investors (also known as unit holders) in proportion of the number of units they own. The levels of diversification are to buy multiple stocks rather than just one stock, different kind of stocks, then adding bonds, then international, and so on. It takes less time as mutual funds automatically diversify in a predetermined category of investments. In the last two decades the mutual funds industry in India has grown in leaps and bounds. This is partly due to the growth in the Indian financial markets and awareness of investors among other factors. Thus, investing in mutual funds has become an immensely popular avenue of both savings and investment for the mid income group of Indian citizens.

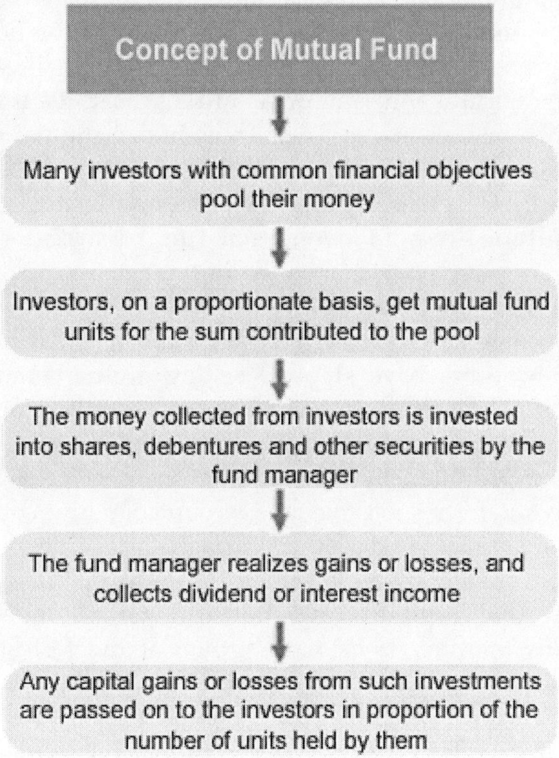

Fig. 1.1: Concept of Mutual Fund

Source: www.personalfn.com *(mutual funds guide 2010)*

Any change in the value of the investments made into capital market instruments (such as shares, debentures etc.) is reflected in the Net Asset Value (NAV) of the scheme. NAV is defined as the market value of the mutual fund scheme's assets net of its liabilities. NAV of a scheme is calculated by dividing the market value of scheme's assets by the total number of units issued to the investors. Mutual Funds in India have emerged as a critical institutional linkage among various financial segments like savings, capital market and the corporate sectors. They provide the much needed impetus to the money markets and stock markets in addition to direct and indirect support to the corporate sector. Above all mutual funds have given a new direction to the flow of personal savings and enabled small and medium investors in the remote rural and semi-urban areas to reap the benefits of the stock market investments. Thus, Indian mutual funds are playing a very crucial developmental role in allocating resources in the emerging market economy. Mutual funds were traditionally sold by mutual fund distributors for commission (which was embedded in the entry load) which was received by them from the mutual fund houses. However, after the abolition of entry load in August 2009, many distributors have stopped selling mutual funds on account of a lack of incentive. SEBI has recently proposed that a distributor would be paid directly by his clients for the advice provided by him and/or the service making distributors more responsible and accountable. Investors can transact in mutual funds either through their mutual fund distributor, directly by approaching the AMC or through an online mutual fund trading platform. Of all investing institutions, mutual funds have grown at the fastest rate due to their operational flexibility and because they provide better returns to the investors and also serve as a sophisticated market clearing agent. Mutual funds invest in a well-diversified portfolio of securities which enables investor to hold a diversified investment portfolio (whether the amount of investment is big or small). Mutual funds diversify in a predetermined category of investments (i.e. growth companies, emerging or mid-size companies, etc). Thus, without spending considerable time and money small investors can enjoy the facility of diversification reducing and spreading the risk factor of investors. Mutual funds are considered as one of the best available investments as compare to others they are very cost efficient and also easy to invest in, thus by pooling money together in a mutual fund, investors can purchase stocks or bonds with much lower trading costs than if they tried to do it on their own. Due to the economies of scale, mutual funds pay lesser transaction costs. These benefits are passed on to the investors. Mutual funds provide the benefit of skilled portfolio management by professional managers, to small investors who otherwise can't afford such expertise or knowledge. Mutual funds provide investors with various schemes with different investment objectives. Investors have the option of investing in a scheme having a correlation between its investment objectives and their own financial goals. These schemes further have different plans/options. Funds provide investors with updated information pertaining to the markets and the schemes. All material facts are disclosed to investors as required by the regulator. Investors also benefit from the convenience and flexibility offered by Mutual funds. Investors can switch their holdings from a debt scheme to an equity scheme and vice-versa. Option of systematic (at regular intervals) investment and withdrawal is also offered to the investors in most open-end schemes. An investor may not be able to sell some of the shares held by him very easily and quickly, whereas units of a mutual fund offer sufficient liquidity. Also the minimum investment in a Mutual fund is relatively smaller than that of shares. Mutual Fund industry is part of a well-regulated investment environment where the interests of the investors are protected by the regulator. All funds are registered with SEBI and complete transparency is forced. Thus, a risk averse investor can expect the market return at a lower cost and lower risk. The stock market fluctuations have less impact over Mutual funds. Mutual funds play a dynamic role in mobilising savings by issuing units and channeling funds in the capital market into productive investment. In this way they further the process of financial intermediation and also provide depth to the market. However, there are some inherent disadvantages of investing in mutual funds. The fund management costs are deducted from total returns earned on the fund's portfolio and only the balance is distributed among investors. Many investors find it difficult to select one option from the plethora of funds/schemes/

plans available thus taking advice from financial planners in order to invest in the right fund to achieve their objectives. Further, the investment portfolio decision is taken by the fund manager. Investors have no right to interfere in the decision-making process of a fund manager, which some investors find as a constraint in achieving their financial objectives.

Some funds don't perform in the market, as their management is not dynamic enough to explore the available opportunity, thus many investors debate over whether or not the so-called professionals are any better than mutual fund or investor himself, for picking up stocks. As funds have small holdings across different companies, high returns from a few investments often don't make much difference on the overall return. This is known as dilution or which is also the result of a successful fund getting too big. When money pours into funds that have had strong success, the manager often has trouble finding a good investment for all the new money. While making decisions about the investor's money, fund managers don't consider their personal tax situation. For example, when a fund manager sells a security, a capital-gain tax is triggered, which affects how profitable the individual is from the sale. It might have been more advantageous for the individual to defer the capital gains liability. These factors make mutual fund investment risky and unpopular.

Inspite of these disadvantages the growth of mutual funds has helped accelerate the development of the capital market, by channeling a growing part of savings of the household sector into equity investments and also by increasing awareness about capital markets among many investors.

HISTORY OF MUTUAL FUNDS

The first mutual fund of the world, The Massachusetts Investors trust was launched in Boston USA in 1924. It was

40 years later in 1963 that a Mutual Fund Institution namely, the Unit Trust of India was launched in India. However, the real growth of Mutual Funds as well as investor awareness has only been since the late 1980s. The primary objective of UTI at that time was to attract the small investors and it was made possible through the collective efforts of the Government of India and the Reserve Bank of India. However, the history of mutual fund industry in India can be better understood dividing it into following phases:

Phase I. Establishment and Growth of Unit Trust of India - 1964–87

Unit Trust of India enjoyed complete monopoly when it was established in the year 1963 by an Act of Parliament. UTI was set up by the Reserve Bank of India and it continued to operate under the regulatory control of the RBI until the two were delinked in 1978 and the entire control was transferred in the hands of Industrial Development Bank of India (IDBI). UTI launched its first scheme in 1964, named as Unit Scheme 1964 (US-64), which attracted the largest number of investors in any single investment scheme over the years. UTI launched more innovative schemes in 1970s and 80s to suit the needs of different investors. It launched ULIP in 1971, six more schemes between 1981 and 1984, Children's Gift Growth Fund and India Fund (India's first offshore fund) in 1986, Mastershare (India's first equity diversified scheme) in 1987 and Monthly Income Schemes (offering assured returns) during 1990s. By the end of 1987, UTI's assets under management grew ten times to Rs 6700 crores.

Phase II. Entry of Public Sector Funds - 1987–1993

The Indian mutual fund industry witnessed a number of public sector players entering the market in the year 1987. In November 1987, SBI Mutual Fund from the State Bank of India became the first non-UTI mutual fund in India. SBI Mutual Fund was later followed by Canbank Mutual Fund

(December, 1987), LIC Mutual Fund (1989), Indian Bank Mutual Fund (November 1989), Bank of India Mutual Fund (June 1990), GIC Mutual Fund (1990) and PNB Mutual Fund (August 1989), Bank of Baroda Mutual Fund (October 1992). By 1993, the assets under management of the industry increased seven times to Rs 47,004 crores. However, UTI remained to be the leader with about 80 per cent market share.

Table 1.1: Overview of Aum by UTI and Public Sector

(Rs in Crores)

1992-93	*Amount Mobilised*	*Assets Under Management*	*Mobilisation as percentage of Gross Domestic Savings*
UTI	11,057	38,247	5.2
Public Sector	1,964	8,757	0.9
Total	**13,021**	**47,004**	**6.1**

Source: personalfn.com

Phase III. Emergence of Private Sector Funds: 1993-96

Private sector funds including foreign fund management companies (most of them entering through joint ventures with Indian promoters) entered the mutual fund industry in 1993, providing a wide range of choice to investors and more competition in the industry. Private funds introduced innovative products, investment techniques and investor-servicing technology. By 1994-95, about 11 private sector funds had launched their schemes. In 1993, the first Mutual Fund Regulations came into being, under which all mutual funds, except UTI were registered and governed. The erstwhile Kothari Pioneer (now merged with Franklin Templeton) was the first private sector mutual fund registered in July 1993. The industry now functions under the revised SEBI (Mutual Fund) Regulations 1996. As at the end of January 2003, there were 33 mutual funds with total assets of Rs 1,21,805 crores. The Unit Trust of India with Rs 44,541 crores of assets under management was way ahead of other mutual funds.

Phase IV. SEBI Regulation - 1996-2004

The mutual fund industry witnessed robust growth and stricter regulation from the SEBI after the year 1996. SEBI (Mutual Funds) Regulations, 1996 was introduced by SEBI that set uniform standards for all mutual funds in India. The Union Budget in 1999 exempted all dividend incomes in the hands of investors from income tax. Various Investor Awareness Programmes were launched during this phase both by SEBI and AMFI, with an objective to educate investors and make them informed about the mutual fund industry. The SEBI regulations, AMFI codes and IRDA regulations have been discussed later. In February 2003, the UTI Act was repealed and UTI was stripped of its special legal status as a trust formed by an Act of Parliament. The primary objective behind this was to bring all mutual fund players on the same level. UTI was reorganised into two parts: 1. The Specified Undertaking, with AUM of Rs 29,835 crores (as on January 2003). The Specified Undertaking of Unit Trust of India, functioning under an administrator and under the rules framed by Government of India and does not come under the purview of the Mutual Fund Regulations. 2. The UTI Mutual Fund, sponsored by SBI, PNB, BOB and LIC. It is registered with SEBI and functions under the Mutual Fund Regulations. With the bifurcation of the erstwhile UTI which had in March 2000 more than Rs 76,000 crores of AUM and with the setting up of a UTI Mutual Fund, conforming to the SEBI Mutual Fund Regulations, and with recent mergers taking place among different private sector funds, the mutual fund industry has entered its current phase of consolidation and growth. As at the end of September, 2004, there were 29 funds, which manage assets of Rs 1,53,108 crores under 421 schemes. Presently, Unit Trust of India operates under the name of UTI Mutual Fund and its past schemes (like US-64, Assured Return Schemes) are being gradually wound up. However, UTI Mutual Fund is still one of the largest players in the industry. During the 1990s Mutual Funds have emerged as an important financial intermediary and institutional investor in India. They have a very strong presence in the savings market today and in fact have mobilised more funds than the Banks did in 1999-2000. As on 31st March 1999, UTI, Public Sector and Private Sector had Rs 53,320, Rs 8292 and Rs 6860 crores of AUM.

Table 1.2: Fund Mobilsed by UTI, Public and Private Sector

Gross Fund Mobilisation (Rs Crores)					
From	*To*	*UTI*	*Public sector*	*Private sector*	*Total*
01-04-98	31-03-99	11,679	1,732	7,966	21,377
01-04-99	31-03-00	13,536	4,039	42,173	59,748
01-04-00	31-03-01	12,413	6,192	74,352	92,957
01-04-01	31-03-02	4,643	13,613	1,46,267	1,64,523
01-04-02	31-Jan-03	5,505	22,923	2,20,551	2,48,979
01-Feb.-03	31-03-03	*	7,259*	58,435	65,694
01-04-03	31-03-04	-	68,558	5,21,632	5,90,190
01-04-04	31-03-05	-	1,03,246	7,36,416	8,39,662
01-04-05	31-03-06	-	1,83,446	9,14,712	10,98,158

Source: personalfn.com

Mutual Funds from Domestic and Foreign Private Sectors have taken away a significant proportion of the market share of UTI and Public Sector Mutual Funds.

Phase V. Growth and Consolidation - 2004 Onwards

The industry has also witnessed several mergers and acquisitions recently, (acquisition of schemes of Alliance Mutual Fund by Birla Sun Life and PNB Mutual Fund by Principal Mutual Fund). Simultaneously, more international mutual fund players have entered India like Fidelity, Franklin Templeton mutual fund etc. This is a continuing phase of growth of the industry through consolidation and entry of new international and private sector players. The growth and success of mutual fund industry depends upon sound financial management of policies and investment practices. It pursues to bring about value addition to the corpus of mutual funds.

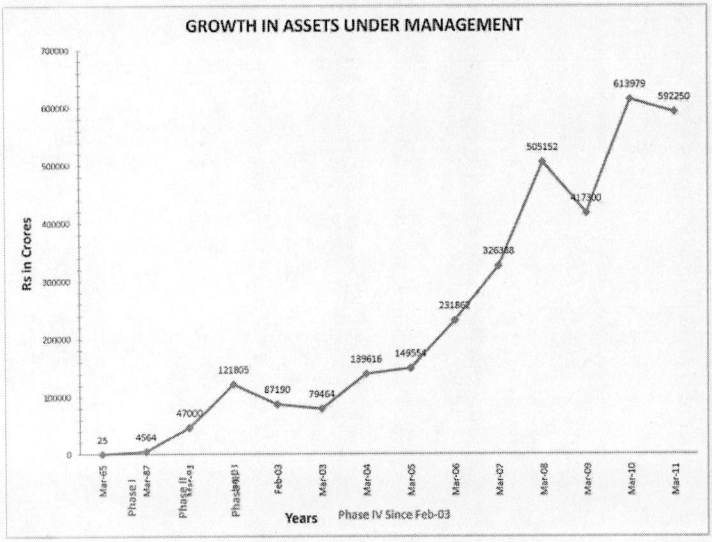

Fig. 1.2: Assets Under Management.

Source: amfiindia.com

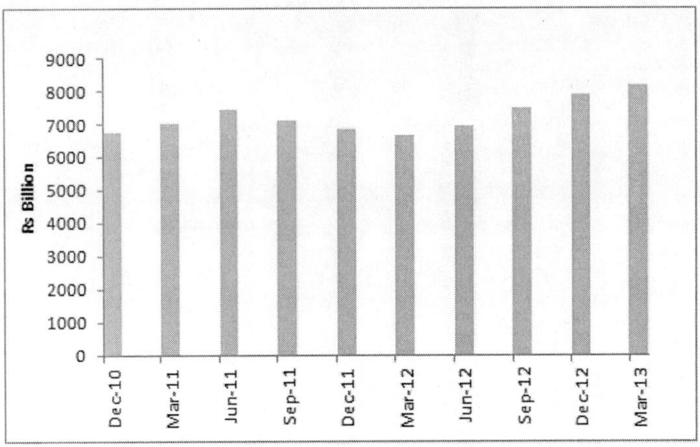

Fig. 1.3: Assets Under Management from December 2010.

Source: www.amfiindia.com

As on 30th June 2015 there were 43 Mutual Funds with an AUM of Rs 190280.96 crore (excluding FoF-domestic but including FoF-overseas).

2

Structure and Types of Mutual Funds in India: Structure of Mutual Fund Industry in India

The Indian mutual fund industry follows a three-tier structure as discussed below:

Sponsor: It's the agency which of its own or in collaboration with other body corporates that complies with the formalities of establishing a mutual fund. SEBI grants permission to start a mutual fund only to corporates of integrity, with significant experience in the financial sector and a certain minimum net worth. The trust is established by a sponsor or more than one sponsor who is like promoter of a company.

Trust: A company is appointed as a Trustee to manage mutual fund. They can dismiss the appointed AMC. It's their responsibility to supervise collection of any income due to be paid to the scheme. Once the Trust is created, it is registered with SEBI, after which point, this Trust is known as the mutual fund. The trustees of the mutual fund hold its property for the benefit of the unit holders. The trustees are vested with the general power of superintendence and direction over AMC. They monitor the performance and compliance of SEBI Regulations by the mutual fund.

Asset Management Company (AMC): The Trustees appoint the AMC, which is established as a legal entity, to manage the investor's money. In return for this money management on behalf of the mutual fund, the AMC is paid a fee for the services provided. The AMC has to be approved by SEBI and it functions under the supervision of its Board of Directors, and also under the direction of the Trustees and the regulatory framework established by SEBI. It is the AMC, which in the name of the Trust, that floats new schemes and manages these schemes by buying and selling securities. Asset Management Company (AMC) approved by SEBI manages the funds by making investments in various types of securities.

Custodian: The mutual fund appoints a custodian to hold the funds securities in safekeeping, settle securities transactions for the fund, collect interest and dividend paid on securities and record information on stock splits and other corporate action. The custodian also participates in a clearing and settlement system through approved depository companies on behalf of mutual funds, in case of dematerialised securities. Custodian, who is registered with SEBI, holds the securities of various schemes of the fund in its custody.

Transfer Agents: Registrar and Transfer Agents (RTAs) maintain the investor's (unit holder's) records, reducing the burden on the AMCs.

SEBI Regulations require that at least two-thirds of the directors of trustee company or board of trustees must be independent i.e. they should not be associated with the sponsors. Also, 50 per cent of the directors of AMC must be independent. All mutual funds are required to be registered with SEBI before they launch any scheme.

When an investor subscribes for the units of a mutual fund, he becomes part owner of the assets of the fund in the same proportion as his contribution amount put up with the corpus (the total amount of the fund). Mutual fund investor is also known as a mutual fund shareholder or a unit holder. Any change in the value of the investments made into capital market instruments (such as shares, debentures etc.) is reflected in the Net Asset Value (NAV) of the scheme. NAV is defined as the market value of the mutual fund scheme's assets net of its liabilities. NAV of a scheme is calculated by dividing the market value of scheme's assets by the total number of units issued to the investors.

The performance of a particular scheme of a mutual fund is denoted by Net Asset Value (NAV). Mutual funds invest the money collected from the investors in securities markets. In simple words, Net Asset Value is the market value of the securities held by the scheme. Since market value of securities changes every day, NAV of a scheme also varies on day to day basis. The NAV per unit is the market value of securities

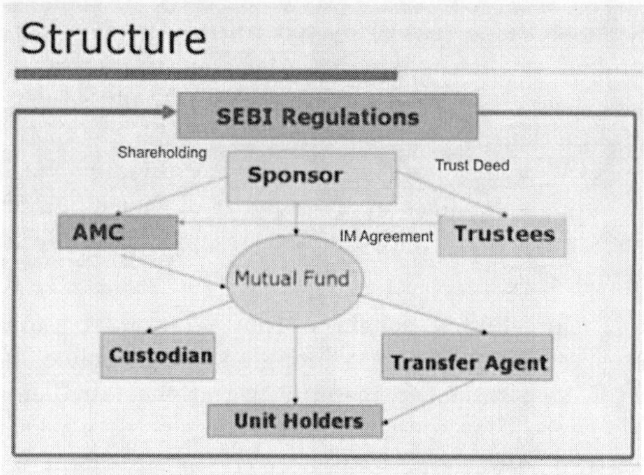

Fig. 2.1: Structure of Mutual Funds in India.

Source: personalfn.com

of a scheme divided by the total number of units of the scheme on any particular date. For example, if the market value of securities of a mutual fund scheme is Rs 200 lakhs and the mutual fund has issued 10 lakhs units of Rs 10 each to the investors, then the NAV per unit of the fund is Rs 20. NAV is required to be disclosed by the mutual funds on a regular basis - daily or weekly - depending on the type of scheme.

TYPES OF MUTUAL FUNDS

A variety of Mutual Fund Schemes exists to cater to the needs such as financial position, risk tolerance and return expectations etc. Investors can choose from over hundreds of mutual funds schemes. An overview of existing schemes is as follows:

(A) BY STRUCTURE

1. Open-Ended Schemes: These schemes are available for subscription all through the year and don't have a fixed maturity. Investors can conveniently buy and sell units at Net Asset Value (NAV) related prices. The key feature of open-end schemes is liquidity. Open-end funds are required to calculate their net asset value (NAV) daily serving as a useful measure of its fair market value on a per-share basis. The NAV of the fund is calculated by dividing the fund's assets minus liabilities by the number of shares outstanding. They are generally traded at the closing price at the end of the market day.

2. Close-Ended Schemes: They have a set number of shares issued to the public through an initial public offering. They have a stipulated maturity period generally between 3 to 15 years. They operate their shares in the stock market by listing. Price determination is done by demand and supply. These are open for subscription during a specified period. Investors can invest in the scheme at the time of the initial public issue and thereafter they can buy or sell the units of the scheme on the stock exchanges where the units are listed. In order to provide an exit route to the investors, some close-ended funds give an option of selling back the units to the mutual fund through periodic repurchase at NAV related prices. SEBI Regulations stipulate that at least one of the two exit routes is provided to the investor i.e. either repurchase facility or through listing on stock exchanges. These mutual funds schemes disclose NAV generally on weekly basis.

3. Interval Schemes: They combine the features of open-ended and close-ended schemes. The units may be traded on the stock exchange or may be open for sale or redemption during pre-determined intervals at NAV related prices.

(B) BY NATURE

1. Equity Fund: They predominantly invest in company stocks, aiming for the increase in the company's value over time. Stocks are often categorised by their market capitalisation (or caps). Equity fund managers employ different styles of stock picking when they make investment decisions for their portfolios. Some fund managers use a value approach to stocks searching for stocks that are undervalued when compared to other similar companies or looking primarily at growth, trying to find stocks that are growing faster than their competitors, or the market as a whole. They have the potential to generate more returns, are meant for a longer time horizon, thus they rank high on the risk-return matrix. These investors are expected to possess appetite for higher risks.

The Equity Funds are sub-classified depending on their ***investment objective,*** as follows,

(a) Diversified Equity Funds: Except for a small portion of investment in liquid money market, diversified equity funds invest mainly in equities without any concentration on a particular sector(s). These funds are well diversified and

reduce sector-specific or company-specific risk. However, like all other funds they too are exposed to equity market risk. One prominent type of diversified equity fund in India is Equity Linked Savings Schemes (ELSS). As per the mandate, a minimum of 90 per cent of investments by ELSS should be in equities at all times. ELSS investors are eligible to claim deduction from taxable income at the time of filing the income tax return. This type of diversified scheme can also be considered as a Tax Saving Mutual Fund.

(b) Specialty Funds: Specialty funds have stated criteria for investments and their portfolio comprises of only those companies that meet their criteria. They are concentrated and thus, are comparatively riskier than diversified funds. There are following types of specialty funds:

(i) Sector Funds: Their exposure is limited to a particular sector (Information Technology, Banking) making them more risky than equity funds that invest in multiple sectors. Also known as thematic funds, they allow investors to place bets on specific industries or sectors, which have strong growth potential. They are more volatile than funds holding a diversified portfolio of securities in many industries. They come in the high risk high reward category and are not suitable for investors having low risk appetite. If a particular sector is doing very well with long-term growth prospects, one should trade in sector funds.

(ii) Foreign Securities Funds: They invest in one or more foreign companies thereby achieving international diversification and hence they are less risky than sector funds. However, they are exposed to foreign exchange rate risk and country risk.

(iii) Option Income Funds: They write options on a large fraction of their portfolio. Proper use of options can reduce volatility, which is otherwise considered as a risky instrument. These funds invest in big, high dividend yielding companies, and then sell options against their stock positions, which generate stable income for investors.

Funds based on capitalisation can also be considered as a type of specialty fund. However, they have been discussed separately.

(c) Growth Funds: The aim of growth funds is to provide capital appreciation over the medium to long-term. Such schemes normally invest a major part of their corpus in equities. Such funds have comparatively high risks. They focus on those companies, which are experiencing significant earnings or revenue growth, rather than companies that pay out dividends. Growth funds tend to look for the fastest-growing companies in the market. Growth managers are willing to take more risk and pay a premium for their stocks in an effort to build a portfolio of companies with above-average earnings momentum or price appreciation. These schemes provide different options to the investors like dividend option, capital appreciation, etc. and the investors may choose an option depending on their preferences.

(d) Aggressive Growth Funds: They provide maximum capital appreciation. They are suitable for investors willing to take a high degree of risk and wait for a long period. They purchase the fastest growing stocks, irrespective of the size, current yield and risks, like undervalued and emerging stocks with the potential for higher growth. Due to these speculative investments Aggressive Growth Funds become more volatile.

(e) Equity Index Funds: They offer market rate of return by investing in a popular index. The portfolio of these funds comprises the same companies that form the index and is constituted in the same proportion as the index. Equity index funds that follow broad indices (S&P CNX Nifty, Sensex) are less risky than equity index funds that follow narrow sectoral indices (BSE BANKEX or CNX Bank Index). Narrow indices are less diversified and therefore, are more risky. The fund makes no effort to beat the index and in fact it merely tries to earn the same return. As per efficient markets concept index funds provide optimum returns in the long run. They don't have to pay for expensive analysts and

frequent trading. They track a broad index which is less volatile than specific stocks or sectors, thereby lessening the risk for investors. Indian indices like the Sensex (30) and the Nifty (50) cover a relatively small number of stocks and ignore many opportunities in the mid-cap sector. Indian markets haven't been thoroughly researched and there is enormous scope to beat the market by sound research.

(f) Value Funds: Value funds are those mutual funds that tend to focus on safety rather than growth, and often choose investments providing dividends as well as capital appreciation. They invest in companies that are undervalued in terms of share prices or are overlooked by the market, either due to poor earnings or investors' changing preference. The main focus of these funds is safety (though they provide long-term growth). Their returns are less volatile and more conservative than growth funds. They are suitable for investors with a moderate risk profile.

(g) Equity Income or Dividend Yield Funds: Their objective to generate high recurring income and steady capital appreciation for investors by investing in those companies which issue high dividends (Power or Utility companies whose share prices fluctuate comparatively lesser than others). They are generally exposed to the lowest risk level as compared to other equity funds.

The Equity Funds can be sub-classified depending on their ***market capitalisation*** as follows:

(a) Large Cap Funds: They seek capital appreciation by investing primarily in stocks of large blue chip companies with above-average prospects for earnings growth. Generally, companies with a market capitalisation in excess of Rs 1000 crore are known large cap companies. Investing in large caps is a lower risk-lower return proposition, because such companies are usually widely researched and information is widely available. Large cap funds invest in those companies that have more potential of earning growth and higher profit.

They are less volatile than mid cap and small cap funds and the near term prospects of large however they offer lower returns than mid cap or small cap funds. But when compared in totality, large cap funds outperform all other funds. Top Large Cap Funds: HDFC Top 200, UTI Large Cap Fund, Franklin India Blue Chip, Kotak 30, DSPML Top 100 Equity, Principal Large Cap Fund, Reliance Growth Fund etc.

(b) Mid Cap Funds: Mid cap funds are those mutual funds, which invest in small/medium sized companies. Those companies that have a market capitalisation between Rs 500 crore and Rs 1,000 crore are classified as medium sized. Small/midsized companies tend to be under researched thus they present an opportunity to invest in a company that is yet to be identified by the market. Such companies offer higher growth potential going forward and therefore an opportunity to benefit from higher than average valuations. Mid cap companies are looked upon as wealth creators and have the potential to join the league of large cap companies. Such companies are nimble, flexible and can adapt to the changes faster. But mid cap funds are very volatile so, caution should be exercised while investing in mid cap mutual funds. Top Mid Cap Funds: Sundaram BNP Paribas Select Midcap, Franklin India Prima Fund, HDFC Capital Builder, Kotak Indian Mid Cap Fund, HSBC Midcap Equity Fund and others.

(c) Small Cap Funds: Small-cap companies have market capitalisation of less than Rs 500 crores. The shares of Small-Cap Companies are not as liquid as of Large-Cap Companies which gives rise to volatility in share prices of these companies and consequently, investment gets risky.

2. Debt/Income Funds: They invest in medium to long-term debt instruments issued by private companies, banks, financial institutions, governments and other entities belonging to various sectors (like infrastructure companies etc.). The focus is to generate a steady stream of income consistent with preservation of capital and liquidity. They invest in fixed income securities, money market instruments, cash and cash equivalents while maintaining a small exposure to the equity markets. They are low risk profile funds. These funds are not affected because of fluctuations in equity markets. However, opportunities of capital appreciation are also limited in such funds. They are subject to credit risk by the issuer at the time of interest or principal payment. To minimise the risk of default, debt funds usually invest in securities from issuers who are rated by credit rating agencies and are considered to be of "Investment Grade". Debt funds that target high returns are more risky.

Based on ***investment objectives,*** there can be following types of debt funds:

(a) Diversified Debt Funds: Debt funds that invest in all securities issued by entities belonging to all sectors of the market are known as diversified debt funds. The best feature of diversified debt funds is that investments are properly diversified into all sectors which results in risk reduction. Any loss incurred, on account of default by a debt issuer, is shared by all investors which further reduces risk for an individual investor.

(b) Focused Debt Funds: They are narrow focus funds that are confined to investments in selective debt securities, issued by companies of a specific sector or industry or origin like sector, specialised and offshore debt funds, funds that invest only in Tax Free Infrastructure or Municipal Bonds. They are more risky as compared to diversified debt funds. Although not yet available in India, these funds are conceivable and may be offered to investors very soon.

(c) High Yield Debt Funds: They prefer securities issued by those issuers who are considered to be of "below investment grade" aiming to earn higher interest returns from these issuers. These funds are more volatile and bear

higher default risk, although they may earn at times higher returns for investors.

(d) Assured Return Funds: These funds come with a lock-in period and offer assurance of annual returns to investors during the lock-in period. Any shortfall in returns is suffered by the sponsors or the AMCs. These funds are generally debt funds and provide investors with a low-risk investment opportunity. However, the security of investments depends upon the net worth of the guarantor (whose name is specified in advance on the offer document). To safeguard the interests of investors, SEBI permits only those funds to offer assured return schemes whose sponsors have adequate net-worth to guarantee returns in the future. Currently, no AMC in India offers assured return schemes to investors, though possible.

(e) Fixed Term Plan Series: They are closed-end schemes having short-term maturity period (of less than one year) that offer a series of plans and issue units to investors at regular intervals. They are not listed on the exchanges. They usually invest in debt/income schemes and target short-term investors aiming to gratify investors by generating some expected returns in a short period.

Debt funds can also be classified as:

(a) Gilt Funds: They invest their corpus in securities issued by Government, popularly known as Government of India debt papers. They carry zero Default risk but have Interest Rate risk.

(b) Income Funds: They invest a major portion into various debt instruments such as bonds, corporate debentures and Government securities.

(c) MIPs: They invest maximum of their total corpus in debt instruments while they take minimum exposure in equities. It gets benefit of both equity and debt market. These scheme ranks slightly high on the risk-return matrix when compared with other debt schemes.

(d) Short-term Plans (STPs): Meant for investment horizon for three to six months, they primarily invest in short-term papers like Certificate of Deposits (CDs) and Commercial Papers (CPs). Some portion of the corpus is also invested in corporate debentures.

(e) Liquid Funds: Also known as Money Market Funds. Investors seeking stability of principal, higher liquidity and shorter investment horizon consider these funds. They have a portfolio of short-term debt instruments - treasury bills, commercial papers, certificate of deposits. Money market funds are of two types which are Institutional Money Market Mutual Funds and Retail Money Market Mutual Funds.

3. Balanced Funds: Also known as hybrid fund, they mostly invest in well trusted companies having sound track record in dividend payments. They are good for risk averse investors interested in exposure to equities. The aim of balanced funds is to provide both growth and regular income as such schemes invest both in equities and fixed income securities in the proportion indicated in their offer documents. These are appropriate for investors looking for moderate growth. They generally invest 40-60 per cent in equity and debt instruments. Such diversified holdings ensure that these funds will manage downturns in the stock market without too much of a loss.

4. Hybrid Funds: Their portfolio blends equities, debts and money market securities. Hybrid funds have an equal proportion of debt and equity in their portfolio. In India they are:

(a) Balanced Funds: It has been discussed previously.

(b) Growth-and-Income Fund: They combine features of growth funds and income funds. They achieve high level of current income, capital appreciation and conservation of capital. Their risk is low. They can be balanced and equity income funds.

(c) Asset Allocation Fund: They have two or more different classes of assets in their portfolio. The main objective is to reduce portfolio risk. Fund managers may switch over to equity if they expect equity market to provide good returns and switch over to debt if they expect debt market to provide better returns. Success of these funds depends upon the skill of a fund manager in anticipating market trends.

5. Commodity Funds: They focus on investing in different commodities (like metals, foodgrains, crude oil etc.) or commodity companies or commodity futures contracts. A commodity fund that invests in a single commodity or a group of commodities is a specialised commodity fund and a commodity fund that invests in all available commodities is a diversified commodity fund and bears less risk than a specialised commodity fund. "Precious Metals Fund" and Gold Funds (investing in gold, gold futures or shares of gold mines) are examples.

6. Real Estate Funds: They invest directly in real estate or lend to real estate developers or invest in shares/ securitised assets of housing finance companies. Their objective may be to generate regular income for or capital appreciation.

7. Exchange Traded Funds: Exchange Traded Funds (ETFs) represent a basket of securities that is traded on an exchange, similar to a stock. Hence, unlike conventional mutual funds, ETFs are listed on a recognised stock exchange and their units are directly traded on stock exchange during the trading hours. In ETFs, since the trading is largely done over stock exchange, there is minimal interaction between investors and the fund house. They provide investors with combined benefits of a closed-end and an open-end mutual fund.

8. Fund of Funds: They invest in other open/closed ended funds, which are performing well. They are good for cautious investors who want to minimise risks. They provide investors with an advantage of diversifying into different mutual fund schemes with even a small amount of investment, which further helps in diversification of risks. However, their expenses are quite high on account of compounding expenses of investments into different mutual fund schemes. Also, since a FoF buys many different funds which themselves invest in many different stocks, it is possible to own the same stock through several different funds and it can be difficult to keep track of the overall holdings. They can be classified into *Mutual fund FoF and Hedge fund FoF.*

(C) BY GEOGRAPHICAL DISTRIBUTION

1. International Mutual Funds: International mutual funds invest in non-domestic securities markets throughout the world mainly in emerging Asian markets, Eastern Europe and Latin America. Some of these markets have generated spectacular returns during the past few years. All these markets are fast growing and that is why they have become an alternative investment destination for many countries. It provides greater portfolio diversification. Fund managers need to keep close watch on foreign currencies and world markets as profitable investments in a rising market can lose money if the foreign currency rises against the dollar.

2. Regional Mutual Fund: It confines itself to investments in securities from a specified geographical area, usually, the fund's local region. The objective is to take advantage of regional growth potential before the national investment community does or to invest in a specific segment of the region's economy, such as banking, energy etc. For the investor, the primary benefit is that he increases his diversification by being exposed to a specific foreign geographical area. They carry more risk as compared to international mutual funds because their investments are less diversified geographically.

(D) BY LOAD STRUCTURE

1. Load Funds: A load fund imposes following types of loads on the investors:

Exit Load (Back-end load) – It is charged on an investor on redemption of his units. It is deducted from the redemption proceeds to an outgoing investor.

Deferred Load - Deferred load is charged to the scheme over a period of time.

2. No-Load Funds: All those funds that do not charge any of the above mentioned loads are known as No-load Funds.

(E) BY TAX TREATMENT

1. Tax Exempt Funds: They enjoy tax exemption. They are normally contributed by middle income group of investors to lessen their burden of tax liability. All open-end equity oriented funds are exempt from distribution tax. Long-term capital gains and dividend income in the hands of investors are tax-free.

2. Non-tax Exempt Funds: They invest in taxable securities. Profits arising out of sale of units by an investor within 12 months of purchase are categorised as short-term capital gains, which are taxable. Sale of units of an equity oriented fund is subject to Securities Transaction Tax (STT). STT is deducted from the redemption proceeds to an investor.

Other Type of Funds

1. Arbitrage Funds: They make risk free profit by buying equity in the cash market and selling them in the future market thereby generating returns.

2. Capital Protection Funds: They guarantee the investor to get their initial investment and also give a better return than a bank deposit. Here generally 60-70 per cent of investment is made in the risk free securities and balance in risky assets.

3. Children Funds: Here parents invest money for the future of their children. Fund managers invest in quality stocks with long time horizon with the motive of long-term capital appreciation through investment in relatively low risk instruments.

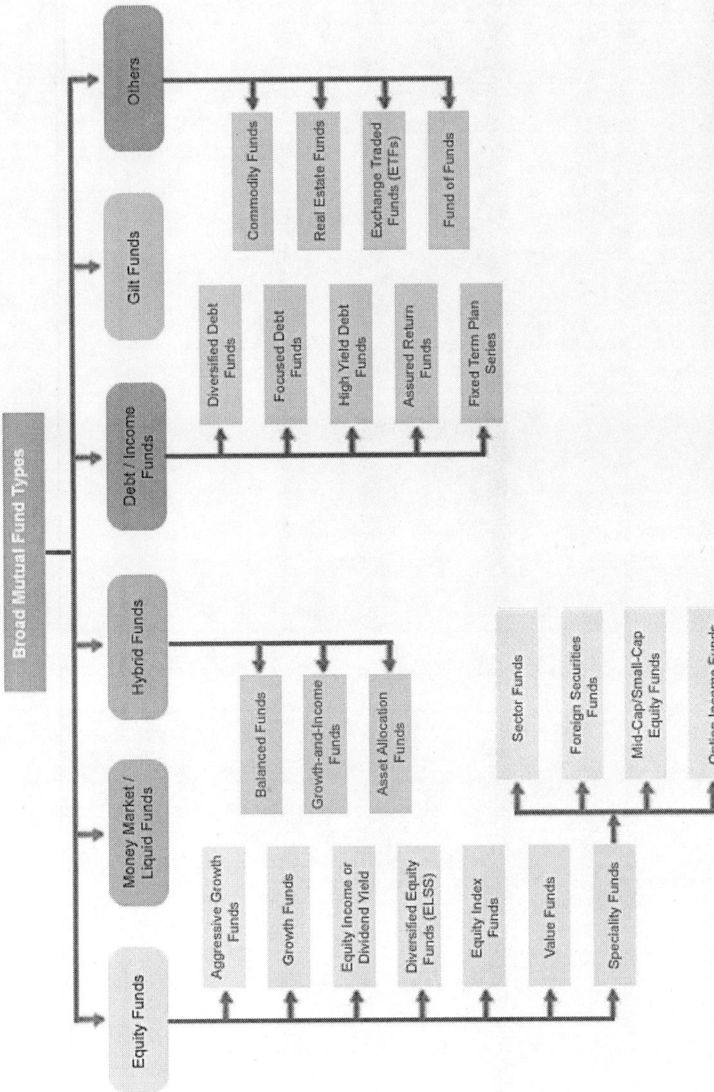

Source: www.personalfn.com

Fig. 2.2: Broad Mutual Fund Types.

3

How are Mutual Funds Regulated in India

The mutual fund industry witnessed robust growth and stricter regulation from the SEBI after the year 1996. To protect the interest of the investors, SEBI formulates policies and regulates the mutual funds. It notified regulations in 1993 (fully revised in 1996) and issued guidelines continuously. MFs promoted by public or private sector and foreign entities are governed by these Regulations. An organisation, to start a mutual fund, requires the approval of SEBI, ensuring quality and credibility check on everyone. SEBI approved Asset Management Company (AMC) manages the funds by making investments in various types of securities. Custodian, registered with SEBI, holds the securities of various schemes of the fund in its custody. According to SEBI Regulations, two-thirds of the directors of Trustee Company or board of trustees must be independent.

(A) Securities and Exchange Board of India (SEBI) Guidelines

The Indian mutual fund industry is undergoing a transformation, adapting to the various regulatory changes that are coming about. In the year 2009, SEBI brought in some sweeping reforms in the mutual fund industry. Some of the key amendments are highlighted.

1. *Entry Load:* In recent years SEBI has focused more on investor protection, introducing a number of regulations to empower retail investors in Mutual Funds ('MFs'). SEBI prohibited the charging of initial issue expenses, which were permitted for closed-ended schemes, and mandating that such MF schemes shall recover sales and distribution expenses through entry load only. Subsequently, w.e.f. August 1, 2009, SEBI banned the entry load that was deducted from the invested amount, and instead allowed customers the right to negotiate and decide commissions directly with distributors based on investor's assessment of various factors and related services to be rendered. This was to bring about more transparency in commissions and encourage long-term investment, making distributors more responsible and accountable.

2. *No Additional Management Fees on schemes launched on "no load" basis:* SEBI has scrapped the additional management fee of one per cent charged by AMCs on schemes launched on a no-load basis leading to a further squeeze in margins earned by the AMC.

3. *Direct Tax Code:* Unlike the extant tax provisions, DTC does not provide for any benefit for investment in equity linked savings scheme, and also proposes to increase the compliance in the hands of MFs by widening the scope of deduction of tax to include payments made to residents. However, it is unclear whether the income earned will be exempt or taxed in the hands of the investors on accrual basis, as stated in the Discussion Paper on the DTC.

4. *Documentation:* In December 2009, SEBI made it mandatory for all AMCs to maintain a copy of full investor documentation including Know Your Customer details, which was earlier maintained by the respective MF distributors who have now been asked to give a copy of the same to the fund houses.

5. *Disclosure of Investor Complaints in the Annual Report:* In order to improve the transparency in the 'grievance redressal mechanism', SEBI has recently issued a circular that requires MFs to include details of investor complaints in their Annual Report as part of the Report of the Trustees, beginning with the annual report for the year 2009-10. Investors can obtain relevant information from the trustees and inspect documents like trust deed, investment management agreement, annual reports, offer documents, etc. They must receive audited annual reports within six months from the financial year end. Equity mutual funds have been asked to play a more active role in corporate governance of the companies they invest in. SEBI has now made it mandatory for funds to disclose whether they voted for or against moves (suggested by companies in which they have invested) such as mergers, demergers, corporate governance issues, appointment and removal of directors. MFs have to disclose it on their website as well as annual reports. SEBI has also asked Mutual Funds to reveal all commission paid (upfront and trail) to its sponsor or associate companies, employees and their relatives. SEBI ordered mutual funds not to disclose the indicative portfolio or indicative yield of their newly launched Fixed Maturity Plans (FMPs), since this was pro-actively used as a tool to miss sell the product to the investors.

6. *Fund of Fund Schemes:* In the past, AMCs had been entering into revenue sharing arrangements with offshore funds in respect of investments made on behalf of Fund of Fund (FoF) schemes, which has now been prohibited by SEBI and they have been prohibited from receiving any revenue by whatever means/ head from the underlying fund.

7. Recommendations to re-visit the eligibility norms of AMCs: SEBI had constituted the "Committee on Review of Eligibility Norms" (CORE) to re-visit the eligibility norms and other functional aspects prescribed for various intermediaries. The key recommendations are relating to increase in the minimum net worth of AMCs from the existing Rs 10 crores to Rs 50 crores, change in the definition of net worth, sponsor to be a regulated entity and change in definition of control. This is to allow only the serious players to enter/remain in the market leading to better governance, thereby boosting investor confidence in the industry.

8. Trading through stock exchange platforms: SEBI has permitted online trading of MF units on recognised stock exchanges. While trading through the stock exchange, the investor would get to know about the validity of his order and the value at which the units would get credited/ redeemed to his account by the end of the day thereby optimising his investment decisions due to the reduced time lag in the movement of funds. This transparency would enable the investor to get a single view of his portfolio across multiple assets like securities, MF units etc. *New Fund Offers (NFOs):* They will only be open for 15 days. (ELSS funds though will continue to stay open for up to 90 days). Earlier, mutual funds would keep an NFO open for 30 days, and the minute they received their first cheque, the money would be directly invested in the market; creating a skewed accounting for those that entered later since they get a fixed NFO price. The market regulator has corrected this by extending Application Supported by Blocked Amount (ASBA) to mutual funds effective starting July 1st 2010. By the ASBA process one can continue to earn interest in the bank account until the NFO closes when the fund manager will be able to invest the money.

9. Dividends: Dividends can now only be paid out of actually realised gains. In case of dividend declaration, investors have a right to receive the dividend within

30 days of declaration. In case the investor fails to claim the redemption proceeds immediately, then the applicable NAV depends upon when the investor claims the redemption proceeds.

10. Redemption: On redemption request by investors, the AMC must dispatch the redemption proceeds within 10 working days of the request. In case the AMC fails to do so, it has to pay an interest @ 15 per cent. This rate may change from time to time subject to regulations.

11. Investor Rights: Investors can wind up a scheme or terminate the AMC if unit holders representing 75 per cent of scheme's assets pass a resolution to that respect. Investors have the right to be informed about changes in the fundamental attributes of a scheme viz. type of scheme, investment objectives and policies and terms of issue and can approach the investor relations officer for grievance redressal or the investor grievance cell of SEBI or sue the trustees.

12. Mutual Fund Distributors: SEBI allowed mutual fund investors to change their mutual fund distributors without obtaining a No Objection Certificate (NOC) from their earlier distributor, thus facilitating investors to shift their distributor without any hassle.

These guidelines set by the SEBI will lead to greater transparency for the common investor and an investable environment that would attract investors with greater faith and confidence.

(B) Association of Mutual Funds in India (AMFI)

Association of Mutual Funds in India (AMFI) was incorporated on 22nd August, 1995, as the apex body of all Asset Management Companies (AMC) which has been registered with SEBI. It functions under the supervision and guidelines of its Board of Directors. It follows the principle of protecting and promoting the interests of mutual funds and their unit holders. The objectives of AMFI are as follows:

1. AMFI maintains high professional and ethical standards in all areas of operation of the industry. It recommends and promotes the top class business practices and code of conduct which is followed by members and related people engaged in the activities of mutual fund and asset management. AMFI is engaged in upgrading professional standards and in promoting best industry practices in diverse areas such as valuation, disclosure, transparency etc. The agencies who are by any means connected or involved in the field of capital markets and financial services also involved in this code of conduct of the association.

2. AMFI interacts with SEBI and works according to SEBIs guidelines in the mutual fund industry. AMFI represents the Government of India, the Reserve Bank of India and other related bodies on matters relating to the Mutual Fund Industry.

3. AMFI develops a team of qualified and trained Agent distributors. It implements a training and certification programme for intermediaries and others engaged in the MF industry.

4. AMFI undertakes all-India awareness programme for investors in order to promote understanding of the concept and working of mutual funds.

5. AMFI disseminates information on Mutual Fund Industry and undertakes studies and researches either directly or in association with other bodies.

(C) Insurance Regulatory Authority of India Regulations

IRDA (Registration of Companies) Regulations, 2000 under Regulation 7 (c) of Chapter II has set certain regulations relating to insurance agencies and Mutual Fund investments.

As Gilt, Government Security and Liquid Mutual Funds, predominantly invest in Government Securities and Money Market instruments, the Authority revised the existing guidelines on investment in Mutual Funds. These investments in Gilt, G Sec and Liquid Mutual Funds would form part of 'Approved Investment' under IRDA (Investment) (Fourth Amendment) Regulations, 2008 (effective from 1st August) as per guidelines listed below. However, these investments should not be used as long-term investments instead of investing directly in Government Securities. Any Investment made in other categories of Mutual Funds, including those which partly invest in Government Securities and Money Market instruments, will fall under 'Other Investments', which in turn shall be subject to the limits prescribed in the guidelines issued under IRDA (Investment) Regulations, 2000 along with the norms.

4

How to Invest in Mutual Funds

FACTORS TO CONSIDER BEFORE INVESTING IN MUTUAL FUNDS

Investors often get confused when it comes to selecting the right fund from the plethora of funds available. There are various aspects within a fund that an investor must carefully consider before short-listing it for making investments. These aspects are as follows:

(A) Performance: If the fund has a well-established track record, the likelihood of it performing well in the future is higher than a fund which has not performed well. Under the performance criteria, one must make a note of the following:

1. *Comparisons:* It is crucial to compare the fund with its benchmark index and its peers, to deduce a meaningful inference. One must be careful while selecting the peers for comparison.

2. *Time period:* It's very important that investors have a long-term horizon if they wish to invest in equity oriented funds. It is important to evaluate the long-term, short-term and market cycle wise performance of the funds.

3. *Returns:* It is one of the important parameters that one must look at while evaluating a fund. In addition to the returns, investors must also look at the risk parameters.

4. *Risk:* Risk is normally measured by Standard Deviation (SD). SD signifies the degree of risk the fund has exposed its investors to. From an investor's perspective, evaluating a fund on risk parameters is important because it will help to check whether the fund's risk profile is in line with their risk profile or not.

5. *Risk-adjusted return:* This is measured by Sharpe Ratio. It signifies how much return a fund has delivered vis-à-vis the risk taken. Higher the Sharpe Ratio better is the fund's performance. From an investor's perspective, it is important because they should choose a fund which has delivered higher risk-adjusted returns. In fact, this ratio tells us whether the high returns of a fund are attributed to good investment decisions, or to higher risk.

6. *Portfolio Concentration:* Funds that have a high concentration in particular stocks or sectors tend to be very risky and volatile. Investors investing in these funds should have a high risk appetite. Ideally, a well diversified fund should hold no more than 40 per cent of its assets in its top 10 stock holdings.

7. *Portfolio Turnover:* The portfolio turnover rate measures the frequency with which stocks are bought and sold. Higher the turnover rate, higher the volatility. The fund might not be able to compensate the investors adequately for the higher risk taken.

(B) Fund Management: The managing team should be experienced in dealing with market fluctuation. One should focus on process-driven fund houses not 'star' fund manager driven.

(C) Costs: There is no reason for an AMC to incur higher costs, other than its desire to have higher margins. The two main costs incurred are:

1. *Expense Ratio:* Annual expenses involved in running the mutual fund include administrative costs, management salary, overheads etc. Expense Ratio is the percentage of assets that go towards these expenses. Every time the fund manager churns his portfolio, he pays a brokerage fee, which is ultimately borne by investors in the form of an Expense Ratio. Higher churning not only leads to higher risk, but also higher cost to the investor.

2. *Exit Load:* An exit load is charged to investors when they sell units of a mutual fund within a particular tenure; most funds charge if the units are sold within a year from the date of purchase. As exit load is a fraction of the NAV, it eats into your investment value. One should invest in a fund with a low expense ratio and stay invested in it for a longer duration.

PROCESS OF BUILDING A MUTUAL FUND PORTFOLIO

Step 1: Process of elimination: One must question the existence of every mutual fund in the portfolio to select the very best funds. It's important to guard against over-diversification.

Step 2: Process of selection: Once the elimination process is performed by the investors diligently enough, the second step will come naturally. For instance, if one has ignored all the sector/thematic funds that leave one with just the well-diversified ones. Likewise, if even those funds that have not completed a 3-Yr track record, you are automatically left with those who have a minimum 3-Yr track record. While selecting mutual funds, one must keep the following points in mind:

1. Investors should have a mix of both large cap as well as mid cap funds, since both have their inherent strengths. When both are well-selected, they can reward the investor handsomely over the long-term. The proportion of investments in large cap funds will depend upon the risk appetite of the investor.

2. Investors should go for both well-managed growth style and value style equity funds. This will help to capitalise on opportunities across the board.
3. Investing in a balanced fund will help in bringing in stability in the portfolio on account of the provision in the investment mandate for investment in debt.

A LIST OF FREQUENTLY ASKED QUESTIONS:

1. Can a mutual fund impose fresh load or increase the load beyond the level mentioned in the offer documents?

Mutual funds cannot increase the load beyond the level mentioned in the offer document. Any change in the load will be applicable only to prospective investments and not to the original investments. In case of imposition of fresh loads or increase in existing loads, the mutual funds are required to amend their offer documents so that the new investors are aware of loads at the time of investments.

2. What is sale or repurchase/redemption price?

The price or NAV a unit holder is charged while investing in an open-ended scheme is called sales price. It may include sales load, if applicable.

Repurchase or redemption price is the price or NAV at which an open-ended scheme purchases or redeems its units from the unit holders. It may include exit load, if applicable.

3. What is an assured return scheme?

Assured return schemes are those schemes that assure a specific return to the unit holders irrespective of performance of the scheme.

A scheme cannot promise returns unless such returns are fully guaranteed by the sponsor or AMC and this is required to be disclosed in the offer document.

Investors should carefully read the offer document whether return is assured for the entire period of the scheme or only for a certain period. Some schemes assure returns one year at a time and they review and change it at the beginning of the next year.

4. Can a mutual fund change the asset allocation while deploying funds of investors?

Considering the market trends, any prudent fund managers can change the asset allocation i.e. he can invest higher or lower percentage of the fund in equity or debt instruments compared to what is disclosed in the offer document. It can be done on a short-term basis on defensive considerations i.e. to protect the NAV. Hence, the fund managers are allowed certain flexibility in altering the asset allocation considering the interest of the investors. In case the mutual fund wants to change the asset allocation on a permanent basis, they are required to inform the unit holders and giving them option to exit the scheme at prevailing NAV without any load.

5. How to invest in a scheme of a mutual fund?

Mutual funds normally come out with an advertisement in newspapers publishing the date of launch of the new schemes. Investors can also contact the agents and distributors of mutual funds who are spread all over the country for necessary information and application forms. Forms can be deposited with mutual funds through the agents and distributors who provide such services. Nowadays, the post offices and banks also distribute the units of mutual funds. However, the investors may please note that the mutual funds schemes being marketed by banks and post offices should not be taken as their own schemes and no assurance of returns is given by them. The only role of banks and post offices is to help in distribution of mutual funds schemes to the investors.

Investors should not be carried away by commission/ gifts given by agents/distributors for investing in a particular scheme. On the other hand they must consider the track record of the mutual fund and should take objective decisions.

6. Can Non-resident Indians (NRIs) invest in mutual funds?

Yes, non-resident Indians can also invest in mutual funds. Necessary details in this respect are given in the offer documents of the schemes. Many Mutual Fund Houses have come up with special schemes to attract NRI investors.

7. How much should one invest in debt or equity oriented schemes?

An investor should take into account his risk taking capacity, age factor, financial position, etc. As already mentioned, the schemes invest in different type of securities as disclosed in the offer documents and offer different returns and risks. Investors may also consult financial experts before taking decisions. Agents and distributors may also help in this regard.

8. How to fill up the application form of a mutual fund scheme?

An investor must mention clearly his name, address, number of units applied for and such other information as required in the application form. He must give his bank account number so as to avoid any fraudulent encashment of any cheque/draft issued by the mutual fund at a later date for the purpose of dividend or repurchase. Any changes in the address, bank account number, etc. at a later date should be informed to the mutual fund immediately.

9. What should an investor look into an offer document?

An abridged offer document, which contains very useful information, is required to be given to the prospective investor by the mutual fund. The application form for subscription to a scheme is an integral part of the offer document. SEBI has prescribed minimum disclosures in the offer document. An investor, before investing in a scheme, should carefully read the offer document. Due care must be given to portions relating to main features of the scheme, risk factors, initial issue expenses and recurring expenses to be charged to the scheme, entry or exit loads, sponsor's track record, educational qualification and work experience of key personnel including fund managers, performance of other schemes launched by the mutual fund in the past, pending litigations and penalties imposed, etc.

10. When will the investor get certificate or statement of account after investing in a mutual fund?

Mutual funds are required to despatch certificates or statements of accounts within six weeks from the date of closure of the initial subscription of the scheme. In case of close-ended schemes, the investors would get either a demat account statement or unit certificates as these are traded in the stock exchanges. In case of open-ended schemes, a statement of account is issued by the mutual fund within 30 days from the date of closure of initial public offer of the scheme. The procedure of repurchase is mentioned in the offer document.

11. How long will it take for transfer of units after purchase from stock markets in case of close-ended schemes?

According to SEBI Regulations, transfer of units is required to be done within thirty days from the date of lodgment of certificates with the mutual fund.

12. As a unit holder, how much time will it take to receive dividends/repurchase proceeds?

A mutual fund is required to despatch to the unit holders the dividend warrants within 30 days of the declaration of the dividend and the redemption or repurchase proceeds within 10 working days from the date of redemption or repurchase request made by the unit holder.

In case of failures to despatch the redemption/repurchase proceeds within the stipulated time period, Asset Management Company is liable to pay interest as specified by SEBI from time to time.

13. Can a mutual fund change the nature of the scheme from the one specified in the offer document?

Yes. However, no change in the nature or terms of the scheme, known as fundamental attributes of the scheme e.g., structure, investment pattern, etc. can be carried out unless a written communication is sent to each unit holder and an advertisement is given in one English daily having nationwide circulation and in a newspaper published in the language of the region where the head office of the mutual fund is situated. The unit holders have the right to exit the scheme at the prevailing NAV without any exit load if they do not want to continue with the scheme. The mutual funds are also required to follow similar procedure while converting the scheme form close-ended to open-ended scheme and in case of change in sponsor.

14. How will an investor come to know about the changes, if any, which may occur in the mutual fund?

There may be changes from time to time in a mutual fund. The mutual funds are required to inform any material changes to their unit holders. Apart from it, many mutual funds send quarterly newsletters to their investors.

At present, offer documents are required to be revised and updated at least once in two years. In the meantime, new investors are informed about the material changes by way of addendum to the offer document till the time offer document is revised and reprinted.

15. How to know the performance of a mutual fund scheme?

The performance of a scheme is reflected in its net asset value (NAV) which is disclosed on daily basis in case of open-ended schemes and on weekly basis in case of close-ended schemes. The NAVs of mutual funds are required to be published in newspapers. The NAVs are also available on the websites of mutual funds. All mutual funds are also required to put their NAVs on the website of Association of Mutual Funds in India (AMFI) www.amfiindia.com and thus the investors can access NAVs of all mutual funds at one place

The mutual funds are also required to publish their performance in the form of half-yearly results which also include their returns/yields over a period of time i.e. last six months, one year, three years, five years and since inception of schemes. Investors can also look into other details like percentage of expenses of total assets as these have an effect on the yield and other useful information in the same half-yearly format.

The mutual funds are also required to send annual report or abridged annual report to the unit holders at the end of the year.

Various studies on mutual fund schemes including yields of different schemes are being published by the financial newspapers on a weekly basis. Apart from these, many research agencies also publish research reports on performance of mutual funds including the ranking of various schemes in terms of their performance. Investors should study these reports and keep themselves informed about the performance of various schemes of different mutual funds.

Investors can compare the performance of their schemes with those of other mutual funds under the same category. They can also compare the performance of equity oriented schemes with the benchmarks like BSE Sensitive Index, S&P CNX Nifty, etc.

On the basis of performance of the mutual funds, the investors should decide when to enter or exit from a mutual fund scheme.

16. How to know where the mutual fund scheme has invested money mobilised from the investors?

The mutual funds are required to disclose full portfolios of all of their schemes on half-yearly basis which are published in the newspapers. Some mutual funds send the portfolios to their unit holders.

The scheme portfolio shows investment made in each security i.e. equity, debentures, money market instruments, government securities, etc. and their quantity, market value and percentage to NAV. These portfolio statements also required to disclose illiquid securities in the portfolio, investment made in rated and unrated debt securities, non-performing assets (NPAs), etc.

Some of the mutual funds send newsletters to the unit holders on quarterly basis which also contain portfolios of the schemes.

17. Is there any difference between investing in a mutual fund and in an initial public offering (IPO) of a company?

Yes, there is a difference. IPOs of companies may open at lower or higher price than the issue price depending on market sentiment and perception of investors. However, in the case of mutual funds, the par value of the units may not rise or fall immediately after allotment. A mutual fund scheme takes sometime to make investment in securities. NAV of the scheme depends on the value of securities in which the funds have been deployed.

18. If schemes in the same category of different mutual funds are available, should one choose a scheme with lower NAV?

Some of the investors have the tendency to prefer a scheme that is available at lower NAV compared to the one available at higher NAV. Sometimes, they prefer a new scheme which is issuing units at Rs 10 whereas the existing schemes in the same category are available at much higher NAVs. Investors may please note that in case of mutual funds schemes, lower or higher NAVs of similar type schemes of different mutual funds have no relevance. On the other hand, investors should choose a scheme based on its merit considering performance track record of the mutual fund, service standards, professional management, etc. This is explained in an example given below:

Example: Suppose scheme A is available at a NAV of Rs 15 and another scheme B at Rs 90. Both schemes are diversified equity oriented schemes. Investor has put Rs 9,000 in each of the two schemes. He would get 600 units (9000/15) in scheme A and 100 units (9000/90) in scheme B. Assuming that the markets go up by 10 per cent and both the schemes perform equally good and it is reflected in their NAVs. NAV of scheme A would go up to Rs 16.50 and that of scheme B to Rs 99. Thus, the market value of investments would be Rs 9,900 (600 × 16.50) in scheme A and it would be the same amount of Rs 9900 in scheme B (100 × 99). The investor would get the same return of 10 per cent on his investment in each of the schemes. Thus, lower or higher NAV of the schemes and allotment of higher or lower number of units within the amount an investor is willing to invest, should not be the factors for making investment decision. Likewise, if a new equity oriented scheme is being offered at Rs 10 and an existing scheme is available for Rs 90, should not be a factor for decision-making by the investor. Similar is the case with income or debt-oriented schemes.

On the other hand, it is likely that the better managed scheme with higher NAV may give higher returns compared to a scheme which is available at lower NAV but is not managed efficiently. Similar is the case of fall in NAVs. Efficiently managed scheme at higher NAV may not fall as much as inefficiently managed scheme with lower NAV.

Therefore, the investor should give more weightage to the professional management of a scheme instead of lower NAV of any scheme. He may get much higher number of units at lower NAV, but the scheme may not give higher returns if it is not managed efficiently.

19. Are the companies having names like mutual benefit the same as mutual funds schemes?

Investors should not assume some companies having the name "mutual benefit" as mutual funds. These companies do not come under the purview of SEBI. On the other hand, mutual funds can mobilise funds from the investors by launching schemes only after getting registered with SEBI as mutual funds.

20. Is the higher net worth of the sponsor a guarantee for better returns?

In the offer document of any mutual fund scheme, financial performance including the net worth of the sponsor for a period of three years is required to be given. The only purpose is that the investors should know the track record of the company which has sponsored the mutual fund. However, higher net worth of the sponsor does not mean that the scheme would give better returns or the sponsor would compensate in case the NAV falls.

21. Where can an investor look out for information on mutual funds?

Almost all the mutual funds have their own websites. Investors can also access the NAVs, half-yearly results and portfolios of all mutual funds at the website of Association of mutual funds in India (AMFI) www.amfiindia.com. AMFI has also published useful literature for the investors.

Investors can log on to the website of SEBI www.sebi.gov.in and go to "Mutual Funds" section for information on SEBI regulations and guidelines, data on mutual funds, draft offer documents filed by mutual funds, addresses of mutual funds, etc. Also, in the annual reports of SEBI available on the website, a lot of information on mutual funds is given.

There are a number of other websites which give a lot of information of various schemes of mutual funds including yields over a period of time. Many newspapers also publish useful information on mutual funds on daily and weekly basis. Investors may approach their agents and distributors to guide them in this regard.

22. Can an investor appoint a nominee for his investment in units of a mutual fund?

Yes. The nomination can be made by individuals applying for/holding units on their own behalf singly or jointly. Non-individuals including society, trust, body corporate, partnership firm, Karta of Hindu Undivided Family, holder of Power of Attorney cannot nominate.

23. If mutual fund scheme is wound up, what happens to money invested?

In case of winding up of a scheme, the mutual funds pay a sum based on prevailing NAV after adjustment of expenses. Unit holders are entitled to receive a report on winding up from the mutual funds which gives all necessary details.

24. How can the investors redress their complaints?

Investors would find the name of contact person in the offer document of the mutual fund scheme that they may approach in case of any query, complaints or grievances. Trustees of a mutual fund monitor the activities of the mutual fund. The names of the directors of asset management company and trustees are also given in the offer documents. Investors should approach the concerned Mutual Fund/ Investor Service Centre of the Mutual Fund with their complaints.

If the complaints remain unresolved, the investors may approach SEBI for facilitating redressal of their complaints. On receipt of complaints, SEBI takes up the matter with the concerned mutual fund and follows up with it regularly.

25. What are the Types of returns?

There are three ways, where the total returns provided by mutual funds can be enjoyed by investors:

- Income is earned from dividends on stocks and interest on bonds. A fund pays out nearly all income it receives over the year to fund owners in the form of a distribution.
- If the fund sells securities that have increased in price, the fund has a capital gain. Most funds also pass on these gains to investors in a distribution.
- If fund holdings increase in price but are not sold by the fund manager, the fund's shares increase in price. You can then sell your mutual fund shares for a profit. Funds will also usually give you a choice either to receive a check for distributions or to reinvest the earnings and get more shares.

26. How to Select an Equity Fund?

(a) Compare a fund with its peers: One of the basic fundamental of benchmarking is to evaluate funds within the same category. For example, if you are evaluating the performance of a thematic fund, say IT based fund, then you should compare its performance with another similar IT based fund. Comparing it with banking sector fund for example will not give the correct picture. Comparing a fund over stock market cycle (boom and bust) will give investors a good idea about how the fund has fared.

(b) Compare returns against those of the benchmark index: Every fund mentions a benchmark index in the Offer

Document. It can be BSE 100, BSE 200, Nifty or any other index. The benchmark index serves as a guidepost for both the fund manager and the investor. Compare how the fund has fared against the benchmark index over a period of three to five years. The funds that have outperformed their benchmark indices during stock market volatility must be given a close look.

(c) Compare against the fund's own performance: Apart from comparing a fund with its peers and benchmark index, investors should evaluate its historical performance. By evaluating a fund against its own historical performance, you can get an idea about consistent performers.

27. In the present scenario of severe volatility in the global and Indian financial markets does it make any difference in investing in mutual funds as compared to traditional financial market instruments?

The market fluctuations will certainly affect the returns generated by the mutual fund schemes as the mutual funds are investing their corpus in diverse financial market instruments. However, the fluctuations in return generated can be smoothened out by the mutual fund investments due to diversification of portfolio.

28. What is a Systematic Investment Plan?

Systematic investment plan as the name suggest allows a user to build an investment portfolio with a small systematic investment at regular intervals. The investor can choose his or her preferred mode of investment as monthly, quarterly or annually and invest the funds according to his or her convenience.

29. Is there any special advantage in investing through Systematic Investment Plans?

Investing in a systematic investment plan allows users to maintain a monthly investment scheme which is far easier to maintain in the long run rather than investing a lump sum amount each year. Investing in systematic investment plans must be considered by all investors who are yet to attain an investment discipline allowing them the convenience to invest a pre-determined short sum every month towards their future.

30. Is there in major risk involved in investing through SIPs?

The biggest risk of investing in through SIPs is that your money moves with the market in an SIP, and when you leave and join at will, you indulge in trying to time the market. When this attempt converts into buying at peaks and selling at the bottom, there is no money to be made, thereby reducing the returns generated to a large extent.

MUTUAL FUNDS AS A FINANCIAL PLANNING TOOL

A financial plan helps an investor in the following ways:

1. Enabling investors to identify his goals and investment needs.
2. Understand the various financial products with respect to their risk, return, liquidity and maturity profile.
3. Combine the features of financial products with the investor's financial needs and determine appropriate mix of investments, technically referred to as asset allocation.
4. Suggest suitable instruments as part of asset allocation.

Mutual fund allows a financial planner (read investor) to enhance the effectiveness of his financial plan in the following fashion:

1. Diversification

Diversification as practiced in financial planning can be done at three levels by assets, investment style and management style.

(a) Diversification of assets – Assets can be diversified on many levels, for example, holding a mix of stocks, bonds and cash. Possibly then by geographic sector taking advantage of global opportunities and the fact that if one economy is weak, another is strong. And then by economic sector, to include a variety of industries, because when one industry is slowing down, another is picking up. Each of these diversifications will serve to increase returns and reduce risk.

(b) Diversification of styles - Each asset class is then diversified into multiple investment styles – such as growth, value, and opportunities.

(c) Diversification of managers - Portfolio returns can be enhanced by using multiple managers with complementary investment styles who react in their own ways to varying market conditions. However, we opine investors not to provide primacy to the fund managers in the diversification criteria.

2. Asset Allocation

Except for the most conservative portfolios which do not hold equities, every portfolio should be diversified to hold all major assets classes:

(a) Cash for security and liquidity, so that one can take advantage of opportunities as they arise

(b) Bonds, to help preserve capital and provide a steady income

(c) Stocks, for growth to help you beat inflation and counter the impact of taxes

(d) Real estate, because of their low correlation with stocks and bonds

(e) Gold, for its ability to be a hedge against uncertainties.

An important inference could be, that one should spend considerable amount of time and energy in choosing a tailor made or customised asset allocation strategy. Once the strategy is in place, then the next important action point would be the instruments to fulfill the role of respective asset classes.

3. Portfolio Strategy

Most portfolios are structured with 5 financial objectives in mind:

(a) Growth

(b) Income

(c) Inflation protection

(d) Peace of mind and preservation of capital

(e) Minimise taxes

A financial planner has to balance the importance of each of these, and keep them in mind as he goes about structuring a portfolio. There is no such thing as an optimal balance that's right for everyone. The balance is a personal choice depending on the relative importance of these factors for a given investor. While doing financial planning through mutual funds, one must try to answer the following questions:

(a) Towards what objective/goal is the investor allocating his money?

Knowing the objective of investing enables the investor to select the right options offered by a mutual fund house. For example, if an individual has a long-term objective, then he may go in for a long-term equity fund and for investors with short-term objectives or needing intermediate returns, a liquid fund is the right option.

(b) What is the time horizon?

Time horizon refers to, when does the investor want to enjoy the fruit of investment? This ascertainment is critical because both, the risk and the reward of investments can vary according to the time horizon. Generally, a longer horizon allows for more aggression in investment. The less time, the more one needs to avoid risk.

(c) What is the risk tolerance of the investor?

There is a risk-reward continuum running from cash to bonds to stocks. Returns are commensurate with the risk someone is willing to tolerate. Risk has other dimensions investor to replace capital. If not earning any income, replacing lost capital will be difficult, which means a more conservative approach. Other considerations could be the present financial situation, estate planning and level of taxation. One other important factor is age. As a general rule, the younger one is, the more aggressive someone can afford to be with their investment portfolio.

This is because the investor has more time to recover from any possible setbacks in the value of the portfolio.

4. Rebalancing

Rebalancing is the action of bringing a portfolio of investments that has deviated away from target asset allocation. The goal of rebalancing is to move the current asset allocation back in line to the originally planned asset allocation. Rebalancing is primarily warranted under conditions where the returns have significantly deviated than expected or to stay in line with market conditions. For example, an equity heavy portfolio needs to be restructured in contraction phases where company profits are hit harder and interest rates move up. It could be done by moving a portion of equity holdings to debt instruments. Mutual funds probably allow the easiest window to rebalancing due to their diversity of offerings.

A case would be help to understand better on rebalancing.

Mr X has planned for his son's marriage in 2020, for which the estimated cost in 2020 would be Rs 1.7 crores. In 2010 he is advised to invest Rs 70,000 in equity and Rs 30,000 in Debt assuming an average return of 12 per cent for equity and five per cent for debt the expected value of investments at year end would be 78,400 for equity and 31,500 for debt. At year end, at eight per cent, the equity markets performed worse than expected and at 14 per cent the debt markets performed better than expected.

Hence, the portfolio value, instead of the planned Rs 109,900 ended up as Rs 109,800.

Consequently, the ratio of debt to equity changed from the original 70:30 to 69:31. To rebalance the portfolio, Mr X has to liquidate his debt holdings by Rs 2,700 and invest in equity and also add Rs 100 cash from his own personal reserves.

5. Tax Efficiency

Where mutual funds score head and shoulder over other instruments in a financial planner's eyes is when it comes to tax efficiency and reduction in transaction charges. Imagine a scenario where a person holds the individual stocks BSE-Sensex in the same proportion as it is meant to be and another person holds a unit of an index fund. The chances are that the Mutual Fund unit holder would be a happier person for the fact that:

(a) The mutual fund unit holder is safe from transaction fees the stockholder might have to pay for using his DEMAT account for equity trading.

(b) The incidence of capital gains tax would be zero for a mutual fund holder as it is the fund which is involved in equity trading and that equity trading is considered primary business and hence is exempt.

(c) Dividends declared by equity-oriented funds (i.e. mutual funds with more than 65 per cent of assets inequities) are tax-free in the hands of investor. There is also no dividend distribution tax applicable on these funds under section 115R. Diversified equity funds, sector funds, balanced funds are examples of equity-oriented funds.

Thus, mutual funds allow the financial planner to align the investment goals on the mantra of:

POINTERS TO INVESTING IN MUTUAL FUNDS

While investing in mutual funds, an investor must primarily broadly look at the following points, which enable them to select the right one:

1. A fund sponsor with integrity

Investors must check the sponsor's (promoter) record in the financial services arena. Apart from a consistent and clean record in financial services, sponsor(s) should have requisite experience and background in managing mutual funds be it in India or overseas.

2. An experienced fund manager

The fund manager must be experienced, which is best reflected in the returns he has generated on funds previously/currently managed by him.

3. A suitable investment philosophy

Every fund manager has his own individual style and investment philosophy. While some managers are aggressive, others are passive. Investors must choose the fund that best reflects and matches his own investment philosophy.

4. The correct fund by nature and category.

5. Fees and charges

Asset management companies (AMC) charge a fee for managing investor monies. In other words, your mutual fund deducts charges and fees from the net asset value (NAV) of the fund. As an investor you must be aware of the fees and charges of the AMC. Two schemes with more or less similar performances would generate different returns if one of the two schemes charges higher fees.

6. The load

An investor may be required to pay a load at the time of selling the units. Again, the returns of two similar performing schemes may vary depending on the load charged by the scheme to the investor.

7. The tax implications

The investor needs to understand the tax implications before investing in mutual fund schemes. Currently, if an investors exits (sells) his equity oriented fund prior to the completion of 12 months of his holding period, he will be liable to pay a short-term capital gains tax @ 15 per cent + 3 per cent education cess. However, where an investor exits (sells) his equity oriented fund after the completion of 12 months of its holding period, he will not be liable to the payment of long-term capital gains tax. The dividend earned on an equity oriented is also exempt from tax.

Tax-saving funds (commonly known as Equity Linked Saving Schemes (ELSS)) offer a tax benefit to the investors under Section 80C of the Income Tax Act 1961.

8. Investor service and transparency

Services offered by mutual funds (MFs) may vary across funds. Some MFs are more investor friendly than others, and offer information at regular intervals. For instance, some funds disclose the expense ratios, an important criterion for fund selection, once a year, some disclose it once every three months, while a few disclose it every month.

9. Fund performance

Every fund is benchmarked against an index like the BSE Sensex, Nifty, BSE 100, BSE 200, CNX 500, etc. The investor must track the fund's performance against the benchmark index. He must also compare its performance with other funds from the same category. He should also see the fund's calendar year performances over the years.

5

The Challenges and Opportunities of Mutual Funds in India

Challenges for Indian Mutual Fund Industry in India

The Indian mutual fund industry finds itself in an economic landscape which has undergone rapid changes over the years. The industry achieved a high water mark when it doubled its AUM from Rs 3.6 trillion in FY2007 to Rs 6.13 trillion in FY2010 – clocking an impressive growth rate of 16.2 per cent per year. Since then the Indian economy (coupled with the emerging economies) has faced a slowdown. From an average GDP growth rate of eight to nine per cent during the 2008-2011 years, the Indian economy was growing at a lackluster 4.8 per cent growth rate in Quarter 2, 2013. Coupled with a steep decline in the value of the Indian rupee, the mutual fund industry now finds itself in a capricious global economic environment. However, there is strong reason to believe that the Indian mutual fund industry has not yet seen its global peak and if proper measures are taken, the industry could get back on its former growth path. The challenges are as follows:

1. Problems related to the investors

All the problems related to the investors are, lack of awareness and poor after sales service to the investors. The investors believed, so far, that the mutual funds promoted by UTI, LIC, and nationalised banks are guaranteed by the Central Government. The majority of the new investors don't understand the concept, operations and advantages of investment in mutual funds before investing.

One of the major reasons behind the under-penetration of mutual funds is the lack of understanding about mutual funds, how they differ from ordinary investments and how they manage to offer superior returns over traditional investments. According to a report on mutual funds investments published by Boston Analytics in 2010, approximately a third of all of respondents from Tier II Indian cities did not know how and where to invest in mutual funds (Boston Analytics, 2010). Most people remain unaware of basic financial concepts such reward (return) to variability (risk) ratio, asset allocation, benefits of diversification, passive-active investment strategies etc.

2. Problems related to working

The inventible funds of the mutual funds increase when sales are more than the redemptions and decrease when the redemptions are more than sales creating the problems of maintaining liquidity. The investors prefer to invest in equity funds during boom period and shift their investments to debt funds during the recession period. The most profitable and high income and appreciation potential stocks during the boom period or at the time of investing funds in such stocks may become illiquid over a period of time. The investors can't take decisions of investment due to unavailability of track records of working. Unless the track records of working of mutual funds is available covering the several stock market booms and crashes, the investors can't judge which schemes or mutual funds are better alternatives for investments.

3. Problems related to performance

The investor prefers safety of the principal amount, regular returns, long-term growth, income tax benefits, etc. The mutual fund schemes have been designed based on the preferences of the investors, changes in stock/capital market, and returns on various instruments and changing profile of the investors. The schemes are framed and conceptualised by the top management of the mutual funds and marketed by their branches and through the agents. The agents and the sales executives of the mutual funds assure higher returns to the investors and paint a rosy picture about the mutual funds while marketing schemes. The mutual funds in our country have been quite wrongly promoted as an alternative to equity investing and created very high expectations in the minds of the investors. The ignorance of the investors about mutual funds coupled with aggressive selling by promising higher returns to the investors have resulted into loss of investors' confidence due to inability to provide higher returns. All mutual funds set a higher target for mobilisation of savings from the investor by launching new schemes and expanding investor base. The agents or distributor of mutual funds are more governed by commissions and incentives they get for selling the schemes and not by the requirements of the investors and quality of the products. They share commissions with the investors and don't explain the risk factors to them.

The investors who invest in growth or equity schemes consider it as an alternative to stock market investing and the investors who invest in debt schemes expect higher returns on their investments than returns on nationalised banks' fixed deposits. The investors expect higher returns and get dissatisfied when they don't receive the expected returns. The NAV of the mutual fund scheme gets discounted on debiting the front-ended load of issue expenses after closure, further discounted on listing and continue to decline on trading due to poor demand for such units due to the poor sentiments of the investors.

The mutual funds are bound to invest the funds as per their investment objectives of each scheme published in the offer document. After the issue is over, it becomes the mandate and the mutual funds have no choice to invest the funds in other securities, which can provide higher returns.

The greater transparency, increased innovations, better services to the investors, liquidity and higher returns will make mutual fund schemes more popular and investors friendly.

4. Lack of Financial Inclusion leading to a skewed structure of participation

While the mutual fund industry continues to be metro and urban centric, the mutual funds are beginning to tap Tier 2 and Tier 3 towns as a vital component to their growth strategy. The contribution of the Top 10 cities to total AUM has gradually declined from approximately 92 per cent in 2005 to approximately 80 per cent currently.

One of the biggest challenges that the mutual fund industry faces is the lack of healthy participation from a large part of the country. This skewed origination of AUM in India is its single biggest challenge and its biggest opportunity at the same time. This under penetration of financial inclusion is not unique to mutual funds, but a deeper structural problem characteristic of the Indian financial sector. More than half of India's population does not have any access to formal banking services. According to 2012 World Bank Global Findex, only 35.23 per cent of respondents in India have an account (either self or together with someone else) at a bank or some other formal financial institution. Even in savings indicators at formal or informal institutions, India continues to be a laggard. Even Bangladesh with a 47 per cent lower per capita Gross Domestic Product (GDP) based on purchasing power parity performs better in financial inclusion parameters.

Mutual fund companies are also required take advantage of the growing opportunity in the commodities market.

5. Lack of Financial Literacy

Most Indian households tend to be extremely risk averse and wary where they invest their hard earned savings. As a result, they are conservative with their savings and tend to invest in 'safe' assets. Investors perceive mutual funds as risky investments (despite the fact that several funds invest in government bonds, thereby being safer than bank deposits) and tend to invest their savings in tangible assets such as gold, jewellery, real estate or fixed deposits in banks. These choices are a result of a mindset which has generally seen investing in stock markets and other market traded securities as akin to gambling. This is reflected by the proportion of savings of Indian households in the financial markets. The gross domestic savings and investment at current market price by households was 22.3 per cent of GDP 2011-12 (RBI Annual Report, 2012). The household investment in physical and financial assets was 14.3 per cent and 8.0 per cent respectively. The investment in shares and debentures as a percentage of gross financial savings by households was 3.6 per cent during 2011-12. The gross financial savings by household in mutual funds is estimated at 2.5 per cent out of total 3.1 per cent in shares/debentures.

6. Distributional Inefficiency

Distributional efficiency and number of agents another challenge that AMCs in India face is increasing the efficiency of their distributional channels. In other words, attracting new investors in small cities does not come cheaply for the Asset Management Companies beyond the top 200 districts by GDP. More money has to be spent on distribution and marketing for getting investments in poorer districts. However, AMCs tend to play safe and seem unwilling to focus on their distribution channels outside the T-15 cities.

Cities beyond Top 20 only comprise around 10 per cent of the industry AUM as per industry practitioners. The retail population residing in Tier 2 and Tier 3 towns, even if aware and willing, are unable to invest in mutual funds owing to limited access to suitable distribution channels and investor servicing. The distribution network of most mutual fund houses is largely focused on the Top 20 cities given the high cost associated with deeper penetration into Tier 2 and Tier 3 towns. However, some of the mutual fund houses have begun focusing on cities beyond the Top 20 by building their branch presence and strengthening distribution reach through non-branch channels.

Rural participation in mutual funds continues to be poor. Such poor penetration has much to do with lack of investor awareness, inefficiencies in fund transfer mechanisms, presence of safer substitutes and cost of establishing presence in smaller areas. Fund houses cannot fight this battle single handedly. They need adequate support in terms of banking infrastructure, distribution services and technological solutions to ensure a sustainable cost-benefit model of growth.

7. Diminishing Talent Pool

The acute shortage of talented resources is slowly but surely showing its impact. The pool of talented people is diminishing and staff costs are soaring. The key challenge is to find a permanent solution to tide over this acute shortage. One possible solution could be for the industry through AMFI to tie up with universities and colleges to offer programmes dedicated to the financial services industry in general and the mutual fund industry in particular, which would cover various critical aspects of the financial services industry ranging from fund management, research, analysis, treasury, operations and accounting.

8. Limited Focus on Increasing Retail Penetration

The Indian mutual fund industry had limited focus on building retail AUM and has only recently stepped up efforts to augment branch presence in Tier 2 and Tier 3 towns. Large ticket size, tax arbitrage available to corporates on investing in money market mutual funds, easy accessibility to institutional customers concentrated in Tier 1 cities are the factors instrumental in mutual fund houses focusing on the institutional segment. Institutional AUM, however, makes the industry vulnerable to the possibility of sudden redemption pressures that impact the fund performance.

9. Limited Innovation in Product Offerings

The Indian mutual fund industry has largely been product-led and not sufficiently customer focused. The popularity of NFO triggered a proliferation of schemes with a large number of non-differentiated products. The industry has had a limited focus on innovation and new product development, thereby catering to the limited needs of the customer. The Indian mutual fund industry offers limited investment options viz. capital guarantee products for the Indian investors, a large majority of whom are risk averse. The Indian market is still to witness the launch of green funds, socially responsible investments, fund of hedge funds, enhanced money market funds, renewable and energy/ climate change funds.

10. Limited Flexibility in Fees and Pricing Structures

The fee structure in the mutual fund industry is not flexible. While the expenses have continuously risen, the management fee levels have remained stagnant. Distributors are compensated for their services through a fixed charge in the form of entry load and additional fees as considered appropriate by the AMC. Regardless of the quality of advice and service provided, the commission payable by the mutual fund customer to the distributors is fixed.

11. Limited Customer Engagement

Mutual fund distributors have been facing questions on their competence, degree of engagement with customer and the value provided to the customer. In the absence of a framework to regulate distributors, both the distributors and the mutual fund houses have exhibited limited interest in continuously engaging with customers post closure of sale as the commissions and incentives had been largely in the form of upfront fees from product sales (although trail commissions have also been paid in limited instances regardless of the service rendered). As a result of the limited engagement, there have been rising instances of mis-selling to customers.

12. Limited Focus of the Public Sector Network on Distribution of Mutual Funds

Public sector banks with a large captive customer base, significant reach beyond the Top 20 cities in semi-urban and rural areas, and the potential to build the retail investor base, have so far played a very limited role in mutual funds distribution. The India Post network operating the largest postal network in the world majority of which is in rural areas, is stated to have 250 post offices selling mutual funds of five AMCs only; further most of the post offices selling mutual funds are located in Tier 1 and Tier 2 cities which are already being catered to, by national level and other distributors. The postal network also serves as a means to facilitate inclusive and equitable growth to all regions and social groups by providing them with access to mutual funds.

What would be the impact of these challenges?

1. Pressures on Margins

To effectively tide over the challenges, fund houses will have to expand their cost budgets which may put pressure on margins in the short run. Reduced margins may have the effect of funds houses flexing their muscles to garner a higher market share of assets under management to enjoy the benefits of economies of scale. This will surely benefit the investors in the long run as they would be able to enjoy better service standards and more product differentiation. Increasing regulations may also bring about an increase in the cost of compliance.

2. Consolidation in the Industry

With more and more new players keen on entering the market, a new wave of consolidation may spark of by way of mergers and acquisitions in the industry.

3. Innovation and Product Differentiation

With competition going up in India and most fund houses offering the same bouquet of products to the investors, product differentiation could take centre stage going forward. Innovative distribution models and service standards would also be a key distinguishing factor amongst players. Agile product design, re-positioning of ETFs (Exchange Traded Funds) and SIPs (Systematic Investment Plans). Better communication of scheme returns on a relative basis to investors is required. The alpha achieved is insufficiently communicated or understood.

4. Increasing Trend on Outsourcing

With the industry facing a shortage of talented resources, there is an increasing trend amongst players to outsource the non-core functions and utilise the limited available resources only for core functions to be performed in house. This is a norm in mature markets for global fund houses which may set a similar trend in our industry as well. Sensing this, more players have entered the fund accounting service provider market in the last one year. As the industry evolves, outsourcing an increasing number of functions to reduce the head-count and increase efficiency might be the norm. All aspects of operating costs must be examined for efficiencies.

A rational look at schemes of an AMC by their management teams is needed to better understand the mix, the cost and the benefits – to the investors as well as to the AMCs.

Following are a few ways in which the challenges of the mutual fund industry can be addressed.

1. Investor Education has to be prioritised to face the biggest challenge facing mutual funds, which is lack of participation. The efforts taken by the industry and AMFI towards investor education are definitely showing results. The media is also making a fair share of its contribution. Today, we have news channels, running dedicated shows for mutual funds, wherein fundamentals of investing in mutual funds are explained and queries of investors are answered by experts. However, the fact remains that in our country mutual funds are sold rather than bought and this trend has been observed uniformly across all classes of investors and for all kinds of products. This is where professional help is required.
2. Fund houses have introduced interesting technological innovations such as transacting through the internet, net asset value updates on mobile phones, unit balance alerts via SMS messages, transacting through ATM cards etc. However, these innovations currently cater to the already pampered urban class of investors. The internet revolution in our country is yet to penetrate to the grass root levels. The per capita usage of internet in our country is still very low compared not only to the developed countries but also as compared to our developing peers. Mobile telephony comparatively has grown exponentially. Herein lays another important challenge for the industry. It is very important to strike the right balance while choosing to invest in technological advancements.

Newer leaner operating structures will have to evolve which will entail the use of technology that helps an AMC (Asset Management Company) reach the retail end user with solutions that enable transactions via platforms such as mobile or online platforms. This will not only give greater direct access but will also help AMCs to better understand investor behaviour and create the appropriate environment and products to move towards long and healthy relationships with the investors.

3. Direct Cash Transfers and linkages with Aadhaar would be a step forward towards the goal of financial inclusion and may prove beneficial to mutual fund houses in the long run. With below poverty households finally coming to own bank accounts, fund houses could use pre-existing bank channels to offer investment opportunities when these people finally start earning saving.

4. It has been shown in past studies that institutional investors (in the form of mutual funds) 'herd' towards small-cap and mid-cap stock which offer growth prospects thereby increasing the depth and breadth of capital markets (Wermers, 1999). Institutional buying and selling of stocks also increases the price-adjustment process in capital markets and under right conditions institutional investors tend to decrease stock price volatility. All these effects are desirables as far as financial markets are concerned.

5. This combination of ignorance, risk-aversion and mutual fund complexity are huge hurdles that AMCs in India will have to overcome if there is to be any increase in retail participation in mutual funds. Investors need to be made to look beyond the traditional avenues of investment through sensitisation and education. In addition to this, campaigns should

be tailored to increase the visibility of debt funds which generally tend to be safer than equity funds.

6. The new AIF (Alternative Investment Fund) guidelines will create opportunities to broaden the revenue base without commensurate cost increases.

The asset management industries in the US and in Japan have had their "401 k" (a type of retirement savings account in the US) moments. In the late 70s market regulators in the US permitted pension funds (later 401K) to invest a portion of their funds (at the discretion of the individual) into mutual fund schemes. This saw a huge upsurge in the AUM of the industry as a whole. Similarly the Japanese asset management industry went on a growth surge around the turn of the century when the pension and retirement funds were permitted to be invested in the asset management schemes. The EPF (Employee Pension Fund) in India is a huge pool of long-term investible funds. These are expected to yield high returns. If the right mechanism were to be created to channelise even a small proportion of the funds to be invested in the Indian mutual fund schemes (specific schemes can be selected if required), it will provide a boost to the industry, apart from maintaining the more important objective of having the funds managed by a regulated sector and by persons with a track record.

A similar impact could be generated by introducing the concept of individual retirement accounts (IRAs). Some of the investment products available are in the nature of retirement benefit plans ([EPF, PPF and now NPS (National Pension Fund) as well as certain insurance products].

Avenues such as EPF are available to only a certain section of the population. To encourage people to save for the post retirement period IRAs can be offered. The investments into such schemes could be self-directed, flexible and in specific circumstances tax deductible. The fund so created could be available tax free (EEE) at the age of retirement. Such a concept exists in the mature western markets such as the US and contributes to about 20 per cent of the assets under management.

The recently announced Rajiv Gandhi Equity Savings Scheme is another opportunity for the mutual fund industry. Given the low financial awareness of such new or first time investors in the far flung regions, it is imperative that these investors are channelised into the markets via mutual funds rather than directly investing into equities themselves.

6

Future of Mutual Funds in India

There is still vast potential in our semi-urban and rural areas where savings are still largely kept as post office and bank deposits. This is a vast untapped market in our country. Thus, building a good distribution network should be paid attention to. New and more aggressive Mutual Funds should try to educate and tap prospective investors in these areas. The new generation of young investors are aware of the various investment avenues and thereby consider mutual funds as an interesting and safer investment option as compared to traditional money market instruments. Thus, mutual funds are expected to grow even further as the Indian Financial Markets become more robust.

Suggestions for Improvement

Here are few suggestions for the improvement of the functioning of Mutual Funds, so that they may continue to grow in the process of resource mobilisation and capital formation. The various suggestions have been divided into three broad categories, viz., (a) Suggestions for the regulatory framework, (b) Suggestions for the Mutual Fund Houses and (c) Suggestions for the Investors.

(a) Suggestions for the Regulatory Framework

Over the years the regulatory framework governing the Mutual Funds has seen significant development keeping pace with the dynamic environment of the Indian Financial Market.

SEBI has emerged as the nodal agency governing all the aspects of the Mutual Fund Industry emphasising on the protection of the investors interest. However, in spite of the constant vigil of SEBI, there are a lot of gray areas which need to be considered, thereby making the regulations applicable and effective in reality. Harmonisation of Policies across Multiple Regulatory Frameworks in the Financial Services Sector would go a long way towards better implementation and thereby effectiveness of the regulations. Few points have been discussed as follows.

1. To create a strong regulatory framework comparable to international standards: India need a comprehensive set of regulations to check the malpractices which have become commonplace today. SEBI should be given more punitive power to make the Mutual Funds operations more transparent. Penal provisions should be provided against key personnel of an AMC or Trustees of Mutual Funds who are found guilty of violating the provisions. The monetary penalties should increase and be comparable to the magnitude of the economic offence. SEBI should seek justification from the AMCs for continuous underperformance of fund(s). SEBI should come out with guidelines to educate investors through various programmes.

2. Regular amendments and updates: SEBI should constantly amend the regulations relating to Mutual Funds thereby covering every aspect of the ever changing industry. The international scenario should also be considered at every step thereby making the regulations comprehensive and exhaustive.

3. To inculcate a culture of Self Regulation: Overregulation may be counter-productive, thus the fund houses and managers should inculcate self-regulation thereby emphasising the protection of investors interest. Educating fund managers in business ethics should be prioritised through the help of SROs like AMFI. It would help if AMFI plays a more proactive role in developing and monitoring mutual funds. AMCs should be more responsible in managing the corpus. To keep pace with the dynamic financial environment, self-regulation has to be an ongoing process.

4. Maintaining an environment of fair play: SEBI has already ensured a level playing field for all in the Mutual Funds Industry. However, regulatory framework to allow niche players to co-exist with players having a diversified product portfolio without raising requirements for minimum net worth. Regulations should be formulated to encourage and support more serious players in the market, who help bring in more investor awareness.

5. Increasing Transparency: Measures should be taken to increase transparency for mutual fund houses, particularly at the retail level. Disclosure requirements should hold consistently across all asset management companies in order to institutionalise greater transparency in the system. Information should be readily available and communicated effectively to investors, for them to take informed decisions. Measures should be initiated to avoid misselling of products, with guidelines communicated to all distributors, whether they are banks, distribution houses or IFAs.

6. Constituting a Steering Committee of Financial Services Regulators under the Ministry of Finance: The Government should constitute a Steering Committee under the aegis of the Ministry of Finance comprising the Financial Services Regulators for mutual funds and capital markets. PSUs should be allowed to invest larger surpluses in mutual funds. Acceptance and Rollout of the Unique Identification Card as a valid document for KYC should be encouraged.

7. Pricing Flexibility: Enable flexibility in regulations to allow customers to pay through varying arrangements based on the method of purchase, degree of service provided and the time frame for payment would encourage a lot of potential investors to benefit from mutual fund investments.

(b) Suggestions for the Mutual Fund Houses

1. Introduction of Customer-Friendly Products and Product Features: Focus on design of products around women, children, low income group and other specific category is the need of the day. This would attract Risk Averse Customers. Innovative products like Pension Funds, Theme based Funds and a wider variety of International Funds would attract potential investors. Encouraging the introduction of customised ETFs for retail and institutional customers would also help in the growth of the investor base. Acceptance and Rollout of the Unique Identification Card as a valid document for KYC would help the investors.

2. Increase in Mutual Fund Penetration through Customer Awareness campaigns: AMCs with support from CII, AMFI and NISMs should roll out customer awareness campaigns and provide infrastructure, content and speakers for running the campaigns on a pan-India basis. Social marketing firms and media companies should design effective and meaningful mass media campaigns in multiple languages using television, hoardings, flyers, street plays and other mechanisms to reach the masses. Creation of the 'Mutual Fund Education Fund'–a common corpus of funds from AMCs and distributors would be beneficial for training the distributors in handling well informed and intelligent investors.

3. Promoting Financial Planning Awareness in Educational Institutions: NISM should be the nodal agency and should work in a collaborative manner with AMCs, CII and AMFI by teaching faculty in schools and colleges across India. The India Post and public sector banks could promote customer awareness by using their infrastructure for conducting awareness programmes and campaigns. Investor associations, self help groups and other affinity groups should facilitate investor workshops in cities and towns across the country.

4. Focus on Increasing Customer Engagement Pre and Post Completion of the Investment: AMCs should focus on enhancing the marketing and advisory capabilities of all distributors so that they win the trust and confidence of customers. Quick and effective grievance redressal should be in place for improving investor confidence in funds. Special Advisory cell can be opened by the AMCs to assist customers in various aspects of investing.

5. Public Sector Thrust into Mutual Funds Distribution and Focus on Strengthening Presence beyond Tier 2 Cities: Training of the Public Sector Employee Base and opening up of the Public Sector Branch Network in Tier 3 and Tier 4 Towns would help in better distribution. Sale of mutual funds through the branch network of India Post, Nationalised Banks, Regional Rural Banks and Cooperative Banks would make mutual funds more accessible. Boosting the presence of Investor Service Centres (ISCs) through R&T Agents in Tier 2 and Tier 3 towns would go a long way in capturing the rural market which is still majorly neglected.

6. Separate Managers for each Fund: Mutual fund houses should allocate only one fund under a Fund Manager. If the fund manager focuses on only one scheme at a time he would be able to allocate the corpus better. However, as lucrative as it may sound, it may not be a very practical option for the Mutual Fund Houses.

7. Increased Transparency in Operations: SEBI has ensured a massive transparency in the operations of Mutual Fund Houses through strict disclosure requirements. This should be considered by the Mutual Fund Houses in the right spirit and they should adhere to this principle by communicating correct information to the investors at regular intervals.

8. Education of Fund Managers: The fund managers should be very well versed with the fluctuations in the financial markets including the influence of international factors. This would make them very cautious in selecting the portfolio thereby incorporating better market timing capability. In the recent global meltdown many fund managers have not been able to optimise their portfolio leading to a fall in the returns of many mutual fund schemes. This has lead to the fall in customer confidence in the managers. Thus, the fund managers should be extremely careful in their stock selection so that the investors' money and faith is well preserved. Fund managers may also discuss some portfolio diversification possibilities with the investors thereby increasing the investors' confidence in the manager.

(9) Advisory services to off-shore funds should be explored further as an area of revenue diversification. More could be done in this direction.

(c) Suggestions for the Investors

1. Investors should weigh their options carefully before investing in any mutual fund: In general before investing in a mutual fund, its performance over at least one complete business cycle should be considered. This period should include a recession or slowdown phase and a boom phase. The track record of the fund managers' efficiency in selecting stocks for the mutual fund portfolio should be considered before investing in mutual funds. Investors with a high risk return appetite should invest in Equity Diversified Open-Ended Mutual fund schemes; however, should carefully study the track record of the fund. The effect of Global Financial Markets and fluctuations in the financial and capital markets should be carefully considered before investing in Indian mutual funds. Mutual funds which invest overseas should be carefully studied before investing in them.

2. Investors should identify the appropriate investment vehicle for themselves: There are a variety of mutual funds available today, catering to the diverse needs of investors. Thus, the investor should also analyse these available funds to best meet their investment objectives. Investors should avoid over exposure to a single segment and should be more open to systematic investment plans. For example, a retiring investor should opt for pension funds. Younger investors can stay in for a longer time and maximise the risk thus, Gold ETFs are a good option as they eliminate counterparty risk and maintenance costs.

3. Having clearly defined objectives: The investor should be clear about what he wants from his investment in the mutual fund. A financial map should be prepared and thereby adhered to in order to reach that objective. Saving early in a regular and systematic way goes a long way towards meeting future financial goals.

4. Tracking the performance of the fund: The investors should constantly track the performance of the fund they have invested in. They should be aware of the returns so that they can sell the fund at the appropriate time. A proper benchmark should be considered appropriate for a particular fund and the performance should be compared with it over time. Investing when prices are low seem to be a good option as the fund would grow, mature and thereby generate better returns in future thereby leading to an increase in price. This would benefit the investor in the long run.

5. Long time investment: It is always better to stay invested for a considerable period of time as in spite of the market fluctuations, the volatility gets neutralised over a longer period of time and maximises the return. Investors should preferably avoid speculation.

6. Gilt Funds for risk averse investors: Gilt funds investing in government papers have medium to long-term maturity period and are less risky than the equity funds. Thus, these are appropriate for the risk averse investors.

7. Equity linked savings scheme for the salaried: As they invest in various companies, the risk factor is low. Tax benefit is also available. Thus, such schemes are suitable for salaried investors.

8. Avoid panicking: During this recent global meltdown a lot of mutual funds performed very badly. This made the investors lose faith in the funds. However, they should not panic in trying times as the markets would hopefully bounce back eventually and the same funds would again perform well. Thus, the investors should hold their investments through the fluctuating times for a longer period of time. This would ultimately reduce the risk and even out the returns at the end.

9. Investment through SIPs: Rather than investing, disinvesting and switching investments at a single point of time, it is prudent to spread the total investment in installments every month. This would average out the fluctuations in unit price of the scheme invested in by the final installment.

10. Disinvesting at the opportune moment: The investor should know when to sell out his investment. If he has invested in more than one MF scheme, then he should sell out the ones which have grown substantially, thereby making some profits out of the investment.

Conclusion

The Indian Mutual Fund Industry, though still in its early stages is growing at an astronomical pace. The growth in the number of young market savvy investors has helped in this development to a large extent. Though the rural areas have not been tapped completely, there is a huge scope for market penetration. With advanced technology and growing investor awareness the mutual fund industry will surely continue its great run in years to come. However, investors should always take proper caution before investing in mutual fund schemes as they are subject to market fluctuations. SEBI and other Government regulatory agencies have made the investment scenario extremely transparent, competitive and investor-friendly. Thus, a well-regulated financial market will further help in consolidating the investors' faith in mutual funds. In the global scenario, Indian Mutual Funds are at a very nascent stage. However, India is one of the fastest growing economies in the world and this growth phase will obviously help the overall financial markets, thereby mutual funds.

Investors should foray into this lucrative avenue of investing and see their money multiply in no time.

7

A Brief History of Global Mutual Funds

Despite being the number one way that many invest for the future, most people know little about the basic history behind mutual funds. Perhaps not as exciting as the birth of exchange traded funds (ETFs), mutual funds' history is exciting in its own right. Spanning several centuries and nations, the basic concepts behind mutual funds are as old as modern trade itself. The idea of pooling capital for investment purposes has been around for a very long time. The history of how mutual funds began and how many of the rudimentary concepts behind these pooled investments got their start are discussed here.

Eighteenth Century: "Unity Creates Strength"

To look at how mutual funds first began, we need to hop in the time machine and go all the way back to 1774. It was here in the Netherlands that the idea of pooling investment capital together in order to own assets was first created. Historians credit a Dutch merchant named Abraham van Ketwich with creating the first "mutual fund." Ketwich created a diversified pooled security specifically designed for citizens of modest means. The *negotiatie* was called Eendragt Maakt Magt, which translates to "unity creates strength," and owned bonds issued by foreign governments and plantation loans in the West Indies.

Ketwich followed up the *negotiatie* with several others, including one that lasted for more than 114 years before being dissolved. Various other merchants and traders in the Netherlands began offering similar vehicles to regular folk. In fact, during the 1780s, there were more than 30 *negotiaties* that owned United States credit issues alone.

Nineteenth Century: Spreading Across Europe

By the time the calendar rolled over to the Nineteenth century, Ketwich's idea had become a European phenomenon. The *negotiatie* had spread across almost the entire continent, especially in England and France. The English offered a few refinements to the structure and used it to help expand the British Empire. The *negotiatie* evolved into the investment trust, which is akin to modern closed-end funds. In 1868, the first "official" investment trust—the Foreign and Colonial Government Trust—was founded in London. Shares of the fund are still traded on the London Stock Exchange today.

From here, the investment trust structure flowed towards and into America. Formed in 1893, The Boston Personal Property Trust became America's first closed-end fund. Shortly after several others would launch, including the important Alexander Fund. This fund was critical in shaping the modern history of mutual funds as it allowed investors to make withdrawals on demand. That feature has many historians calling the Alexander fund the very first mutual fund.

Twentieth Century: The Start of "Real" Mutual Funds

The roaring '20s saw the introduction of the first official open-ended mutual fund. On March 21st, 1924, the Massachusetts Investors Trust (MITTX) was created. The key distinction of this fund was that open-ended mutual funds must buy back their shares from their investors at the end of every business day. The creation of MITTX essentially gave birth to mutual fund industry as we know it today.

The late '20s saw a flurry of mutual fund activity including some notable firsts. State Street launched its first fund, while Scudder, Stevens and Clark would launch the first no-load fund in 1928. Perhaps the biggest advancement would come from the creation of the Wellington Fund. Wellington—which is now part of Vanguard—was the first mutual fund to own stocks and bonds in one ticker. By the end of 1929, there were 19 open-ended mutual funds and roughly 700 closed-end funds in the US.

But all good things must come to an end. The stock market crash of 1929 and resulting Great Depression put the kibosh on the mutual fund industry. That is until the creation of the Securities and Exchange Commission (SEC), the passage of the Securities Act of 1933, and the enactment of the Securities Exchange Act of 1934. These events saw several important safeguards designed to protect investors put in place, including quarterly filings with the SEC as well as requiring that a prospectus be made available for investors.

Modern Times: Index Funds, IRAs and ETFs

The mutual fund industry really got cooking after World War II ended and America began to boom during the 1950s. By 1951, there were more than 100 mutual funds operating and more than 150 additional funds were created over the next two decades. The 1960s saw the birth of aggressive growth funds, which bet on high tech stocks, while the 1970s and 1980s saw some of the biggest contributions to mutual funds' history.

One of the biggest contributions was the creation of the index fund – a mutual fund that would hold all the stocks of a particular market measure. William Fouse and John McQuown of Wells Fargo established the first index fund in

1971. However, it was Vanguard's John Bogle who made it memorable back in 1974 by offering it to retail investors. The First Index Investment Trust—based on the S&P 500 Index—allowed Mom & Pop investors to own the entire market. The first money market fund—The Reserve Fund—debuted in 1971, while 1976 saw the first municipal bond launch. The 1990s saw the rise of the superstar fund manager, as people like Bill Miller and Peter Lynch became driving forces at the funds they managed.

Powering the expansion of mutual funds during this time had been the creation of various retirement and tax vehicles such as the IRA and 401(K) accounts. These accounts helped to replace traditional pensions at many companies. As such, money from investors of all sizes and walks of life poured directly into mutual funds.

Today, the evolution of mutual funds continues with the creation of the exchange traded fund (ETF). In 1993, Nathan Most developed a way for investors to trade index funds throughout the day. He dubbed his fund the Standard & Poor's Depository Receipts (SPDRs -pronounced spiders) and based it off the S&P 500 Index. The SPDR S&P 500 (SPY) kicked off the ETF revolution and is still one of the most successful funds.

With more than 14,000 mutual funds available to investors today, it just goes to show how successful the idea of pooling small amounts of capital to own stocks and bonds can be. Mutual funds continue to evolve and will continue to be a major backbone in how retail investors build wealth.

COMPARATIVE STUDY OF MUTUAL FUNDS OF DIFFERENT COUNTRIES

1. General Commonalities and Issues of Mutual Funds During the Late twentieth Century: One of the most interesting financial phenomena of the 1990s was the explosive growth of mutual funds. This was particularly true in the

United States where total net assets of mutual funds grew from USD 1.6 trillion in 1992 to 5.5 trillion in 1998, equivalent to an average annual rate of growth of 22.4 per cent. With the exception of some East Asian countries (including Japan), it was also true of most other countries around the world.

The 15 countries that are members of the European Union witnessed an increase in their total mutual fund assets from USD 1 trillion in 1992 to 2.6 trillion in 1998 (average annual growth rate of 17.7 per cent). Among EU member countries, Greece recorded the highest growth rate at 78 per cent, followed by Italy at 48 per cent and Belgium, Denmark, Finland and Ireland, all with growth rates of around 35 per cent. Some developing countries, such as, for example, Morocco, registered even higher growth rates, but from much smaller starting points.

In the United States, not only did mutual fund assets grow explosively over this period, but household ownership of mutual funds also experienced rapid growth. Survey estimates reported by the Investment Company Institute (the trade association of US mutual funds) show that the proportion of US households owning mutual funds grew from six per cent in 1980 to 27 per cent in 1992 and 44 per cent in 1998 (ICI, 2002).

The global growth of mutual funds was fuelled by the increasing globalisation of finance and expanding presence of large multinational financial groups in a large number of countries and by the strong performance of equity and bond markets throughout most of the 1990s. A third factor was probably the demographic aging that characterises the populations of most high and middle-income countries and the search of financial instruments that are safe and liquid but also promise high long-term returns by growing numbers of investors. It is also important to note that this growth occurred contemporaneously with a period of high growth in market capitalisations around the world, fueled in part by the technology/internet boom. For example, at the height of the bubble in March 2000, the market capitalisation of US publicly traded internet stocks was estimated to be US $1.3 trillion (as compared to a valuation of US $843 billion in June 2000). Over the period of our sample, 1991-1999, the market capitalisation in the US increased by over 300 per cent, from a base of 68 per cent of GDP to over 180 per cent of GDP. Although we suggest that many factors contributed to the global growth of mutual funds, the proportion of US households owning mutual funds continued to increase after 1998 and reached 52 per cent in 2001, before falling back slightly to 49.6 per cent in 2002 (ICI, 2002). The popular interest and visibility of equity market performance certainly helped contribute to the increased popularity of mutual fund products.

Seen as financial institutions that serve the needs of households, the growth of mutual funds is likely to be determined by a number of factors.

- First and foremost is the level of income and wealth of the residents of a country. Conceptually, investing in mutual funds, like purchasing life insurance and saving for retirement, should be seen as a luxury good with a positive income elasticity of demand. In practice, however, the relationship between per capita income (used as an indicator of economic development and wealth) and holdings of mutual fund assets (expressed as a percentage of national income) is not always positive.
- The availability or not of substitutes as well as complements also greatly affects the growth of mutual fund assets. Houses are distant substitutes of mutual fund shares in household wealth but most other instruments are either close substitutes or close complements, in some cases both at the same time. Bank deposits, both the traditional form of checking accounts and savings deposits and the more modern money market deposit accounts, are close substitutes

of money market mutual funds. The interest rate spread between bank deposits and money market funds would be expected to play an important part in determining the demand for money market mutual funds.

- The role of bonds, equities and contractual savings (savings with life insurance and pension funds) is more complex. At the level of individual investors, marketable securities are substitutes of mutual fund shares. Demand for mutual funds would depend on their cost-efficiency in offering portfolio diversification and professional management. But at the aggregate level, mutual fund shares and marketable securities look more like complements. As already noted, Mutual funds need well-developed markets for bonds and equities for their successful operation. Given the importance of complementarities between mutual funds and securities markets, indicators of investor confidence in market integrity, liquidity and efficiency tend to acquire major significance and to outweigh the impact of income and wealth.
- Contractual savings and mutual funds would also be expected to be substitutes, at least at the margin. However, the growing tendency of insurance companies and pension funds to offer products that are either directly linked to mutual funds or have many similar features has created increasing complementarities between the two types of instruments.
- The regulation of the investments of pension funds and insurance companies could also affect the growth of mutual funds. The impact of contractual savings institutions on mutual fund growth would be smaller in countries where they are compelled to invest in government bonds. In contrast, freedom to invest in

mutual funds or "funds of funds" would stimulate the development of the mutual fund industry.

- The demand for mutual funds would be expected to respond to differences in the level and volatility of real returns on mutual funds and alternative instruments. The challenge here lies in constructing good indicators of rates of return and their volatility and allowing for differences in the time horizons and responses of mutual fund investors. Return differentials are also affected by tax policies and financial regulation. In several countries, investing in mutual funds enjoys a significant tax incentive in the form of a rate of withholding tax that is lower than the marginal tax rate of wealthy investors. This often explains the strong demand for bond mutual funds in countries where securities markets are not well developed. In addition, demand for mutual funds may be distorted by indirect taxes (VAT or transaction taxes) that are imposed on other financial instruments or on transactions by other financial institutions but from which mutual funds are exempt. In Brazil, the exemption of mutual funds from the tax on financial transactions has been a major factor behind the creation of exclusive mutual funds for company pension funds that, in turn, has contributed to the rapid development of the Brazilian mutual fund industry.

- In several countries, including in particular the United States and France, the growth of money market mutual funds has been stimulated by the imposition of tight restrictions on the interest rate that banks could pay on retail deposits. Such Regulation Q-type restrictions tend to have a ratchet effect on the growth of mutual funds. Their removal does not result in a reversal of the process, because once money market mutual funds have taken hold, investors are unlikely to revert to their banks, unless the latter can offer some attractive service or benefit that mutual funds cannot match.

- A factor of major importance that would be of universal relevance and would explain the growth of mutual funds in many countries is the advent of electronic technology and the concomitant large reduction in the cost of operating a large number of accounts and an even larger volume of transactions. This has made mutual funds, especially money market funds, more competitive vis-à-vis banks.

- A final factor that may affect the growth of mutual funds in a particular country is the "proximity" of a better developed or tax advantaged overseas centre offering mutual fund investments to foreign investors. The countries with large offshore business, such as Luxembourg, Ireland and Switzerland in Europe or Hong Kong and Singapore in Asia, have a negative effect on the growth of mutual funds in their neighbouring countries. However, it is difficult to estimate the impact of such proximity since this depends not only on geographical distance but also on cultural and other factors. For instance, the large presence of German banks in Luxembourg is likely to have a bigger restraining impact on the growth of mutual funds in Germany compared to other neighbouring European countries. When combined with an unfriendly regulatory regime (as was the case in Germany before the 1990s), the negative impact can be very large as well as difficult to reverse after domestic regulations are relaxed.

- Mutual funds are more advanced in countries with better developed capital markets (reflecting investor confidence in market integrity, liquidity and efficiency and a greater supply of investable securities) and market-based financial systems. Higher market returns and liquidity and lower volatility have also contributed to mutual fund growth.

- Openness to trade and a high share of high-tech exports are significant factors in high income countries, while per capita income and strong banking systems are related to mutual fund development in middle-income countries. Legal origin is significantly correlated with mutual fund development. Equity funds are more advanced in common law countries, while bond funds are more developed in countries with civil law systems.
- Restrictions on competing products, namely limits on interest rates on sight and retail time deposits of banks, have been a significant determinant of the growth of money market and (short-term) bond mutual funds. Such restrictions have probably played the role of catalyst in many countries and have had a ratchet effect. Their removal has not reversed mutual fund progress.

Structure and Growth Patterns

The first mutual funds in the form of closed-end investment trusts appeared during the last quarter of the nineteenth century. The first open-end mutual fund was created in Boston in 1924. Mutual funds of both the closed and open-end varieties experienced hectic growth in the 1920s, but they suffered a major setback from mismanagement and fraud as well as from the stock market crash of 1929. Between 1930 and 1970 mutual funds grew relatively little, although there was an upsurge of interest in equity funds during the stock market boom of the early and mid 1960s. However, this was reversed in the 1970s following the first oil crisis and the poor performance of equity markets. The collapse of International Overseas Services, a fraudulent fund management group, in the late 1960s contributed to the loss of investor confidence in mutual funds.

A major product innovation occurred in the 1970s with the launching of money market mutual funds. These specialised in investing in money market instruments and competed with banks by offering market-related returns and lower spread than traditional bank deposits, while ensuring liquidity and ease of access. Money market mutual funds were launched in the United States in the 1970s in response to the regulatory restrictions that prohibited US banks from paying market rates of interest on their retail deposits at a time when high inflation was pushing market rates to very high levels compared to the ceilings imposed on banks. They also achieved high levels of development in other countries with rigid restrictions on bank deposit rates, such as France, Greece and Japan. But even in the absence of regulatory distortions, money market mutual funds, once invented, tend to grow to meet the demand from sophisticated investors who need a convenient place for parking their liquid investment balances.

Growth of equity and bond funds resumed in the early 1980s as macroeconomic performance and equity markets started to improve. But growth did not become explosive until the early 1990s. It is still unclear why investors started to change their financial asset allocations so drastically after 1990. In the United States, the widening of bank spreads as commercial banks attempted to rebuild their capital following their disastrous results of the late 1980s may have provided an early stimulus to equity funds. As the gap between returns on bank deposits and returns on equity funds widened considerably, investors showed an increasing preference for equity funds.

In the United States, the increased demand for mutual funds reflected a broader pickup in demand for financial assets, buoyed by rising equity prices, low and stable interest rates, and subdued inflation. The expansion of retirement savings plans, both the employer sponsored 401(k) plans and individual retirement accounts (IRAs), provided additional stimulus.

Assets of retirement savings plans invested in mutual funds rose from one-fifth of all fund assets in the early

1990s to more than one-third by the end of the decade. The response of the industry, both by expanding the number and variety of mutual funds and by lowering the cost of acquiring and holding mutual funds, was another contributing factor.

In Europe and other regions, the growth of equity funds lagged somewhat behind, both because equity markets were less well established outside Anglo-American countries and because the operating costs of mutual funds continued to be relatively high. But bond funds experienced steady growth as governments favoured the development of long-term bond markets and provided incentives for investments in mutual funds.

Anglo-American countries, where mutual funds were already well developed in the early 1990s, registered growth rates of between 20 and 30 per cent per year in the late nineties. In Europe, some countries, such as Greece and Italy, experienced very rapid growth, while others, most notably France, recorded low growth. Among middle-income countries, Morocco, Argentina, Hungary and Tunisia achieved very high growth from low starting points. Except for Hungary, where mutual funds are increasingly integrated into the European market, the experience of mutual funds in the other three countries has suffered in later years.

The United States is in a class of its own in the development of mutual funds. Following their spectacular growth in the 1990s mutual fund assets rose from the equivalent of 26 per cent of GDP in 1992 to 65 per cent in 1998. Only in Hong Kong (China) do mutual funds come anywhere near this level, having grown from 16 per cent of GDP in 1992 to 52 per cent in 1998. In Canada and several European countries (Spain, France, Italy and Austria) mutual fund assets correspond to between 30 and 40 per cent of GDP. Several European countries, including Belgium, Greece, the Netherlands, Portugal, Switzerland, Sweden and the

United Kingdom, have mutual fund assets ranging between 20 and 30 per cent of GDP.

In continental Europe, Denmark, Finland, Germany and Norway continue to have relatively underdeveloped mutual fund sectors. In the case of Germany, this is partly offset by two factors: the strong presence of closed-end funds and the use of mutual funds based in Luxembourg by many German investors, mostly for tax reasons. The effect of Luxembourg on the size of German mutual funds is likely to be much greater than on mutual funds in other European countries because of the prominent role played by leading German banks in the Luxembourg market.

An interesting feature of the European market is the growing strength of mutual funds in several countries with unfunded social security systems (Austria, Belgium, France, Greece, Italy, Portugal and Spain). Some of these countries have also experienced strong growth of their life insurance industries. For instance, French life insurance assets exceeded 55 per cent of GDP in 1997, a level that is much higher than in Canada, Germany or the United States and close to the levels prevailing in the Netherlands, Switzerland and the United Kingdom. This provides indirect evidence that the saving public is responding to various tax incentives to accumulate long-term savings as a defense against the likely future inability of their national social security systems to honour promised benefits in full.

Among Anglo-American countries, which generally have well-developed securities markets and common law traditions, Australia, New Zealand and South Africa are notable for their relatively underdeveloped mutual fund industries with total assets around 10 per cent of GDP. However, in all three countries mutual funds experienced considerable growth during the 1990s. The presence of a well-developed contractual savings industry in South Africa and the continuing credibility of tax-financed universal pensions in Australia and New Zealand are clearly relevant factors. As already noted, inclusion of the compulsory pension funds, which are mostly based on DC plans, causes a very large increase in the reported Australian statistics.

In East Asia, the experience of Japan is worth noting. Since the collapse of the Tokyo stock market in 1990, the mutual fund industry has stagnated. Total assets under management declined in relation to GDP from nine to eight per cent. Mutual funds were better developed in Korea at the beginning of the decade with assets corresponding to 28 per cent of GDP. They subsequently rose further to 32 per cent of GDP by 1994 but suffered a major setback in the aftermath of the East Asian financial crisis of 1997 when they fell to less than 20 per cent of GDP.

Mutual funds in Malaysia grew aggressively in the first half of the 1990s, rising from 10 to 24 per cent of GDP but plummeted to nine per cent of GDP in 1997. Among other middle-income countries Brazil has the most developed mutual fund sector with assets corresponding to over 13 per cent of GDP. In most other developing countries mutual fund assets are close to, or lower than, five per cent of GDP. Like Korea and Malaysia, mutual funds in Mexico fell in 1994 in the aftermath of the Tequila crisis. In several developing countries, including Argentina, Chile, Morocco and Tunisia, mutual funds grew at spectacular rates, although from non-existent bases.

Countries vary considerably in the structure of their mutual fund industries

- Five countries are characterised by a predominance of equity funds. Using average data for the period 1992-98, the United Kingdom (89 per cent) and South Africa (79 per cent) show the highest allocation to equity funds, most probably a result of the response of investors to the high levels of inflation of the 1970s and early 1980s. Even though inflation declined to low or moderate levels in the 1990s, a ratchet effect may be at play. Once investors switch into equity funds, they are unlikely to return to bond funds as long as equity returns are higher in real terms and their volatility is not intolerably high. Sweden (74), Hong Kong (66) and Switzerland (63) are the other three countries where equity funds represent more than 60 per cent of the total assets of mutual funds.

- There are then several countries where equity funds represent between 40 and 60 per cent of the total. These include Thailand (59), Denmark (52), Norway (49), Canada (48), the Netherlands (46), the United States (44) and Finland (42). The low relative level of equity funds in the United States does not represent a weakness of US equity funds or markets, but rather a relatively strong presence of other types of funds, including in particular money market mutual funds.
- Balanced funds, which invest in both equities and debt instruments, may distort the relevance of these ratios. While in most countries (e.g. Morocco, India, the Czech Republic, Tunisia and several continental European countries) balanced funds are heavily invested in bonds, in a number of countries they may be more "balanced" or even "tilted" in favour of equities. This is likely to be the case in Australia, Ireland and New Zealand, partly explaining why equity funds in these Anglo-American countries represent less than 40 per cent of total mutual fund assets.
- In the majority of countries in continental Europe, Eastern Europe, Latin America, Asia, and the Middle East and North Africa mutual fund investors show a strong preference for fixed income funds, either long-term bonds or short-term money market instruments. In several developing and transition countries, bond instruments have short maturities and thus there is

practically little difference between bond and money market funds. However, in the countries of Southern Europe (France, Greece, Italy, Spain and Portugal) as well as Australia, Japan, Norway and the United States, the strong relative presence of money market mutual funds is notable. This seems to be connected with the imposition of restrictive regulations on the payment of interest on checking accounts and other short-term bank deposits that all these countries have imposed for prolonged periods. Even though such regulations (like the infamous regulation Q in the United States) have been withdrawn over time, once established money market mutual funds have continued to thrive.

- The strong presence of fixed income funds (and corresponding weakness of equity funds) in Latin American and Eastern European countries that have reformed their social security and pension systems (e.g. Argentina, Chile, Hungary, and Poland) has important implications for the regulation of asset allocations by the pension funds. Arguments that absent restrictive investment regulations, pension funds would place a higher proportion of their assets in equities are not supported by the experience of mutual funds, which are free from such investment restrictions. In fact, given the strong preference of the investing public for fixed income instruments and the structural weaknesses of local equity markets, it is likely that without any investment rules, pension funds would have invested an even smaller proportion of their assets in corporate equities.
- Equity funds are very large in Hong Kong and the United States, where they exceed 30 per cent of GDP. In the United States, equity funds reflect the strong preference of the investing public for corporate equities, although this may weaken after the price reversals

suffered by equity markets in the past couple of years. The net assets of equity funds ranged between 10 and 20 per cent of GDP in a small number of countries, including Belgium, Canada, Netherlands, Sweden, Switzerland and the United Kingdom. In most of Continental Europe equity funds were underdeveloped in 1998, although they were growing rapidly in France, Italy and Spain.

- Equity funds have a very small presence in most middle-income countries, even in Brazil and Chile where the equity markets are relatively well developed. This may be explained by a combination of factors: lack of confidence in the integrity of local markets; low risk tolerance of investors; and use of overseas mutual funds by wealthier and more sophisticated investors. The low level of equity funds in Australia and New Zealand may also be explained by the ready access that residents of these countries have to overseas mutual funds, operating in offshore centres, such as Hong Kong and Singapore as well as the United States and the United Kingdom.

- Bond funds are well developed in a number of Continental European countries, such as Austria, France and Italy where government bond markets are large. They are also well established in the United States, which has large government, corporate and mortgage bond markets, and Brazil. Outside these countries, bond funds have a relatively strong presence in Denmark, Greece, Hong Kong, Portugal and Switzerland. They are notably weak in most Anglo-American countries.

- Balanced funds control a large share of the mutual fund sector in several countries. In the Czech Republic, India, Ireland, Morocco and Poland they have close to or over 50 per cent of the total. In Belgium, Israel, New Zealand and Tunisia their share ranges between

25 and 40 per cent. However, in relation to national income, balanced funds are relatively large in only a few countries, including Austria, Belgium, Canada, France, Hong Kong (China), Ireland and Spain. In these countries the total assets of balanced funds correspond to between 5 and 10 per cent of GDP. Balanced funds invest heavily in bonds in some countries (notably the Czech Republic, Morocco and Tunisia); while in others they adopt more diversified investment strategies.

- Money market mutual funds have grown impressively in France, Greece, Spain and the United States. The total assets of money market mutual funds represent close to or more than 10 per cent of GDP in these countries. There are some countries (e.g. Australia and Japan) where money market mutual funds have a significant share of over 25 per cent of the mutual fund sector but their total assets are not large in relation to national income.
- The insignificant growth of money market mutual funds in the United Kingdom is notable. UK banks and building societies have been free from restrictions on the payment of interest on sight and retail time deposits. Despite the prevalence of securities markets and the active trading needs of investors and market participants, neither institutional nor retail investors have shown a preference for parking their liquid funds in money market mutual funds. This seems to be in sharp contrast to the prevailing pattern in the United States.

During the 1990s, mutual funds grew explosively in most countries and regions around the world. In high-income countries, mutual fund assets expanded from 10 to 24 per cent of GDP over this period and in middle-income countries they first grew from four to eight per cent but then fell back to four per cent of GDP after the East Asian crisis. This reversal was mostly caused by the experience of Asian countries. In general, mutual funds are more advanced in countries with better developed and more stable capital markets (reflecting investor confidence in market integrity, liquidity and profitability and a greater supply of investable securities). Equity funds dominate in Anglo-American countries and bond funds in most of Continental Europe and in middle-income countries. In developed countries, investors are concerned with market microstructure; for example, equity funds are significantly smaller in countries with higher market volatility and weaker accounting standards. In comparison, in developing countries macroeconomic factor appear most important; for example, bond fund development in developing countries is significantly related to higher GDP per capita and lower interest rates. However, in both developed and developing countries, lower country risk and higher investor confidence leads to greater fund development. In addition, restrictions on competing savings products may have acted as a catalyst for the development of money market and (short-term) bond funds.

2. MUTUAL FUNDS IN UNITED STATES OF AMERICA

Mutual funds have become an important intermediary between households and financial markets, particularly the equity market. By providing liquid, low cost shares in a diversified portfolio of financial assets selected by professional money managers, mutual funds have enabled an increasing number of households to enter financial markets. Indeed, about half of all US households currently own shares in a mutual fund.

Since 1990, total mutual fund assets have increased nearly seven-fold, and the assets of mutual funds that invest in stocks have grown even more, expanding nearly twenty-fold. Over the same period, mutual fund assets have come to account for a larger share of household wealth. Moreover, a greater proportion of US households now own stock, in large part because of their investments in mutual funds. Much of this growth has come in households' retirement assets, as developments in pension plans and other tax preferred retirement accounts have increasingly made it possible for households to control more of their retirement asset portfolios—and households have tended to invest a significant portion of their retirement assets in mutual funds.

As the popularity of mutual funds as an investment vehicle has grown, so too has their importance in financial markets. Mutual funds currently hold about one-fifth of publicly traded US corporate equities. Thus, the investment behaviour of mutual fund shareholders could, in theory, influence equity market prices. For example, if fund shareholders were to request large redemptions from their accounts when faced with a sharp decline in equity prices, mutual fund managers might be forced to sell some of the funds' equity holdings in the slumping market, exacerbating the decline. In recent years, however, mutual fund shareholders as a group have not tended to flee from their equity investments when confronted with sharp temporary drops in equity prices. Indeed, there is some evidence that shareholder restraint in requesting redemptions has been greater recently than during earlier periods of market turbulence. Mutual fund investors could also distort equity prices if their enthusiasm for investing in mutual funds were to go beyond general market assessments of fundamentals and tolerance for risk, pushing equity prices temporarily above the level that other equity market participants would tend to settle on. We present evidence, however, indicating that mutual fund investors, like other market investors, have been trading primarily in response to new information and other factors that influence the value of stocks. Thus, in general, we find little evidence that mutual fund investors have been a destabilising force in the US equity market in recent years.

GROWTH OF MUTUAL FUND ASSETS

Millions of dollars, 2007–2014[2]								
		Equity			*Bond*			
	Total	*Total*	*Domestic*	*Global/ International*	*Total*	*Domestic taxable*	*Domestic municipal*	*Global/ International*
2007	$28,369	$24,608	$4,949	$19,659	$3,761	$1,966	-$880	$2,675
2008	-22,298	-8,739	-7,052	-1,687	-13,560	-6,770	-6,089	-700
2009	-3,259	-2,520	-2,366	-154	-739	-788	-238	287
2010	5,430	2,054	1,995	59	3,376	1,900	1,119	357
2011	6,018	4,466	3,206	1,260	1,551	724	825	2
2012	11,315	2,953	2,840	113	8,362	3,249	3,032	2,081
2013	13,742	3,554	4,097	-543	10,188	3,921	-155	6,423
2014	4,766	4,339	3,844	494	427	105	533	-212

Assets under management at mutual funds have grown substantially over the past fifteen years. At the end of August 2000, mutual funds held about $71D2 trillion in assets, making them the largest type of financial institution (as measured by assets under management), even larger than commercial banks. Most of the recent growth has come in assets invested in *equity mutual funds*, that is, mutual funds that specialise in investing in the shares of publicly traded firms. At the end of August 2000, equity funds held more than 60 per cent of all mutual fund assets, or more than $41D2 trillion.

The next largest group—*money market mutual funds*, which invest in very short-term liquid assets such as commercial paper and Treasury bills—held less than $2 trillion in assets. *Bond funds*—which invest in corporate, treasury, government agency, and foreign bonds—and *hybrid funds*—which invest in a mix of stocks and bonds—held about $1 trillion in assets combined.

Mutual funds that invest primarily in the shares of corporations based in the United States are by far the largest type of equity mutual fund. These *domestic equity funds* hold more than 85 per cent of the assets of all equity mutual funds. *International equity funds,* which invest primarily in the shares of non-US companies, account for the remainder. In 1999, 81 per cent of total mutual fund assets were held by households.

The remainder were held by institutional investors—businesses, fiduciaries, and other organisations. Institutional investors are much more likely to invest in money market funds than in long-term funds (equity, hybrid, and bond) and at the end of August 2000 held less than 10 per cent of the assets of equity funds. Thus, almost all mutual fund assets invested in the equity market are owned by households.

Mutual fund assets grow because investors, on net, decide to put more of their financial assets into mutual funds or because the underlying financial securities held by the funds increase in value, or a combination of these two factors. Over the 1990s, total mutual fund assets grew at an annual rate of more than 21 per cent. More than half the growth came from fund performance, that is, from the net appreciation in value of the securities held in the funds and from the reinvestment of dividends and interest earned by the securities held in the funds. Mutual fund performance has been robust in recent years, primarily because equity funds have benefited from the stock market boom. Net new cash flows accounted for 40 per cent of mutual fund asset growth over the 1990s.

Recently, average monthly net new cash flows into mutual funds have been dominated by flows into equity funds. Since 1994, net new cash flows from households into equity funds have greatly outpaced those into all other types of mutual funds.

Modern mutual funds were introduced in 1924. Equity funds were the most popular type of fund until 1979, when the assets of money market funds surpassed those of equity funds. Money market funds dominated equity funds throughout the 1980s, and by 1985, bond fund assets had also grown beyond those of equity funds. It was not until 1993 that equity funds regained their current position as the largest type of mutual fund.

In contrast, approximately 40 per cent of money market fund assets are held in institutional accounts, with the remainder in retail accounts. The share of money market fund assets held by institutional shareholders has increased greatly in recent years, as many businesses and other organisations have decided that having their liquid assets managed by mutual funds is more cost-effective than managing them internally.

The Asian financial crisis and the Russian debt default prompted a "flight to safety" in 1998, and mutual fund investors reduced their investments in stocks and increased their investments in lower-risk money funds and short-term bond funds. That episode proved to be only temporary, and mutual fund investors returned vigorously to equity funds, increasing the pace of net new cash flows into those funds to a record level over the first eight months of 2000. Over the same period, however, households were, on balance, net sellers of directly held equities. Thus, at least part of the cash flows into equity mutual funds may represent a shift in household preferences toward holding a smaller portion of their equity portfolio in directly held stocks and a larger portion in indirect holdings via equity funds.

In recent years, the flow of net new investment into equity funds has been greatest for domestic equity funds, with a much smaller flow going into international equity funds. From 1996 to 1998, net new investment in domestic equity funds was split fairly evenly between *capital appreciation funds*—which hold stocks whose return is mainly from capital gains—and *total return funds*—which hold stocks that return a mix of capital gains and dividend income. In 1999, however, the pace of net new flows into capital appreciation funds picked up substantially relative to both the pace of the preceding few years and the pace of flows into total return funds, which fell off appreciably. Through August, net new flows into capital appreciation funds in 2000 were at a pace more than twice that of 1999, whereas total return funds experienced net outflows. Over the same period in which the composition of equity fund flows was shifting, the relative share prices of technology firms were booming. From late 1998 until mid-2000, the six-month moving average of increases in the Nasdaq composite index, which is dominated by technology firms, was markedly greater than the increases in the Wilshire 5000 index of the total stock market. Capital appreciation equity funds are more likely than total return equity funds to hold the shares of technology companies.

Thus, households were directing more of their net new investment into capital appreciation funds, which hold a greater share of their portfolio in technology stocks, at the same time the share prices of technology firms were generally outperforming the share prices of other publicly traded firms.

The volatility of equity prices has also increased recently. Greater equity price volatility, everything else constant, might be expected to temper risk-averse households' appetite for equity mutual funds. However, not only did domestic equity fund flows accelerate through August 2000, but they were increasingly targeted toward relatively riskier capital appreciation funds. Taken together, these developments might suggest that there is a relationship between equity fund flows.

From 1995 to 1999, households, on net, sold an average of about $329 billion worth of directly held corporate equities annually. In the first half of 2000, households sold, on net, $513 billion of directly held corporate equities, at an annual rate.

Indirect equity holdings include holdings through mutual funds and also through employer-sponsored defined contribution accounts, personal trust accounts, and annuity accounts at life insurance companies.

MUTUAL FUNDS AND HOUSEHOLD ASSETS

The share of households' financial assets kept in mutual funds roughly doubled over the past decade, approaching 20 per cent at the end of 1999; nearly all the increase was in long-term funds. Domestic equity funds accounted for most of the increase in long-term funds, both because their assets appreciated at a greater rate than most other financial assets and because they became the preferred type of fund for new mutual fund investments. Net additions to household wealth, as measured by the US personal saving rate, have declined dramatically over the past fifteen years, even as the popularity of mutual fund investing has grown. As a result, the share of household saving done through mutual funds has been rising. The share of *gross financial saving*—households' acquisition of financial assets, net of capital gains—allocated to mutual funds rose from about 15 per cent in 1985 to about 70 per cent in 1999. If this trend continues, mutual funds will represent an increasing share of households' financial assets over time, even if the performance of mutual funds is equivalent to that of households' other financial assets. Mutual funds' share of aggregate household financial assets has grown in part because an increasing percentage of US households are investing in mutual funds. In June 2000, an estimated 50 million households, or about half of all US households, owned shares in at least one mutual fund.

After averaging around nine per cent from 1950 through 1985, the US personal savings rate has fallen to lower than 1D2 per cent in 2000. The Federal Reserve Board's flow of funds accounts calculate personal saving in several ways. One measure is households' net acquisition of financial and housing assets less their increase in liabilities. Gross financial saving, which excludes the acquisition of housing assets and liabilities, is the component of this measure of personal saving that is most relevant to households' mutual fund decisions.

In 1984, fewer than 12 per cent of all US households owned shares in a mutual fund; by 1992, the proportion had grown to 27 per cent.

Higher-income households are more likely than lower-income households to have financial assets, and they have greater financial asset holdings. Thus, they are also more likely to own mutual fund shares. Nevertheless, mutual funds provide access to financial markets for households at all income levels. Indeed, almost 40 per cent of mutual fund shareholders have an annual household income of less than $50,000. Investors who have relatively low levels of income and financial assets generally find investing directly in stocks and bonds more difficult because of high minimum investment requirements and higher fees for small investments.

The likelihood of owning shares in a mutual fund peaks between the ages of 45 and 54, when most heads of household are working, and declines at later ages, when a greater proportion have retired. This pattern may reflect, at least in part, the importance of mutual funds for retirement saving. Because relatively widespread acceptance of mutual funds as an investment option is still a rather recent phenomenon, this pattern may also reflect generational factors. Younger generations, which have grown up with a well-established mutual fund industry, may be more willing to invest in these funds than older generations, which grew up less familiar with market investments and more likely to rely on bank deposits and insurance contracts.

Equity funds are the most popular type of mutual fund, with more than one-third of all US households owning shares in such a fund. Indeed, for each income and age group, more households invest in equity funds than in hybrid, bond, or money market funds.

The percentage of households that directly or indirectly own stock in publicly traded companies increased dramatically over the past decade, rising from less than one-third of all households in 1989 across all but the highest income levels, households are more likely to own stock indirectly and in retirement accounts than directly outside of retirement accounts. In 1998, only 19 per cent of households owned stock directly outside of a retirement account whereas 30 per cent owned stock indirectly (often through a mutual fund) or in a retirement account. For many households, retirement accounts are an important point of access to the equity market; 49 per cent of all households owned some type of retirement account in 1998, up from 35 per cent in 1989.

MUTUAL FUNDS AND RETIREMENT ASSETS

Over the past two decades, the growth of individual retirement accounts (IRAs) and a shift from defined benefit to defined contribution pension plans have given households considerably more control over the portfolio allocation of their retirement assets. At the same time, mutual funds have become an increasingly important component of households' retirement accounts. IRAs generally feature tax-deductible annual contributions and tax-free accrual of investment earnings. Once the account holder reaches age 59, 1D2, assets withdrawn from the IRA are taxed as ordinary income; in addition, a tax penalty is usually imposed on assets withdrawn before that age. Traditional IRAs were established in 1974, but because they were available only to workers not covered by an employer-provided pension, they were not common. In 1981, eligibility was extended to all workers and the annual tax-deductible contribution limits were increased. IRAs subsequently became quite popular. The Tax Reform Act of 1986 retained universal eligibility and the tax-free accrual of investment earnings for IRAs but restricted the tax deductibility of contributions for higher-income households that were covered by an employer-provided pension plan; subsequently, annual contributions to traditional IRAs dropped substantially. Legislation enacted in 1997 introduced Roth IRAs, which permit non-tax deductible contributions. All distributions from these accounts are untaxed, assuming that certain early withdrawal restrictions are not violated. Roth IRAs have renewed investor interest in IRAs. Several types of employer-sponsored IRAs are available to self-employed individuals and employees of small businesses; they are similar to tax-deductible traditional IRAs but typically have higher contribution limits.

IRA ownership has grown considerably over the two decades since the accounts became universally available. In June 2000, 41 per cent of all US households owned at least one type of IRA. Of those households that owned an IRA, 78 per cent held a traditional IRA, 24 per cent a Roth IRA, and 17 per cent an employer-sponsored IRA. As ownership was growing, mutual funds were becoming an increasingly important institution for the management of IRA assets, holding almost half of those assets in 1999.

Households have also gained greater control over the investment of their pension assets. Employer sponsored pension plans have increasingly shifted away from traditional defined benefit plans, which plan assets are invested, toward defined contribution plans, which usually give employees considerable discretion in the investment of those assets. In 1980, defined benefit plans held more than 70 per cent of the assets in all private pension funds. As defined contribution plans became more popular, their assets grew, so that they now hold 55 per cent of all private pension assets. This shift in private pension assets has been important to mutual funds because defined contribution plans are much more likely to use mutual funds to manage their assets. The percentage of working households (that is, households with at least one employed adult) that are covered by a pension and have a defined contribution plan has also risen. In 1989, 40 per cent of working households with a pension were covered by only a defined benefit plan, and another 31 per cent were covered by both a defined benefit and a defined contribution plan; only 30 per cent were covered solely by a defined contribution plan. By 1998, 57 per cent of working households with pension coverage had only a defined contribution plan, and another 25 per cent were covered by both types of plans; only 18 per cent were covered solely by a defined benefit plan. As defined contribution plans became more common, the percentage that were 401(k) plans rose, reaching 78 per cent in 1998, making them the most popular type of plan.

Like IRAs, 401(k) plans feature tax-deductible contributions, tax-free accrual of investment returns, annual contribution limits, and restrictions on withdrawals. Employees who separate from a firm sponsoring a plan before retirement age must pay income taxes on the withdrawn funds at ordinary rates; in addition, they also face a tax penalty unless they roll the funds over into an IRA or another 401(k) account.

Unlike IRAs, 401(k) plans are available only to employees of firms that choose to sponsor the plans. Employers may also make tax-deductible contributions to employees' accounts, and total contribution limits are generally higher for 401(k) plans than for IRAs. Also, employers select the investment options available in 401(k) plans; as a result, the number of options is typically more limited than in an IRA. In 1998, the typical 401(k) plan offered six to nine investment options. These options usually included equity, bond, and money market funds. More than 70 per cent of the plans offered an equity fund option, making it the most popular option offered by sponsoring employers.

Total retirement assets increased three-fold over the past decade, to almost $13 trillion in 1999.

Mutual funds have played an increasingly important role in this growth, accounting for almost one-fifth of total retirement assets in 1999. Moreover, retirement assets held within mutual funds have risen significantly relative to total mutual fund assets, accounting for 35 per cent of total fund assets in 1999. Households have chosen to allocate the bulk of the retirement assets they hold in mutual funds to equities, thus bolstering the total share of mutual fund assets allocated to equity funds.

In 1999, 73 per cent of mutual fund IRA assets and 81 per cent of mutual fund defined contribution pension plan assets were invested in equity funds. Retirement account assets in mutual funds are much more likely than non-retirement-account assets in mutual funds to be devoted to equity investments. The growing role of retirement assets in households' equity mutual fund holdings might be expected to affect mutual fund shareholders' investment behaviour.

One reason is that households take a longer term perspective with the funds they have invested in retirement accounts. In this view, these households would be less likely to trade frequently and, in particular, less likely to redeem their equity fund shares in response to temporary stock-price declines.

Another approach is that households switch more frequently between equity funds and money market or bond funds because the earnings in retirement accounts, including capital gains, are not taxed. In this view, households with equity funds in retirement accounts would be more likely to trade frequently and, in particular, more likely to redeem their equity fund shares in response to stock-price declines.

MUTUAL FUNDS AND FINANCIAL MARKETS

Mutual funds hold about 20 per cent of the publicly traded stocks of US corporations. This proportion not only is much greater than it was a decade ago, but it also is larger than the proportion of the bond market held by mutual funds. The growing importance of mutual funds in the US equity market increases the possibility that households' decisions to invest new cash in, or request redemptions from, equity mutual funds significantly affect equity prices. This possibility can be evaluated by looking at the relationship between domestic equity fund flows and equity prices. Net new flows into domestic equity funds as a percentage of the value of the US stock market have tended to increase over the past fifteen years. The monthly per cent change in the Wilshire 5000 index of stock prices over the same period shows that while equity fund flows were becoming more stable, equity prices were becoming more volatile. A related development is that the response of mutual fund investors to large market declines—specifically, the equity price declines in October 1987, August 1990, and August 1998—has become progressively smaller. In October 1987, when the Wilshire index fell more than 20 per cent (the worst monthly performance for the stock market since World War II), domestic equity funds experienced net outflows of more than $6 billion. This outflow amounted to 0.2 per cent of the total value of the stock market, or just fewer than three per cent of domestic equity fund assets; this was the largest monthly outflow as a percentage of fund assets to date. Indeed, domestic equity funds experienced outflows in fourteen of the sixteen months following the October crash, outflows that summed to a net total of more than $18 billion. All told, mutual fund shareholders withdrew more than 11 per cent of domestic equity fund assets in the aftermath of the October 1987 episode. The next large decline in stock prices occurred in August 1990, when the Wilshire index fell about 10 per cent in the wake of concerns about the Gulf War in Kuwait and Iraq. In that month, mutual fund shareholders withdrew about $21D2 billion from domestic equity funds, which amounted to less than 0.1 per cent of the value of the stock market, or about one per cent of domestic equity fund assets. Outflows from August through September 1990 were only $3 billion, or a little more than one per cent of fund assets. Although the Wilshire index fell half as far in August 1990 as it had in October 1987, fund withdrawals during the 1990 episode were less than half those during the 1987 episode.

Domestic equity funds did not experience a net monthly outflow again until August 1998, when the Wilshire index declined 15 per cent in the midst of the Asian financial market crisis and Russian bond defaults. Shareholders in domestic equity funds requested net redemptions of about $61D2 billion in that month, an amount equal to about 0.3 per cent of total domestic equity fund assets. Domestic equity fund inflows resumed the following month. Thus, redemptions in August 1998 were substantially smaller, as a percentage of assets, than those in August 1990, even though the stock price decline in 1998 was greater.

Although investors have withdrawn money from domestic equity funds during severe market declines, mutual fund managers have not necessarily had to sell stocks immediately to cover redemptions. In addition to holding stocks, equity funds also hold safe, liquid money market assets, usually referred to as "cash." The proportion of a mutual fund's total assets held in cash is known as the *cash ratio*. To the extent that net outflows can be met by cash on hand, they need not translate into forced sales of equities by fund managers. The asset-weighted mean cash ratio for all domestic equity funds has generally been trending down and recently stood a little above four per cent. Despite the decline, funds have had, on average, more than enough cash on hand to cover monthly redemptions throughout the past fifteen years. Moreover, the frequency and magnitude of net redemptions from equity funds, as a percentage of assets, have diminished over time.

A fund's cash holdings are not its only means of meeting a short-term episode of redemptions without selling some of its equity portfolio. Many families of mutual funds now have committed lines of credit to help meet unexpectedly large temporary outflows. Also, some large fund families have been allowed by the Securities and Exchange Commission to borrow between funds. Thus, an outflow from an equity fund, for example, could be covered by borrowing at a fair market rate from another fund in the family that is receiving inflows—say, a bond or money fund.

Credit lines and fund-family borrowing agreements can serve as additional buffers that, along with those traditionally provided by funds' liquid assets, help equity fund managers avoid having to sell equities in a slumping market. However, temporary periods of sharp equity price declines may not be the only time equity fund shareholders' behaviour could have affected equity prices. Equity fund flows may have had more subtle effects on equity prices— effects that may have been small and that may have appeared only with a delay. Evidence of these effects can be sought by calculating correlation coefficients that measure the strength and direction of the co-movement of equity mutual fund flows and changes in equity prices over time. Analysis of these correlation coefficients can give some indication of whether equity mutual fund flows cause changes in equity market prices, or the other way around, or neither.

As would be expected, given that cash has flowed out of domestic equity funds in months with steep stock market declines, fund flows and stock price changes have a positive contemporaneous correlation, averaging about 0.6 for the period since 1984. This contemporaneous correlation is statistically significant, although it has declined over time, from 0.7 in the mid-1980s to below 0.25 more recently. Thus, as an increasing proportion of equity mutual funds were being held in retirement accounts, flows to equity mutual funds were becoming less sensitive to market performance. This positive contemporaneous correlation says little about the direction of causality (if any) between domestic equity fund flows and equity price changes. Three causal relationships are possible: price changes could cause flows, flows could cause price changes, or both flows and price changes could react to new information that affects the market's perceived value of stocks. Exploring the alternative hypotheses associated with these relationships requires an examination of the effect of lagged price changes on current flows and of lagged flows on current price changes.

Investment Company Assets in 2014

US-Registered investment companies (The term investment companies or US investment companies will be used at times throughout this book in place of US-registered investment companies. US-registered investment companies are open-end mutual funds, closed-end funds, exchange-traded funds, and unit investment trusts) managed $18.2 trillion in assets at year-end 2014, $1.1 trillion more than at year-end 2013. US stocks returned more than 10 per cent in 2014, contributing to the increase in total net assets of funds invested in domestic equity markets. International stock markets, by contrast, fell on average, putting downward pressure on the assets of funds invested in international equities. The strengthening of the US dollar against the euro also lowered the dollar value of euro-denominated securities, and thus the value of equity and bond funds holding euro-denominated assets.

The US mutual fund and exchange-traded fund (ETF) markets—with $17.8 trillion in assets under management at year-end 2014—remained the largest in the world, accounting for 53 per cent of the $33.4 trillion in mutual fund and ETF assets worldwide.

The majority of US mutual fund and ETF assets at year-end 2014 were in long-term funds, with equity funds comprising 56 per cent. Within equity funds, domestic funds (those that invest primarily in shares of US corporations) held 42 per cent of total assets and world funds (those that invest primarily in shares of non-US corporations) accounted for 14 per cent. Bond funds held 21 per cent of US mutual fund and ETF assets. Money market funds, hybrid funds, and other funds—such as those that invest primarily in commodities—held the remainder (23 per cent).

Mutual funds reported $102 billion in net inflows in 2014, while other registered investment companies also recorded positive net inflows. On net, investors added $96 billion to long-term mutual funds. Money market funds accounted for the other $6 billion. Mutual fund shareholders reinvested $216 billion in income dividends and $381 billion in capital gains distributions that mutual funds paid out during the year. Investor demand for ETFs continued to thrive with net share issuance (including reinvested dividends) totalling $241 billion in 2014. Unit investment Trusts (UITs) had new deposits of $66 billion, up 18 per cent from 2013, and closed-end funds issued $5 billion in new shares, on net.

Table 7.1: US-Registered Investment Companies

Investment Company Total Net Assets by Type Billions of dollars; year-end, 1997–2014

Mutual funds[1]	$	*Closed-end funds*[2] $	*ETFs*[3] $	*UITs* $	*Total*[4] $
1997	4,468	152	7	85	4,711
1998	5,525	156	16	94	5,790
1999	6,846	147	34	92	7,119
2000	6,965	143	66	74	7,247
2001	6,975	141	83	49	7,248
2002	6,383	159	102	36	6,680
2003	7,402	214	151	36	7,803
2004	8,096	253	228	37	8,614
2005	8,891	276	301	41	9,509
2006	10,398	297	423	50	11,168
2007	12,000	312	608	53	12,974
2008	9,603	184	531	29	10,347
2009	11,113	223	777	38	12,151
2010	11,833	238	992	51	13,113
2011	11,632	242	1,048	60	12,982
2012	13,052	264	1,337	72	14,725
2013	15,035	279	1,675	87	17,075
2014	15,852	289	1,974	101	18,217

1. Mutual fund data include only mutual funds that report statistical information to the Investment Company Institute, and do not include mutual funds that invest primarily in other mutual funds.
2. Closed-end fund data include preferred share classes.
3. ETF data prior to 2001 were provided by Strategic Insight Simfund. ETF data include investment companies not registered under the Investment Company Act of 1940 and exclude ETFs that primarily invest in other ETFs.
4. Total investment company assets include mutual fund holdings of closed-end funds and ETFs.

Note: Data are for investment companies that report statistical information to the Investment Company Institute. Assets of these companies are 98 per cent of investor assets. Components may not add to the total because of rounding.

Source: Investment Company Institute and Strategic Insight Simfund.

Americans' Continued Reliance on Investment Companies

Households make up the largest group of investors in funds, and registered investment companies managed 24 per cent of household financial assets at year-end 2014. As households have come to rely more on funds over the past decade, their demand for directly held equities and bonds has fallen. Household demand for directly held bonds (which had outflows of $455 billion in 2014) has been weak since the financial crisis. Bond funds recorded moderate inflows in 2014, with investors injecting $44 billion. Overall, households invested an additional $416 billion in long-term registered investment companies in 2014. From 2005 to 2014, households invested an annual average of $379 billion, on net, in long-term registered investment companies, with net investments each year except 2008. In contrast, directly held equities and bonds had average annual net sales of $433 billion.

The growth of individual retirement accounts (IRAs) and defined contribution (DC) plans, particularly 401(k) plans, explains some of the increased household reliance on investment companies during the past two decades. At year-end 2014, households had 9.9 per cent of their financial assets in 401(k) and other DC retirement plans, up from 7.0 per cent in 1994. Mutual funds managed 55 per cent of the assets in these plans in 2014, more than double the 22 per cent in 1994. IRAs made up 10.9 per cent of household financial assets at year-end 2014, with mutual funds managing 48 per cent of IRA assets that year. Mutual funds also managed $1.2 trillion in variable annuities outside retirement accounts, as well as $5.7 trillion of assets in taxable household accounts.

Businesses and other institutional investors also rely on funds. Many institutions use money market funds to manage some of their cash and short-term assets. Non-financial businesses held 23 per cent of their cash in money market funds at year-end 2014. Institutional investors also have contributed to growing demand for ETFs. Investment managers, including mutual funds and pension funds, use ETFs to manage liquidity—helping them manage their investor flows and remain fully invested in the market. Asset managers also use ETFs as part of their investment strategies, including as a hedge against their exposure to equity markets.

Role of Investment Companies in Financial Markets

Investment companies have been among the largest investors in the domestic financial markets for much of the past 20 years. They held a large portion of the outstanding shares of US-issued equities and money market securities at year-end 2014. Investment companies as a whole were one of the largest groups of investors in US companies that year, holding 30 per cent of their outstanding stock at year-end 2014.

Mutual funds remained the largest investors in the US commercial paper market—an important source of short-term funding for major corporations around the world. From year-end 2013 to year-end 2014, mutual funds' share of outstanding commercial paper remained steady at 46 per cent. Money market funds accounted for most of mutual fund commercial paper holdings, and mutual fund holdings of commercial paper tend to fluctuate with investor demand for prime money market funds and the supply of commercial paper.

At year-end 2014, investment companies held 26 per cent of tax-exempt debt issued by US municipalities, a fairly stable share despite the increased supply of tax-exempt debt since 2007. Funds held 11 per cent of US Treasury and government agency securities at year-end 2014. In the corporate bond market at year-end 2014, funds' share of outstanding corporate debt securities remained at the same level (19 per cent) as at year-end 2013.

Types of Intermediaries and Number of Investment Companies

A variety of financial services companies offer registered funds in the United States. At year-end 2014, 80 per cent of fund complexes were independent fund advisers, and these firms managed 66 per cent of investment company assets. Other types of fund complexes in the US market include non-US fund advisers, insurance companies, banks, thrifts, and brokerage firms.

In 2014, 867 financial firms from around the world competed in the US market to provide investment management services to fund investors. In the 1980s and 1990s, low barriers to entry attracted many new fund sponsors. But in the early 2000s, increased competition among these sponsors and pressure from other financial products reversed those gains. From year-end 2004 to year-end 2009, 248 fund sponsors left the business but just 238 entered, for a net loss of 10 sponsors. Larger fund sponsors acquiring smaller ones, fund sponsors liquidating funds and leaving the business, and several large sponsors selling their fund advisory businesses played a major role in the decline. The number of fund companies retaining assets and attracting new investments generally has been lower since 2000 than in the 1990s.

This steady turnover and merger activity has contributed to somewhat greater concentration of regulated fund assets managed by the largest fund complexes. The share of assets managed by the five largest firms rose from 32 per cent in 2000 to 43 per cent in 2014, and the share managed by the 10 largest firms increased from 44 to 55 per cent. Most of the increase in market share occurred at the expense of the middle tier of firms—those ranked from 11 to 25 whose market share fell from 25 per cent in 2000 to 19 per cent in 2014.

Two other factors also contributed to rising industry concentration. First, the growing popularity of index funds increased concentration, because the 10 largest fund complexes manage most of the assets in index mutual funds. Actively managed domestic equity mutual funds incurred outflows for nine consecutive years, thus reducing market share for middle-tier firms, while index domestic equity funds had inflows in each of these years. Second, strong inflows over the past decade to bond funds, which are fewer in number and have fewer fund sponsors than equity mutual funds, helped boost the share of assets managed by large fund complexes that offer bond funds.

Nevertheless, in recent years, the number of sponsors has risen once again as the economy and financial markets have recovered, with a net increase of 185 from year-end 2009 to year-end 2014 (394 entering and 209 leaving). Many of the entering firms took advantage of the series trust— a cost-effective management solution in which the fund's sponsor arranges for a third party to provide certain services (e.g., audit, trustee, some legal) through a turnkey setup. The series trust allows the sponsor to focus more on managing portfolios and gathering assets, and its operating costs are spread across the funds in the trust.

Macroeconomic conditions and competitive dynamics also affect the number of funds offered in any given year. Fund sponsors create new funds to meet investor demand, and they merge or liquidate those that do not attract sufficient investor interest. A total of 654 funds opened in 2014, a slight fall from the year before and below the 2007 peak of 726, but near the 2004–2014 average. The rate of fund mergers and liquidations declined significantly from 428 in 2013 to 362 in 2014, which led to the largest annual net increase in the number of mutual funds in more than 10 years.

RECENT TRENDS IN 2014

With nearly $16 trillion in assets, the US mutual fund industry remained the largest in the world at year-end 2014. Total net assets increased by $818 billion from the level at year-end 2013, boosted primarily by appreciation in stock and bond prices. Net new cash flow into all types of mutual funds totalled $102 billion in 2014. Investor demand appeared to be driven, in large part, by improving economic conditions in the United States, lower long-term interest rates, and the demographics of the US population. Equity, bond, and hybrid funds each recorded modest net inflows in 2014, while index funds received substantial inflows.

Investor Demand for US Mutual Funds

Investor demand for mutual funds is influenced by a variety of factors, not least of which is funds' ability to assist investors in achieving their investment objectives. For example, US households rely on equity, bond, and hybrid mutual funds to meet long-term personal financial objectives such as preparing for retirement. US households, as well as businesses and other institutional investors, use money market funds as cash management tools because they provide a high degree of liquidity and competitive short-term yields. Changing demographics and investors' reactions to US and worldwide economic and financial conditions play important roles in determining how demand for specific types of mutual funds—and for mutual funds in general—evolves.

US Mutual Fund Assets

The majority of US mutual fund assets at year-end 2014 were in long-term funds, with equity funds alone comprising 52 per cent of total US mutual fund assets. Bond funds are the second-largest category, with 22 per cent of assets. Money market funds (17 per cent) and hybrid funds (nine per cent) held the remainder.

Investors in US Mutual Funds

Demand for mutual funds is, in part, related to the types of investors who hold mutual fund shares. Retail investors (i.e., households) held the vast majority (89 per cent) of the nearly $16 trillion in mutual fund assets. The proportion of assets held by retail investors is even higher (95 per cent) among mutual fund assets in long-term funds (i.e., equity, bond, or hybrid funds). Retail investors also held substantial assets ($1.7 trillion) in money market funds, but that amounts to a relatively small share (12 per cent) of their total mutual fund assets.

In contrast, institutional investors such as non-financial businesses, financial institutions, and non-profit organisations held a relatively small portion of mutual fund assets. At year-end 2014, institutions held about 11 per cent of mutual fund assets. One of the primary reasons institutions use mutual funds is to help manage cash balances. Sixty-two per cent of the $1.7 trillion that institutions held in mutual funds was in money market funds.

Developments in Mutual Fund Flows

Overall demand for mutual funds as measured by net new cash flow—new fund sales less redemptions plus net exchanges—slowed in 2014. Lower demand for equity, hybrid, and money market mutual funds was only partly offset by greater demand for bond funds. Overall, mutual funds had a net cash inflow of $102 billion in 2014, down from $175 billion in 2013. In 2014, investors added $96 billion, on net, to long-term funds, and $6 billion, on net, to money market funds. Movements in long-term interest rates, global economic conditions, evolving investment preferences, and ongoing demographic trends appeared to influence mutual fund flows in 2014.

The Global Economy and Financial Markets in 2014

Despite a slow start, the US economy turned in a moderately good performance in 2014. Gross domestic product (GDP) contracted by 2.1 per cent in the first quarter as a "polar vortex" of cold weather chilled the economy in the East and Midwest. Growth bounced back dramatically in the next two quarters, with GDP expanding at a

5 per cent annual rate in the third quarter, the strongest pace since the third quarter of 2003. For the full year, GDP advanced 2.4 per cent, the fastest pace since 2010.

Consumer spending, which comprises roughly 70 per cent of GDP, increased by 2.5 per cent in 2014. Consumer confidence was buoyed by continued improvement in the housing market, lower unemployment, and declining energy prices. Home prices rose five per cent in 2014, building on an 11 per cent jump in 2013. Steady improvement in the job market shaved a percentage point from the unemployment rate, which finished the year at 5.6 per cent, down from its recession peak of 10.0 per cent in 2009. Despite this progress, the labour market continued to face paltry wage gains and difficulty absorbing workers who dropped out of the labour force during the recession.

Meanwhile, sharply falling oil and gasoline prices helped put more money in consumers' pockets. Inflation worries remained subdued as the Consumer Price Index finished the year up a mere 0.7 per cent, with the core rate up only 1.6 per cent.

With the economy on firmer footing, the Federal Reserve decided to begin reducing its most recent round of large scale purchases of long-term Treasury and mortgage-backed bonds. While this might have been expected to put upward pressure on long-term interest rates, they fell steadily over the course of 2014. Yields on 10-year Treasury bonds fell from 2.9 per cent at the beginning of 2014 to 2.2 per cent by year-end. Market participants cited a variety of domestic and global factors as possibly contributing to this trend, including lower expectations for long-term economic growth, the federal funds rate, and inflation.

The recovering US economy spurred a three per cent increase in after-tax corporate profits in 2014, building on growth of six per cent in 2013. That, along with few growth opportunities elsewhere in the world, helped drive the total return on the S&P 500 to 14 per cent for the year. Stock prices faltered briefly in October amid concerns about a possible "triple dip" recession in Europe, lower oil prices, and the 2014 Ebola epidemic. A second, smaller dip in worldwide stock prices occurred in mid-December over concerns that plunging oil prices might damage oil producing economies, push Europe into deflation, and threaten the US energy renaissance.

US stock and bond markets performed well in 2014, in part, because overseas growth remained disappointing—buttressing demand for US securities. Economic growth in China slowed to seven per cent and the euro zone economy approached a near stall as possible deflation again became a concern. European stock prices were down 10 per cent for the year. In December 2014, the European Central Bank announced its intention to start its own quantitative easing in 2015. As a result of these factors, plus similar easing in Japan, the value of the dollar rose 14 per cent relative to both the euro and the yen in 2014. Finally, at the end of 2014, European markets faced renewed concern about Greece, and speculation that it might be forced out of the euro zone, with unknown consequences for the European financial system.

Long-Term Mutual Fund Flows

Given continued improvement in the US economy and positive market returns, investors added a modest $96 billion in net new cash flow to equity, bond, and hybrid funds in 2014.

While flows into long-term mutual funds are correlated with market returns, flows tend to be moderate as a percentage of assets even during episodes of market turmoil. Several factors may contribute to this phenomenon. One factor is that households own the vast majority of US long-term mutual fund assets and individual investors generally respond less strongly to market events than do institutional investors. Most notably, households often use mutual funds to save for the long-term, such as for college or retirement. Many of these investors make stable contributions through periodic payroll deductions, even during periods of market stress. In addition, many long-term fund shareholders seek the advice of financial advisers, who may provide a steadying influence during market downturns. These factors are amplified by the fact that there are more than 90 million investors in mutual funds. Thus, fund investors are bound to have a wide range of views on market conditions and how best to respond to those conditions to meet their individual goals. As a result, even during months when funds see significant net outflows, some investors continue to make purchases of fund shares.

Equity Mutual Funds

Net inflows to equity funds tend to rise with stock prices and net outflows tend to occur when stock prices fall. The return on the MSCI All Country World Total Return Index, a measure of returns (including dividend payments) on global stock markets, was five per cent in 2014 and 23 per cent in 2013. At the same time, equity mutual funds received net inflows totalling $25 billion in 2014, down substantially from $160 billion in 2013. Flows to equity funds varied substantially throughout 2014. Equity funds received net inflows of $59 billion in the first four months of the year. As the year progressed, flows waned and turned negative. For example, equity funds experienced net outflows of $24 billion in December.

Outflows from equity funds late in the year were likely related, in part, to market volatility. The Chicago Board Options Exchange Volatility Index (VIX), which tracks the volatility of the S&P 500 index, is a widely used measure of market risk. Values greater than 30 typically reflect a high degree of investor fear and values less than 20 are associated with a period of market calm. In 2014, the daily VIX averaged just 14, but peaked at 26 in October and 24 in December. By comparison, during 2013, when equity funds had strong inflows throughout the year, the VIX never closed above 21. Lower stock market volatility during the early part of 2014 likely helped sustain demand for equity mutual funds.

Investors in the United States increasingly have diversified their portfolios toward equity mutual funds that invest significantly or primarily in foreign markets (world equity funds). Over the past 10 years; world equity funds received net inflows of $639 billion, while domestic equity mutual funds experienced net outflows totalling $647 billion over the same period. In 2013, this pattern subsided temporarily and domestic equity funds had their first positive net flow since 2005. In 2014, despite a stronger US dollar, outflows from domestic equity funds resumed: world equity funds received $85 billion of net new cash while domestic equity funds experienced net redemptions of $60 billion.

The strong demand for world equity funds over the past decade also likely reflects the high returns that have been realised in overseas markets. Between 2003 and 2010, international stocks performed better than domestic stocks, returning an average of 13 per cent per year compared with eight per cent for domestic stocks. In 2013 and 2014, however, US stocks significantly outperformed international stocks. In 2014 alone, the total return on the Wilshire 5000 index (float-adjusted), an index of US stock market performance, was 13 per cent, while the total return on international stocks was -3 per cent. This sharp rise in the market values of US stocks has driven up price-to-earnings ratios on major domestic indexes. For example, at the start of 2013, the price-to-earnings ratio† for the S&P 500 was 22. By the end of 2014, this value had risen steadily to 27—roughly equal to the 20-year average. When price-to-earnings ratios are low compared with historical averages, investors may view stocks as undervalued and shift assets into equity funds.

This may help explain why the demand for domestic equity funds declined in 2014.

Bond Mutual Funds

Bond fund flows are typically correlated with the performance of bonds, which, in turn, is primarily driven by the US interest rate environment. In 2014, as long-term interest rates declined, bond prices, which are inversely related to interest rates, rose. This boosted returns on bonds and bond funds. Bond funds experienced net inflows of $44 billion in 2014, compared with net outflows of $71 billion the prior year.

As 2014 progressed, investors interpreted low inflation, economic headwinds from overseas and continued slack in labour markets as signals that rates would stay at low levels for the near future. Consequently, compared with the prior year, bond fund investors became less concerned with mitigating capital losses associated with rising long-term interest rates, which resulted in lower demand for bond funds with shorter durations. In particular, short-and ultra short-term bond funds experienced $21 billion in net inflows in 2014, down from $32 billion in 2013. Meanwhile, long-duration bond funds—such as those whose investment mandates focus on mid- to long-term Treasury bonds, corporate bonds, or mortgage-backed securities—experienced inflows in 2014. Investors put $94 billion, on net, into these fund types in 2014, after redeeming $50 billion on net in 2013. Investors redeemed $44 billion, on net, from high-yield bond funds in 2014. Nearly all of these outflows occurred after June, when the Fed raised concerns about overheating in the high-yield bond market.

Despite several periods of market turmoil, bond funds have experienced inflows through most of the past decade. Bond funds received $1.9 trillion in net inflows and reinvested dividends since 2005. A number of factors have helped sustain this long-term demand for bond funds.

The aging of the US population has played an important role in boosting inflows to bond funds. Surveys indicate that willingness to take investment risk declines as investor's age. In a 2014 survey of households, 25 per cent of those aged 35 to 49 indicated that they were willing to take above-average or substantial investment risk. In comparison, only 12 per cent of those aged 65 and older were willing to take such risks.

Older investors also tend to have higher account balances because they have had more time to accumulate savings and take advantage of compounding. For example, in 2014, households in which the head was younger than 35 held just six per cent of households' mutual fund assets, whereas households headed by 55 to 64 year-olds held 25 per cent of households' mutual fund assets. Larger mutual fund holdings of older age groups, combined with the tendency of investors to shift toward fixed-income products as they approach retirement, implies an underlying demand for bond funds by older investors.

The continued popularity of target date mutual funds also has helped maintain demand for bond funds. Target date mutual funds invest in a changing mix of equities and fixed-income investments. As the fund approaches and passes its target date (which is usually specified in the fund's name), the fund gradually reallocates assets away from equities toward bonds. Target date mutual funds usually invest through a fund-of-funds approach, meaning they primarily hold and invest in shares of other equity and bond mutual funds. Over the past 10 years, target date mutual funds have garnered inflows of $433 billion. In 2014, target date mutual funds had net inflows of $45 billion and ended the year with assets of $703 billion. The growing investor interest in these funds likely reflects their automatic rebalancing features as well as their inclusion as an investment option in many defined contribution plans. Also, following the adoption of the Pension Protection Act of 2006, many defined contribution plans have selected target date funds as a default option for the investments of newly enrolled plan participants.

Hybrid Mutual Funds

With the exception of 2008, hybrid funds have seen inflows every year in the past decade. Hybrid funds, also called asset allocation funds or balanced funds, invest in a mix of stocks and bonds. The fund's prospectus may specify the asset allocation that the fund seeks to maintain, such as investing approximately 60 per cent of the fund's assets in equities and 40 per cent in bonds. This approach offers a way to balance the potential capital appreciation of stocks with the income and relative stability of bonds over the long-term. The fund's portfolio may be periodically rebalanced to bring the fund's asset allocation more in line with prospectus objectives, which could be necessary following capital gains or losses in the stock or bond markets.

Hybrid funds have become an increasingly popular way to help investors achieve a managed, balanced portfolio of stocks and bonds. Over the past eight years, investors have added $436 billion in net new cash and reinvested dividends to these funds. In 2014, investors added $27 billion in net new cash flow to hybrid funds.

The Development of Alternative Strategies Funds

Equity, hybrid, and bond funds offering "alternative strategies" have attracted considerable inflows in recent years. In many ways, the 2008 crisis evoked a desire among investors to broaden their portfolios and lower the correlation of their investments with the market. In response, fund sponsors created funds that provide an alternative to the long-only strategies of most regulated funds. By creating limited amounts of leverage and investing in a variety of financial securities and instruments, including derivatives, these funds permit investors to gain exposure to strategies and sectors that might be difficult for them to obtain otherwise. Many of these funds also provide investors a means of hedging against declines in various market sectors.

Alternative strategies often involve hedging long positions using options and holding short positions in securities and sectors that appear overvalued. For example, "long/short" strategies seek to provide investors with above-market returns by buying certain securities long (with the expectation that they will increase in value) and selling other securities short (with the expectation that they will decrease in value). Selling short is often employed as part of a "market neutral" strategy, in which the fund attempts to provide positive returns that are independent of market fluctuations. Another strategy, often referred to as a "relative-value" strategy, seeks to take advantage of price differentials between related financial instruments. For example, a fund may track a pair of related securities with historically high correlations and, when the prices of the two securities diverge, buy the lower-valued security and short the other until prices converge again. "Event-driven" strategies also seek lower correlations with equity markets through arbitrage opportunities, specifically those triggered by corporate events (such as mergers, restructurings, liquidations, and new product offerings). Finally, a "macro" strategy seeks to profit from anticipated changes in economic policies that may affect relative currency values, interest rates, and stock index levels.

These strategies have resonated with investors. Assets in alternative strategies mutual funds reached $170 billion at year-end 2014, nearly triple that from five years earlier ($58 billion in 2009). Ninety-nine per cent of these assets are invested in funds with equity exposure (i.e., in either hybrid or equity alternative strategies mutual funds). Since the start of 2007, alternative strategies mutual funds garnered $124 billion in net new cash and reinvested dividends.

The Growing Popularity of Index Funds

Index funds also remained popular with investors. Of households that owned mutual funds, 31 per cent owned at least one equity index mutual fund in 2014. As of year-end 2014, 382 index funds managed total net assets of $2.1 trillion. Demand for index mutual funds remained strong in 2014, with investors adding $148 billion in net new cash flow to these funds. Of the new money that flowed to index mutual funds, 41 per cent was invested in funds tied to domestic stock indexes, 26 per cent went to funds tied to world stock indexes, and another 33 per cent was invested in funds tied to bond or hybrid indexes, such as those commonly used to benchmark target date mutual fund performance. Net new cash flow into index domestic equity mutual funds grew from $52 billion in 2013 to $61 billion in 2014, a 17 per cent increase.

Index equity mutual funds accounted for the bulk of index mutual fund assets at year-end 2014. Eighty-two per cent of index mutual fund assets were invested in funds that track the S&P 500 or other domestic or international stock indexes. Mutual funds indexed to the S&P 500 managed 33 per cent of all assets invested in index mutual funds. The share of assets invested in index equity mutual funds relative to all equity mutual funds' assets moved up to 20 per cent in 2014.

Index domestic equity mutual funds and index-based exchange-traded funds (ETFs), which are discussed in detail in Chapter 3, have benefited from this trend toward more index-oriented investment products. From 2007 through 2014, index domestic equity mutual funds and ETFs received $1 trillion in net new cash and reinvested dividends. Index-based domestic equity ETFs have grown particularly quickly—attracting almost twice the flows of index domestic equity mutual funds since 2007. In contrast, actively managed domestic equity mutual funds experienced a net outflow of $659 billion, including reinvested dividends, from 2007 to 2014.

Demand for Money Market Funds

In 2014, money market funds received a modest $6 billion in net inflows. However, similar to the demand for long-term funds, demand for money market funds was not uniform throughout 2014. In particular, outflows from money market funds were concentrated in the first four months of 2014, during which investors redeemed $143 billion, on net. Tax payments by corporations in mid-March and individuals in mid-April were likely key drivers behind these redemptions. Outflows abated and money market funds received net inflows of $164 billion over the second half of the year. Most of these flows went to institutional share classes of money market funds.

Institutional money market funds—used by businesses, pension funds, state and local governments, and other large-account investors—had a net inflow of $37 billion in 2014, following a net inflow of $27 billion in 2013. Some of the cash generated by rising corporate profits was likely held in money market funds and bank deposits.

Institutions rely more heavily on money market mutual funds to manage their cash today than they did in the early 1990s. For example, in 2008, US nonfinancial businesses held 37 per cent of their cash balances in money market funds, up from just six per cent in 1990. While this portion has declined since the 2007–2008 financial crisis, it remains substantial, measuring 23 per cent in 2014. Part of this increased demand reflects the outsourcing of institutions' cash management activities, which were commonly done in-house, to asset managers. Depending on the size of the cash position, the asset manager may create a separate account for an institutional client with direct ownership of money market instruments or they may invest some of the cash in money market funds.

Individual investors tend to withdraw cash from money market funds when the difference between yields on money market funds and interest rates on bank deposits narrows or becomes negative. Because of Federal Reserve monetary policy, short-term interest rates remained near zero in 2014. Yields on money market funds, which track short-term open market instruments such as Treasury bills, also hovered near zero and remained below yields on money market deposit accounts offered by banks. Retail money market funds, which principally are sold to individual investors, saw a net outflow of $31 billion in 2014, following a net outflow of $12 billion in 2013.

Recent Reforms to Money Market Funds

The US Securities and Exchange Commission (SEC) has amended Rule 2a-7, a regulation governing money market funds, several times since 1983, placing greater limits on the maturity and credit quality of the securities that the funds hold, adding diversification requirements, requiring minimum levels of liquidity for the funds, and increasing their disclosure requirements.

In response to the financial crisis, the SEC significantly reformed Rule 2a-7 in 2010. Among other things, these reforms required money market funds to hold a certain amount of liquidity and imposed stricter maturity limits. One outcome of these provisions is that prime funds have become more like government money market funds. To a significant degree, prime funds adjusted to the SEC's 2010 amendments to Rule 2a-7 by adding to their holdings of Treasury and agency securities. They also boosted their assets in repurchase agreements (repos). A repo can be thought of as a short-term collateralised loan, such as to a bank or other financial intermediary. Repos are collateralised—typically by Treasury and agency securities—to ensure that the loan is repaid. Prime fund holdings of Treasury and agency securities and repos have risen substantially as a share of the fund portfolios, from 12 per cent in May 2007 to a peak of 36 per cent in November 2012.

In December 2014, this share was 31 per cent of prime fund assets, still more than double the value prior to the financial crisis and subsequent reforms.

In July 2014, the SEC adopted additional rules for money market funds, further limiting the use of amortised cost for institutional funds that invest in non-government securities, and requiring that such funds price their shares to the nearest one-hundredth of a cent. Additionally, under the July 2014 rules, non-government money market fund boards can impose liquidity fees and gates (a temporary suspension of redemptions) when a fund's weekly liquid assets fall below 30 per cent of its total assets (the regulatory minimum). The final rules also include additional diversification, disclosure, and stress testing requirements, as well as updated reporting by money market funds. Because the new rules will not be fully implemented until late 2016, it is not yet clear how the SEC's 2014 rules will affect investor demand for money market funds.

What is an ETF?

An ETF is a pooled investment vehicle with shares that can be bought and sold throughout the day on a stock exchange at a market-determined price. Investors may buy or sell ETF shares through a broker or in a brokerage account just as they would the shares of any publicly traded company. In the United States, most ETFs are structured as open-end investment companies (open-end funds) or unit investment trusts, but some ETFs—primarily those investing in commodities, currencies, and futures—have different structures.

ETFs have been available as an investment product for more than 20 years in the United States. The first ETF—a broad-based domestic equity fund tracking the S&P 500 index—was introduced in 1993 after a fund sponsor received US Securities and Exchange Commission (SEC) exemptive relief from various provisions of the Investment Company

Act of 1940 that would not otherwise allow the ETF structure. Until 2008, SEC exemptive relief was granted only to ETFs that tracked designated indexes. These ETFs, commonly referred to as index-based ETFs, are designed to track the performance of their specified indexes or, in some cases, a multiple of or an inverse (or a multiple of an inverse) of their indexes.

In early 2008, the SEC first granted exemptive relief to several fund sponsors to offer fully transparent, actively managed ETFs meeting certain requirements. Each business day, these actively managed ETFs must disclose on their publicly available websites the identities and weightings of the component securities and other assets held by the ETF. Actively managed ETFs do not seek to track the return of a particular index. Instead, an actively managed ETF's investment adviser, like that of an actively managed mutual fund, creates a unique mix of investments to meet a particular investment objective and policy.

US ETF Assets

The US ETF market—with 1,411 funds and nearly $2.0 trillion in assets under management at year-end 2014—remained the largest in the world, accounting for 73 per cent of the $2.7 trillion in ETF assets worldwide.

The vast majority of assets in US-ETFs are in funds registered with and regulated by the SEC under the Investment Company Act of 1940. At year-end 2014, about three per cent of assets were held in ETFs that are not registered with or regulated by the SEC under the Investment Company Act of 1940; these ETFs invest primarily in commodities, currencies, and futures. Non–1940 Act ETFs that invest in commodity or currency futures are regulated by the Commodity Futures Trading Commission (CFTC) under the Commodity Exchange Act and by the SEC under the Securities Act of 1933. Those that invest solely in physical commodities or currencies are regulated by the SEC under the Securities Act of 1933.

ETFs and Mutual Funds

A 1940 Act ETF is similar to a mutual fund in that it offers investors a proportionate share in a pool of stocks, bonds, and other assets. It is most commonly structured as an open-end investment company and is governed by the Investment Company Act of 1940. Like a mutual fund, an ETF is required to post the mark-to-market NAV of its portfolio at the end of each trading day and must conform to the main investor protection mechanisms of the Investment Company Act, including limitations on leverage, daily valuation and liquidity requirements, prohibitions on transactions with affiliates, and rigorous disclosure obligations. Also like mutual funds, creations and redemptions of ETF shares are aggregated and executed just once per day at NAV. Despite these similarities, key features differentiate ETFs from mutual funds.

Key Differences

One major difference is that retail investors buy and sell ETF shares on the secondary market (stock exchange) through a broker-dealer, much like they would any other type of stock. In contrast, mutual fund shares are not listed on stock exchanges, but are purchased and sold by the fund company. Retail investors buy and sell mutual fund shares through a variety of distribution channels, including through investment professionals—full-service brokers, independent financial planners, bank or savings institution representatives, or insurance agents—or directly from a fund company or discount broker.

Pricing also differs between mutual funds and ETFs. Mutual funds are "forward priced," which means that although investors can place orders to buy or sell shares throughout the day, all orders placed during the day will receive the same price—the NAV—the next time it is computed. Most mutual funds calculate their NAV as of 4:00 p.m. eastern time because that is the time US stock exchanges typically close. In contrast, the price of an ETF share is continuously determined on a stock exchange. Consequently, the price at which investors buy and sell ETF shares on the secondary market may not necessarily equal the NAV of the portfolio of securities in the ETF. Two investors selling the same ETF shares at different times on the same day may receive different prices for their shares, both of which may differ from the ETF's NAV.

Demand for ETFs

In the past decade, demand for ETFs has increased as institutional investors have found ETFs to be a convenient vehicle for participating in, or hedging against, broad movements in the stock market. Increased awareness of these investment vehicles by retail investors and their financial advisers also has influenced demand for ETFs. Assets in ETFs accounted for about 11 per cent of total net assets managed by investment companies at year-end 2014. Net issuance of ETF shares reached a record $241 billion.

In 2014, changes in investor demand for specific types of ETFs were likely related to relative performance across the stock, bond, and commodity markets. Continued gains in major US stock indexes and declining long-term interest rates in the United States spurred demand for domestic equity and bond ETFs. Net issuance of broad-based domestic equity ETFs increased to $102 billion in 2014 from $99 billion in 2013 and domestic sector equity ETFs experienced net issuance of $41 billion in 2014, up from $34 billion in 2013. In contrast, demand for global and international equity ETFs slowed in 2014 with $47 billion in net issuance, down from $63 billion in 2013. Bond and hybrid ETFs saw net issuance of $53 billion in 2014, up from $13 billion in 2013, and commodity ETFs had net redemptions of $1 billion in 2014, compared with net redemptions of $30 billion in 2013.

ETFs have been available for the past 20 years, and in that time, large-cap domestic equity ETFs have accounted for the largest proportion of all ETF assets—28 per cent, or $556 billion, at year-end 2014.Solid performance in international stock markets and strong investor demand over the past six years has made global/international equity ETFs the second-largest category with 21 per cent ($415 billion) of all ETF assets. Bond and hybrid ETFs accounted for 15 per cent ($299 billion) of all ETF assets.

Table 7.2: Number of ETFs

	2003–2014		
	Created	*Liquidated/Merged*	*Total at year-end*
2003	10	4	119
2004	35	2	152
2005	52	0	204
2006	156	1	359
2007	270	0	629
2008	149	50	728
2009	120	49	797*
2010	177	51	923
2011	226	15	1,134
2012	141	81	1,194
2013	143	46	1,294*
2014	176	59	1,411

* The difference between the number of ETFs created and liquidated may not equal the difference between the total numbers of ETFs at year-end because of conversions. In 2009, two ETFs converted from holding securities directly to investing primarily in other ETFs. In 2013, three ETFs converted from investing primarily in other ETFs to holding securities directly.

Note: ETF data include ETFs not registered under the Investment Company Act of 1940 but exclude ETFs that invest primarily in other ETFs.

Increased investor demand for ETFs led to a rapid increase in the number of ETFs created by fund sponsors in the past decade. From year-end 2003 to year-end 2014, 1,645 ETFs were created—the peak years came in 2007, with 270 new funds, and 2011, with 226 new funds. In 2014, 176 ETFs were created. Few ETFs had been liquidated until 2008 when market pressures appeared to come into play and sponsors began liquidating ETFs that had failed to gather sufficient assets. Liquidations occurred primarily among ETFs tracking virtually identical indexes, those focusing on specialty or niche indexes, or those using alternative weighting methodologies. In 2012, the number of liquidations jumped to 81 as two sponsors exited the index-based ETF market. In 2014, 59 ETFs were liquidated. On net, there were 117 more ETFs at year-end 2014 than at year-end 2013, bringing the total number of ETFs to 1,411.

As demand for ETFs has grown, ETF sponsors have offered not only a greater number of funds, but a greater variety, including ETFs investing in particular market sectors, industries, or commodities (either directly or through the futures market). At year-end 2014, there were 318 commodity and domestic sector equity ETFs, with commodity ETFs representing the largest category at 26 per cent. The second-largest category, natural resource ETFs, which hold securities of publicly traded companies involved in mining or production of natural resources, accounted for 17 per cent of the total number of sector and commodity ETFs. Commodity and domestic sector equity ETFs altogether held $324 billion in assets. Although commodity ETFs remained the largest category in this group with 18 per cent of net assets at year-end 2014, their share was down from 24 per cent at year-end 2013. Tepid demand for commodity ETFs and weakness in gold and silver prices were the primary drivers behind the drop in commodity ETF assets in 2014.

ETF sponsors continued building on recent innovations by launching additional actively managed ETFs. During 2014, 53 actively managed ETFs were launched, bringing the total number of actively managed ETFs to 111, with nearly $17 billion in assets at year-end.

Characteristics of ETF-Owning Households

An estimated 5.2 million, or four per cent of, US households held ETFs in mid-2014. Of households that owned mutual funds, an estimated nine per cent also owned ETFs. ETF-owning households tended to include affluent, experienced investors who owned a range of equity and fixed-income investments. In mid-2014, 93 per cent of ETF-owning households also owned equity mutual funds, individual stocks, or variable annuities. Sixty-five per cent of households that owned ETFs also held bond mutual funds, bonds, or fixed annuities. In addition, 41 per cent of ETF-owning households owned investment real estate.

Table 7.3: ETF-Owning Households Held a Broad Range of Investments

Percentage of ETF-owning households holding each type of investment, mid-2014	
Equity mutual funds, individual equities, or variable annuities (total)	93
Bond mutual funds, individual bonds, or fixed annuities (total)	65
Mutual funds (total)	89
Equity	85
Bond	53
Hybrid	46
Money market	60
Individual equities	73
Individual bonds	23
Fixed or variable annuities	28
Investment real estate	41

Note: Multiple responses are included.

Some characteristics of retail ETF owners are similar to those of households that own mutual funds and those that own stocks directly. For instance, households that owned ETFs—like households owning mutual funds and those owning individual equities—tended to have household incomes above the national median and to own at least one defined contribution (DC) retirement plan account. However, ETF-owning households also exhibit some characteristics that distinguish them from other households. For example, ETF-owning households tended to have higher incomes and greater household financial assets; they were also more likely to own an individual retirement account (IRA) than households that own mutual funds and those that own individual equities.

Table 7.4: Characteristics of ETF-Owning Households

Mid-2014				
	All US households	*Households owning ETFs*	*Households owning mutual funds*	*Households owning individual equities*
Median				
Age of head of household[1]	51	51	51	53
Household income[2]	$50,000	$110,000	$85,000	$90,000
Household financial assets[3]	$75,500	$500,000	$200,000	$330,000
Percentage of households				
Household primary or co-decision maker for saving and investing				
Married or living with a partner	58	73	73	72
Widowed	9	4	5	7
Four-year college degree or more	32	64	49	52
Employed (full- or part-time)	60	72	77	72
Retired from lifetime occupation	28	28	23	29
Household owns				
IRA(s)	34	75	62	63
DC retirement plan account(s)	46	74	85	72

1. Age is based on the sole or co-decision maker for household saving and investing.
2. Total reported is household income before taxes in 2013.
3. Household financial assets include assets in employer-sponsored retirement plans but exclude the household's primary residence.

ETF-owning households also exhibit more willingness to take investment risk. Forty-nine per cent of ETF-owning households were willing to take substantial or above-average investment risk for substantial or above-average gain in 2014, compared with 21 per cent of all US households and 31 per cent of mutual fund-owning households. This result may be explained by the predominance of equity ETFs, which make up 82 per cent of ETF total net assets. Investors who are more willing to take investment risk may be more likely to invest in equities.

Total Assets of Closed-End Funds

At year-end 2014, 568 closed-end funds had total assets of $289 billion. The number of closed-end funds available to investor's remains below its peak of 662 at the end of 2007 due to the effects of mergers, liquidations, and conversions. Although total assets at year-end 2014 were up nearly 4 per cent ($10 billion) from year-end 2013, they have not fully recovered to the 2007 peak of $312 billion. Three factors have limited the growth in both the assets and the number of closed-end funds in recent years. First, several closed-end funds have repurchased shares through tender offers over the past few years, reducing the number of outstanding shares and the size of assets under management. Second, a few closed-end funds have liquidated each year and others have converted into open-end mutual funds or ETFs. Third, closed-end fund preferred share assets have declined since the financial crisis of 2008.

Historically, bond funds have accounted for a large share of assets in closed-end funds. A decade ago, 68 per cent of all closed-end fund assets were held in bond funds with the remainder held in equity funds. At year-end 2014, assets in bond closed-end funds were $170 billion, or 59 per cent of closed-end fund assets. Equity closed-end fund assets totalled $119 billion, or 41 per cent of closed-end fund assets. These relative shares have shifted, in part because cumulative net issuance of equity closed-end fund shares has exceeded that of bond fund shares over the past eight years. In addition, total returns on US stocks averaged 8.1 per cent annually from year-end 2004 to year-end 2014, while total returns on bonds† averaged 4.8 per cent annually.

Net Issuance of Closed-End Funds

Net issuance of closed-end fund shares slowed substantially to $4.8 billion in 2014 from $13.7 billion in 2013, as investor demand for bond closed-end funds waned. Net issuance of bond closed-end funds fell to $427 million in 2014 from $10.2 billion in 2013. In contrast, demand for equity closed-end funds strengthened further in 2014 with net issuance amounting to $4.3 billion, up from $3.6 billion in 2013 and $3.0 billion in 2012. As in the previous six years, net issuance of domestic equity closed-end funds accounted for the bulk of the equity fund net issuance.

Table 7.5: Closed-End Fund Net Share Issuance[1]

Millions of dollars, 2007–2014(2)								
		Equity			*Bond*			
	Total	*Total*	*Domestic*	*Global/ International*	*Total*	*Domestic taxable*	*Domestic municipal*	*Global/ International*
2007	$28,369	$24,608	$4,949	$19,659	$3,761	$1,966	-$880	$2,675
2008	-22,298	-8,739	-7,052	-1,687	-13,560	-6,770	-6,089	-700
2009	-3,259	-2,520	-2,366	-154	-739	-788	-238	287
2010	5,430	2,054	1,995	59	3,376	1,900	1,119	357
2011	6,018	4,466	3,206	1,260	1,551	724	825	2
2012	11,315	2,953	2,840	113	8,362	3,249	3,032	2,081
2013	13,742	3,554	4,097	-543	10,188	3,921	-155	6,423
2014	4,766	4,339	3,844	494	427	105	533	-212

1. Dollar value of gross issuance (proceeds from initial and additional public offerings of shares) minus gross redemptions of shares (share repurchases and fund liquidations). A positive number indicates that gross issuance exceeded gross redemptions. A negative number indicates that gross redemptions exceeded gross issuance.
2. Data are not available for years prior to 2007.

Note: Components may not add to the total because of rounding.

Closed-End Fund Distributions

In 2014, closed-end funds distributed $17.1 billion to shareholders. Closed-end funds may make distributions to shareholders from three possible sources: income from interest and dividends, realised capital gains, and return of capital. Income from interest and dividends made up 75 per cent of closed-end fund distributions, with the majority of income distributions paid by bond closed-end funds. Return of capital comprised 13 per cent of closed-end fund distributions, and capital gains distributions accounted for 11 per cent.

Closed-End Fund Leverage

Closed-end funds have the ability, subject to strict regulatory limits, to use leverage as part of their investment strategy. The use of leverage by a closed-end fund can allow it to achieve higher long-term returns, but also increases risk and the likelihood of share price volatility. Closed-end fund leverage can be classified as either structural leverage or portfolio leverage. At year-end 2014, at least 372 funds, accounting for 65 per cent of closed-end funds, were using structural leverage, certain types of portfolio leverage (tender option bonds or reverse repurchase agreements), or both as a part of their investment strategy.

Structural leverage, the most common type, affects the closed-end fund's capital structure by increasing the fund's portfolio assets. Types of closed-end fund structural leverage include borrowing and issuing debt and preferred shares. At the end of 2014, 319 funds had a total of $50.7 billion in structural leverage, with a little more than half (53 per cent) of those assets from preferred shares. Forty-seven per cent of closed-end fund structural leverage was other structural leverage. The average leverage ratio* across those closed-end funds employing structural leverage was 26.0 per cent at year-end 2014. Among bond funds employing structural leverage, the average leverage ratio was somewhat higher

(28.2 per cent) than that of equity funds (19.4 per cent) employing structural leverage.

Portfolio leverage is leverage that results from particular portfolio investments, such as certain types of derivatives, reverse repurchase agreements, and tender option bonds. At the end of 2014, 195 closed-end funds had $20.0 billion outstanding in reverse repurchase agreements and tender option bonds.

Characteristics of Households Owning Closed-End Funds

An estimated 3.4 million US households owned closed-end funds in mid-2014.These households tended to include affluent, experienced investors who owned a range of equity and fixed-income investments. In mid-2014, 92 per cent of households owning closed-end funds also owned equity mutual funds, individual stocks, or variable annuities. Sixty-eight per cent of households that owned closed-end funds also held bonds, bond mutual funds, or fixed annuities. In addition, 43 per cent of these households owned investment real estate.

Table 7.6: Closed-End Fund Investors Owned a Broad Range of Investments

Percentage of closed-end fund–owning households holding each type of investment, mid-2014	
Equity mutual funds, individual equities, or variable annuities (total)	92
Bond mutual funds, individual bonds, or fixed annuities (total)	68
Mutual funds (total)	89
Equity	85
Bond	51
Hybrid	44
Money market	66
Individual equities	72
Individual bonds	31
Fixed or variable annuities	36
Investment real estate	43

Note: Multiple responses are included.

Because a large number of households that owned closed-end funds also owned individual equities and mutual funds, the characteristics of closed-end fund owners were similar in many respects to those of individual equity and mutual fund owners. For instance, households that owned closed-end funds (like individual equity- and mutual fund-owning households) were more likely than all households to be headed by college-educated individuals and had household incomes above the national median.

Table 7.7: Closed-End Fund Investors Had Above-Average Household Incomes and Financial Assets

	Mid-2014			
	All U.S. Households	*Households owning closed-end funds*	*Households owning mutual funds*	*Households owning individual equities*
Median				
Age of head of household[1]	51	51	51	53
Household income[2]	$50,000	$100,000	$85,000	$90,000
Household financial assets[3]	$75,500	$350,000	$200,000	$330,000
Percentage of households				
Household primary or co-decision maker for saving and investing				
Married or living with a partner	58	69	73	72
Widowed	9	10	5	7
Four-year college degree or more	32	53	49	52
Employed (full- or part-time)	60	69	77	72
Retired from lifetime occupation	28	33	23	29
Household owns				
IRA(s)	34	72	62	63
DC retirement plan account(s)	46	68	85	72

1. Age is based on the sole or co-decision maker for household saving and investing.
2. Total reported is household income before taxes in 2013.
3. Household financial assets include assets in employer-sponsored retirement plans but exclude the household's primary residence.

Nonetheless, households that owned closed-end funds exhibited certain characteristics distinguishing them from mutual fund-owning households. For example, households with closed-end funds tended to have significantly greater household financial assets. Thirty-three per cent of closed-end fund-owning households were retired from their lifetime occupations, compared with 23 per cent of households owning mutual funds.

Individual and Household Ownership of Mutual Funds

In mid-2014, an estimated 90 million individual investors owned mutual funds—and at year-end, these investors held 89 per cent of total mutual fund assets, directly or through retirement plans. Household ownership of mutual funds has remained steady since 2000. Altogether, 43 per cent of US households—or about 53.2 million—owned mutual funds in mid-2014, slightly below the 2000–2014 average of about 45 per cent. Mutual funds were a major component of many US households' financial holdings in mid-2014. Among households owning mutual funds; the median amount invested in mutual funds was $103,000. Nearly three-quarters of individuals heading households that owned mutual funds were married or living with a partner, nearly half were college graduates, and more than three-quarters worked full-or part-time.

Table 7.8: Characteristics of Mutual Fund Investors

Mid-2014
How many people own mutual funds?
90.4 million individuals
53.2 million US households
Who are they?
51 is the median age of the head of household
73 per cent are married or living with a partner
49 per cent are college graduates
77 per cent are employed (full- or part-time)
12 per cent are Silent or GI Generation (born 1904 to 1945)

contd...

contd...

42 per cent are Baby Boomers (born 1946 to 1964)
31 per cent are Generation X (born 1965 to 1980)
15 per cent are Millennial Generation (born 1981 to 2004)
$85,000 is the median household income
What do they own?
$200,000 is the median household financial assets
$103,000 is the median mutual fund assets
68 per cent hold more than half of their financial assets in mutual funds
62 per cent own IRAs
85 per cent own DC retirement plan accounts
4 mutual funds is the median number owned
86 per cent own equity funds
When and how did they make their first mutual fund purchase?
47 per cent bought their first mutual fund before 1995
64 per cent purchased their first mutual fund through an employer-sponsored retirement plan
Why do they invest?
91 per cent are saving for retirement
49 per cent are saving for emergencies
49 per cent hold mutual funds to reduce taxable income
23 per cent are saving for education

Sources: Investment Company Institute and US Census Bureau. See *ICI Research Perspective*, "Ownership of Mutual Funds, Shareholder Sentiment, and Use of the Internet, 2014"; *ICI Research Perspective*, "Characteristics of Mutual Fund Investors, 2014"; and *ICI Research Report*, "Profile of Mutual Fund Shareholders, 2014."

Mutual Fund Ownership by Age and Income

Mutual fund ownership in mid-2014 was greatest among households in their peak earning and saving years—between the ages of 35 and 64—at about 50 per cent. Thirty-four per cent of households younger than 35 owned mutual funds, the same as for households aged 65 or older.

Among mutual fund-owning households in mid-2014, 42 per cent were headed by members of the Baby Boom Generation (head of household born between 1946 and 1964), 31 per cent were headed by members of Generation X (born between 1965 and 1980), 15 per cent were headed by members of the Millennial Generation (born between 1981 and 2004), and 12 per cent were headed by members of the Silent and GI Generations (born between 1904 and 1945). Heads of mutual fund-owning households had a median age of 51 years.

Not only were Baby Boomers the largest shareholder group in mid-2014, they also held the largest percentage of households' mutual fund assets, at 51 per cent. Households headed by members of Generation X (31 per cent), the Silent and GI Generations (13 per cent), and the Millennial Generation (5 per cent) held the rest.

Households with higher annual incomes are more likely to own mutual funds than those with lower annual incomes. In mid-2014, 67 per cent of US households with annual income of $50,000 or more owned mutual funds, compared with 18 per cent of households with annual income of less than $50,000. In fact, lower-income households tend to have fewer saving than higher-income households. The typical household with less than $50,000 in annual income had only $12,000 in savings and investments, while the typical household with annual income of $50,000 or more held $190,000 in savings and investments.

US households owning mutual funds had a range of annual incomes in mid-2014: 20 per cent had annual income of less than $50,000; 21 per cent had between $50,000 and $74,999; 19 per cent had between $75,000 and $99,999; and the remaining 40 per cent had $100,000 or more. The median income of mutual fund-owning households in mid-2014 was $85,000.

Savings Goals of Mutual Fund Investors

Mutual funds play a key role in the savings goals of US households—both long- and short-term. In mid-2014, 91 per cent of mutual fund-owning households indicated that saving for retirement was one of their financial goals, and 74 per cent said it was their primary financial goal. However, retirement is not the only financial goal for mutual fund-owning households—49 per cent reported saving for emergencies as a goal; 49 per cent reported reducing taxable income as a goal; and 23 per cent reported saving for education as a goal.

Where Investors Own Mutual Funds

The importance that mutual fund-owning households place on retirement saving is reflected in where they own their funds—94 per cent of these households held mutual fund shares inside employer-sponsored retirement plans, individual retirement accounts (IRAs), and other tax-deferred accounts in mid-2014. It also is reflected in the type of funds they choose, with households more likely to invest their retirement assets in long-term mutual funds than in money market funds. Indeed, defined contribution (DC) retirement plan and IRA assets held in equity, bond, and hybrid mutual funds totalled $6.9 trillion at year-end 2014, or 53 per cent of those funds' assets industry wide. By contrast, DC retirement plan and IRA assets in money market funds totalled just $364 billion, or 13 per cent of those funds' assets industry wide.

As 401(k) and other employer-sponsored DC retirement plans have grown more popular, the percentage of households that make their first foray into mutual fund investing inside these plans has increased. Among the households that bought their first mutual fund shares in 2005 or later, 68 per cent did so inside an employer-sponsored retirement plan. Among those that bought their first mutual fund shares before 1990, only 57 per cent did so inside an employer-sponsored retirement plan.

In mid-2014, 82 per cent of mutual fund-owning households held funds inside employer-sponsored retirement plans, with 43 per cent owning funds only inside such plans. Fifty-seven per cent of mutual fund-owning households held funds outside employer-sponsored retirement accounts, with

18 per cent owning funds only outside such plans. For mutual fund-owning households without funds in employer-sponsored retirement plans, 59 per cent held funds in traditional or Roth Erasing many cases, these IRAs held assets rolled over from 401(k) plans or other employer-sponsored retirement plans (either defined benefit or DC plans).

Sources of Mutual Fund Purchases

Households owning mutual funds outside employer-sponsored retirement plans buy their fund shares through a variety of sources. In mid-2014, 80 per cent of these households owned funds purchased with the help of an investment professional, including registered investment advisers, full-service brokers, independent financial planners, bank and savings institution representatives, insurance agents, and accountants. Forty per cent of these households owned funds purchased solely with the help of an investment professional, while another 40 per cent owned funds purchased from investment professionals and directly from fund companies, fund supermarkets, or discount brokers. Thirteen per cent solely owned funds purchased directly from fund companies, fund supermarkets, or discount brokers.

In mid-2014, about 46 per cent of mutual fund-owning households held mutual funds through multiple sources: 15 per cent held mutual funds both inside employer-sponsored retirement plans and through investment professionals; five per cent held mutual funds both inside employer-sponsored retirement plans and directly from fund companies, fund supermarkets, or discount brokers; and seven per cent held mutual funds through investment professionals and directly from fund companies, fund supermarkets, or discount brokers. Sixteen per cent owned mutual funds through all three source categories. Another three per cent owned funds inside and outside employer-sponsored retirement plans, without specifying their outside purchase source. When owning funds through only one source category, the most common source was employer-sponsored retirement plans, at 43 per cent.

At year-end 2014, mutual funds held in DC plans and IRAs accounted for $7.3 trillion, or 29 per cent of, the $24.7 trillion US retirement market. The $7.3 trillion made up 46 per cent of total mutual fund assets at year-end 2014.DC plans and IRAs held 53 per cent of total assets in long-term mutual funds, but a much smaller share of total assets in money market funds (13 per cent). Similarly, mutual funds held in DC plans and IRAs accounted for 55 per cent of household long-term mutual funds but only 22 per cent of household money market funds.

Shareholder Sentiment, Willingness to Take Investment Risk and Confidence

Each year, ICI surveys US households about a variety of topics, including shareholder sentiment. In mid-2014, 68 per cent of mutual fund-owning households familiar with mutual fund companies had "very" or "somewhat" favourable impressions of fund companies, the same as in 2013. The share of mutual fund-owning households with "very" favourable impressions of fund companies, meanwhile, increased from 13 per cent to 17 per cent.

Among all US households, the percentage willing to take above-average or substantial investment risk tends to move with stock market performance. US households tend to become less tolerant of investment risk following periods of poor stock market performance. For example, willingness to take above-average or substantial investment risk fell from 23 per cent in mid-2008, just before the 2007–2008 financial crisis hit, to 19 per cent in mid-2009. Not until mid-2013, more than four years after the stock market bottomed out, did willingness to take investment risk rebound.

Households owning mutual funds are far more willing to take investment risk than other households. In mid-2014, 31 per cent of households owning mutual funds were willing to take above-average or substantial investment risk, more than twice the 13 per cent of households not owning mutual funds.

Table 7.9: Characteristics of Mutual Fund Owners

Internet Access is Nearly Universal Among Mutual Fund–Owning Households Percentage of households with Internet access, mid-2014			
	All US house-holds	*Mutual fund-owning households*	*Households with DC plans*[1]
Age of head of household[2]			
Younger than 35	86	96	96
35 to 49	88	95	95
50 to 64	81	95	93
65 or older	60	86	84
Education level			
High school diploma or less	63	84	84
Some college or associate's degree	85	95	94
College or postgraduate degree	92	97	97
Household income[3]			
Less than $50,000	65	84	82
$50,000 to $99,999	90	94	95
$100,000 to $149,999	95	98	98
$150,000 or more	94	98	98
Total	**79**	**94**	**93**

1. DC plans include 401(k), 403(b), 457, and other DC plans.
2. Age is based on the sole or co-decision maker for household saving and investing.
3. Total reported is household income before taxes in 2013.

Note: Internet access includes access to the Internet at home, work, or some other location.

Source: ICI Annual Mutual Fund Shareholder Tracking Survey. See *ICI Research Perspective*, "Ownership of Mutual Funds, Shareholder Sentiment, and Use of the Internet, 2014."

As with their impressions of fund companies, shareholders' confidence that mutual funds are helping them reach their financial goals declined in the wake of the financial crisis. In mid-2009, 72 per cent of mutual fund shareholders said they were confident in mutual funds' ability to help them achieve their financial goals, down from 85 per cent the year before. From mid-2010 through mid-2014, about eight in 10 mutual fund-owning households said they were confident in mutual funds' ability to help them achieve their financial goals, with more than 20 per cent saying they were "very" confident.

TRENDS IN MUTUAL FUND EXPENSES

Mutual fund investors incur two primary types of expenses and fees: ongoing expenses and sales loads. Ongoing expenses cover portfolio management, fund administration, daily fund accounting and pricing, shareholder services (such as call centers and websites), distribution charges (known as 12b-1 fees), and other operating costs. These expenses are included in a fund's expense ratio—the fund's annual expenses expressed as a percentage of its assets. Since expenses are paid from fund assets, investors pay these expenses indirectly. Sales loads are paid at the time of share purchase (front-end loads), when shares are redeemed (back-end loads), or over time (level loads).

On an asset-weighted basis, average expense ratios incurred by mutual fund investors have fallen substantially. In 2000, equity fund investors incurred expense ratios of 99 basis points, on average, or 99 cents for every $100 invested. By 2014, that average had fallen to 70 basis points, a decline of 29 per cent. Hybrid and bond fund ratios also have declined. The average hybrid fund expense ratio fell from 89 basis points in 2000 to 78 basis points in 2014, a reduction of 12 per cent. In addition, the average bond fund expense ratio fell from 76 basis points in 2000 to 57 basis points in 2014, a decline of 25 per cent.

Understanding the Decline in Fund Expense Ratios

Several factors help account for the steep drop in expense ratios. First, expense ratios often vary inversely with fund assets. Some fund costs included in expense ratios—such as transfer agency fees, accounting and audit fees, and directors' fees—are more or less fixed in dollar terms. That means that when a fund's assets rise, these costs contribute less to a fund's expense ratio. Thus, if the assets of a fixed sample of funds rise over time, the sample's average expense ratio tends to fall.

Mutual fund expenses also have fallen because of economies of scale and competition. Investor demand for mutual fund services has increased dramatically in recent years. From 1990 to 2014, the number of households owning mutual funds more than doubled—from 23.4 million to 53.2 million. All else equal, this sharp increase in demand would tend to boost fund expense ratios. Any such tendency, however, was mitigated by downward pressure on expense ratios—from competition among existing fund sponsors, new fund sponsors entering the industry, competition from products such as exchange-traded funds (ETFs), and economies of scale resulting from the growth in fund assets.

Finally, shareholders tend to invest in funds with below-average expense ratios. The simple average expense ratio of equity funds (the average for all equity funds offered for sale) was 133 basis points in 2014. The asset-weighted average expense ratio for equity funds (the average shareholders actually paid) was far lower—just 70 basis points.

Another way to illustrate this tendency is to examine how investors allocate their assets across funds. At year-end 2014, equity funds with expense ratios in the lowest quartile held 74 per cent of equity funds' total net assets, while those with expense ratios in the upper three quartiles held only 26 per cent. This pattern holds for actively managed equity funds, index equity funds, and target date funds (funds that adjust their portfolios, typically more toward fixed income, as the fund approaches and passes its target date). Index equity funds with expense ratios in the lowest quartile held 85 per cent of index equity fund assets at year-end 2014.

Index Mutual Fund Expenses

Growth in index mutual funds has contributed to the decline in equity and bond fund expense ratios. Index fund assets have grown substantially in recent years, from $384 billion in 2000 to $2.1 trillion in 2014. Investor demand for index bond funds and index hybrid funds has grown in the past few years, but as of December 2014, 82 per cent of index fund assets were invested in index equity funds.

Index funds tend to have lower-than-average expense ratios for several reasons. The first is their approach to portfolio management. An index fund generally seeks to mimic the returns on a given index. Under this approach, often referred to as passive management, portfolio managers buy and hold all, or a representative sample of, the securities in their target indexes.

By contrast, under an active management approach, managers have discretion to increase or reduce their exposure to the sectors or securities in their investment mandates. This approach offers investors the chance to enjoy superior returns. However, it also entails more-intensive analysis of securities or sectors, which can be costly.

A second reason index funds tend to have below-average expense ratios is their investment focus. Historically, the assets of index equity funds have been concentrated most heavily in "large-cap blend" funds that target US large-cap indexes, notably the S&P 500. Assets of actively managed funds, on the other hand, have been divided among stocks of varying levels of market capitalisation, international regions, or specialised business sectors. Managing portfolios of mid- or small-cap, international, or sector stocks is generally acknowledged to be more expensive than managing portfolios of US large-cap stocks.

Third, index funds are larger on average than actively managed funds, which help reduce fund expense ratios through economies of scale. In 2014, the average index equity fund had $5.0 billion in assets, more than triple the $1.5 billion for the average actively managed equity fund.

Finally, index fund investors who hire financial professionals might pay for that service out-of-pocket, rather than through the fund's expense ratio. Actively managed funds more commonly bundle those costs in the fund's expense ratio, through a 12b-1 fee.

These reasons, among others, help explain why index funds generally have lower expense ratios than actively managed funds. Note, however, that both index and actively managed funds have contributed to the decline in mutual funds' overall average expense ratios. The average expense ratios incurred by investors in both index and actively managed funds have fallen—and by roughly the same amount. From 2000 to 2014, the average expense ratio of index equity funds fell 16 basis points, similar to the decline of 20 basis points in the expenses of actively managed equity funds. Over the same period, the average expense ratio of index bond funds and actively managed bond funds fell 10 basis points and 15 basis points, respectively.

In part, the downward trend in the average expense ratios of both index and actively managed funds reflects investors' tendency to buy lower-cost funds. Investor demand for index funds is disproportionately concentrated in the very lowest-cost funds. In 2014, for example, 69 per cent of index equity fund assets were held in funds with expense ratios that were among the lowest 10 per cent of all index equity funds. This phenomenon is not unique to index funds, however; the proportion of assets in the lowest-cost actively managed funds is also high.

Understanding Differences in the Expense Ratios of Mutual Funds

Like the prices of most goods and services, the expenses of individual mutual funds differ considerably across the array of available products. The expense ratios of individual funds depend on many factors, including investment objective, fund assets, and payments to intermediaries.

Fund Investment Objective

Fund expenses vary by investment objective. For example, bond and money market funds tend to have lower expense ratios than equity funds. Among equity funds, expense ratios

Table 7.10: Expense Ratios for Selected Investment Objectives

Basis points, 2014					
Investment objective	*10th percentile*	*Median*	*90th percentile*	*Asset-weighted average*	*Simple average*
Equity funds[1]	72	125	208	70	133
Growth	74	120	200	82	128
Sector	79	135	216	81	141
Value	73	118	196	80	125
Blend	45	108	189	46	112
World	88	139	220	86	146
Hybrid funds[1]	70	124	205	78	133
Bond funds[1]	48	86	165	57	98
Taxable	47	90	172	57	99
Municipal	50	80	157	56	93
Money market funds[1]	6	10	21	13	12
Memo					
Target date funds[2]	49	94	161	57	99
Index equity funds[1]	8	44	156	11	70

1. Data exclude mutual funds available as investment choices in variable annuities and mutual funds that invest primarily in other mutual funds.
2. Data include mutual funds that invest primarily in other mutual funds, but exclude mutual funds available as investment choices in variable annuities. Ninety-seven per cent of these funds invest primarily in other mutual funds.

Source: Investment Company Institute and Lipper.

tend to be higher for funds that specialise in a given sector—such as healthcare or real estate—or those that invest in equities around the world, because such funds tend to cost more to manage. Even within a particular investment objective, fund expense ratios can vary considerably. For example, 10 per cent of equity funds that focus on growth stocks have expense ratios of 74 basis points or less, while another 10 per cent have expense ratios of 200 basis points or more. This variation reflects, among other things, the fact that some growth funds focus more on small- or mid-cap stocks and others focus more on large-cap stocks. This is important because portfolios of small and mid-cap stocks tend to cost more to manage.

Mutual Fund Fee Structures

Mutual funds often are categorised by the class of shares that fund sponsors offer, primarily load or no-load classes. Load classes generally serve investors who buy shares through financial professionals; no-load classes usually serve investors who buy shares without the assistance of a financial professional or who choose to compensate their financial professional separately. Funds sold through financial professionals typically offer more than one share class in order to provide investors with alternative ways to pay for financial services.

12b-1 Fees

Since 1980, when the US Securities and Exchange Commission adopted Rule 12b-1 under the Investment Company Act of 1940, funds and their shareholders have had the flexibility to compensate financial professionals and other financial intermediaries through asset-based fees. These distribution fees, known as 12b-1 fees, enable investors to pay indirectly for some or all of the services they receive from financial professionals (such as their broker) and other financial intermediaries (such as retirement plan record keepers and discount brokerage firms). Funds also use 12b-1 fees to a very limited extent to help defray advertising and marketing costs.

Load Share Classes

Load share classes include a sales load, a 12b-1 fee, or both. Sales loads and 12b-1 fees are used to compensate brokers and other financial professionals for their services.

Front-end load shares, which are predominantly Class A shares, were the traditional way investors compensated financial professionals for assistance. These shares generally charge a sales load—a percentage of the sales price or offering price—at the time of purchase. They also generally have a 12b-1 fee, often 0.25 per cent (25 basis points). Front-end load shares are used in employer-sponsored retirement plans sometimes, but fund sponsors typically waive the sales load for purchases made through such retirement plans. Additionally, front-end load fees often decline as the size of an investor's initial purchase rises (called *breakpoint discounts*), and many fund providers offer discounted load fees when an investor has total balances exceeding a given amount in that provider's funds.

Back-end load shares, often called Class B shares, typically do not have a front-end load. Investors using back-end load shares pay for services provided by financial professionals through a combination of an annual 12b-1 fee and a contingent deferred sales load (CDSL). The CDSL is paid if fund shares are redeemed before a given number of years of ownership. Back-end load shares usually convert after a specified number of years to a share class with a lower 12b-1 fee (for example, Class A shares). The assets in back-end load shares have declined substantially in recent years.

Level-load shares, which include Class C shares, generally do not have front-end loads. Investors in this share class compensate financial advisers with an annual 12b-1 fee (typically one per cent) and a CDSL (also typically one per cent) that shareholders pay if they sell their shares within a year of purchase.

No-Load Share Classes

No-load share classes have no front-end load or CDSL, and have a 12b-1 fee of 0.25 per cent (25 basis points) or less. Originally, no-load share classes were sold directly by mutual fund sponsors to investors. Now, investors can purchase no-load funds through employer-sponsored retirement plans, mutual fund supermarkets, discount brokerage firms, and bank trust departments, as well as directly from mutual fund sponsors. Some financial professionals who charge investors separately for their services, rather than through a load or 12b-1 fee, help investors select a portfolio of no-load funds.

Mutual Fund Load Fees

Many mutual fund investors engage an investment professional, such as a broker, an investment adviser, or a financial planner. Among households owning mutual fund shares outside employer-sponsored retirement plans, 80 per cent own fund shares through investment professionals. These professionals can provide many benefits to investors, such as helping them identify financial goals, analysing an existing financial portfolio, determining an appropriate asset allocation, and (depending on the type of financial professional) providing investment advice or recommendations to help investors achieve their financial goals. The investment professional also may provide ongoing services, such as responding to investors' inquiries or periodically reviewing and rebalancing their portfolios.

Thirty years ago, fund shareholders usually compensated financial advisers through a front-end load—a one-time, up-front payment for current and future services. That structure has since changed significantly.

One important outcome of the changing distribution structure has been a marked decline in load fees paid by mutual fund investors. The maximum front-end load fee that shareholders might pay for investing in mutual funds has changed little since 1990. But front-end load fees that investors actually paid have declined markedly, from nearly 4 per cent in 1990 to less than 1 per cent in 2014.This in part reflects the increasing role of mutual funds in helping investors save for retirement. Funds that normally charge front-end load fees often waive load fees on purchases made through defined contribution (DC) plans, such as 401(k) plans. Also, front-end load funds offer volume discounts, that is, waiving or reducing load fees for large initial or cumulative purchases.

Table 7.11: Front-End Sales Loads That Investors Pay Are Well Below the Maximum Front-End Sales Loads That Funds Charge

	Percentage of purchase amount, selected years					
	Maximum front-end sales load[1]			*Average front-end sales load that investors actually paid*[2]		
	Equity	*Hybrid*	*Bond*	*Equity*	*Hybrid*	*Bond*
1990	5.0	5.0	4.6	3.9	3.8	3.5
1995	4.8	4.7	4.1	2.5	2.4	2.1
2000	5.2	5.1	4.2	1.4	1.4	1.1
2005	5.3	5.3	4.0	1.3	1.3	1.0
2010	5.4	5.2	3.9	1.0	1.0	0.8
2014	5.4	5.2	3.8	0.9	0.9	0.7

1. The maximum front-end sales load is a simple average of the highest front-end load that funds may charge as set forth in their prospectuses.
2. The simple average front-end sales load that investors actually paid is the total front-end sales loads that funds collected divided by the total maximum loads that the funds could have collected based on their new sales that year. This ratio is then multiplied by each fund's maximum sales load. The resulting value is then averaged across all funds.

Note: Data exclude mutual funds available as investment choices in variable annuities and mutual funds that invest primarily in other mutual funds.

Sources: Investment Company Institute, Lipper, and Strategic Insight Simfund.

Another important element in the changing distribution structure of mutual funds has been a shift toward asset-based fees, which are assessed as a percentage of the assets that the financial professional helps an investor manage. Brokers and other financial professionals who sell mutual funds increasingly have been compensated through these fees. An investor may pay an asset-based fee indirectly through a fund's 12b-1 fee, which is included in the fund's expense ratio, or directly (out-of-pocket) to the financial professional, in which case it is not included in the fund's expense ratio.

Table 7.12: Nearly All Net New Cash Flow Was in No-Load Institutional Share Classes

	Billions of dollars, 2005–2014									
	2005	*2006*	*2007*	*2008*	*2009*	*2010*	*2011*	*2012*	*2013*	*2014*
All long-term mutual funds	*$192*	*$227*	*$224*	*-$225*	*$389*	*$243*	*$28*	*$198*	*$160*	*$96*
Load	12	18	-2	-156	9	-62	-129	-77	-63	-175
Front-end[1]	41	44	18	-105	2	-56	-100	-67	-56	-159
Back-end[2]	-47	-47	-42	-39	-24	-27	-23	-16	-11	-9
Level[3]	18	22	25	-13	31	21	-6	6	-2	-4
Other[4]	(*)	(*)	(*)	(*)	(*)	(*)	(*)	-1	(*)	-3
Unclassified	-1	-1	-2	(*)	(*)	(*)	(*)	(*)	6	(*)
No-load[5]	139	156	165	-73	324	265	170	300	265	341
Retail	65	71	59	-103	139	55	-46	21	33	113
Institutional	73	84	106	30	185	210	215	279	232	228
Variable annuities	18	24	25	-26	29	7	-21	-28	-54	-66
"R" share classes[6]	24	29	37	30	27	33	9	3	11	-4

1. Front-end load > 1 per cent. Primarily includes Class A shares; includes sales where front-end loads are waived.
2. Front-end load = 0 per cent and contingent deferred sales load (CDSL) > 2 per cent. Primarily includes Class B shares.
3. Front-end load d" 1 per cent, CDSL d" 2 per cent, and 12b-1 fee > 0.25 per cent. Primarily includes Class C shares; excludes institutional share classes.
4. All other load share classes not classified as front-end load, back-end load, or level load.
5. Front-end load = 0 per cent, CDSL = 0 per cent, and 12b-1 fee d" 0.25 per cent.
6. "R" shares include assets in any share class that ICI designates as a "retirement share class." These share classes are sold predominantly to employer-sponsored retirement plans. However, other share classes—including retail and institutional share classes—also contain investments made through 401(k) plans or IRAs. (*) = inflow or outflow of less than $0.5 billion

Note: Components may not add to the totals because of rounding. Data exclude mutual funds that invest primarily in other mutual funds.

Source: Investment Company Institute and Lipper.

In part because of the shift toward asset-based fees (either through the fund or out-of-pocket), the market shares of front-end and back-end load share classes have declined in recent years, while those in no-load share classes have increased substantially. For example, from year-end 2005 to year-end 2014, front-end and back-end load share classes had net outflows totalling $717 billion; in addition, their share of long-term mutual fund assets fell from 29 per cent to 16 per cent.

Table 7.13: Total Net Assets of Long-Term Mutual Funds are Concentrated in No-Load Share Classes

Billions of dollars, 2005–2014

	2005	2006	2007	2008	2009	2010	2011	2012	2013	2014
All long-term mutual funds	$6,865	$8,060	$8,914	$5,771	$7,797	$9,029	$8,940	$10,359	$12,316	$13,127
Load	2,313	2,630	2,795	1,722	2,185	2,352	2,176	2,362	2,658	2,634
Front-end[1]	1,728	2,027	2,190	1,374	1,750	1,882	1,751	1,893	2,148	2,116
Back-end[2]	271	241	204	102	98	78	50	39	32	24
Level[3]	287	340	379	237	328	381	367	417	459	480
Other[4]	17	15	10	7	8	8	7	11	10	11
Unclassified	9	8	13	2	2	4	2	2	8	3
No-load[5]	3,427	4,073	4,587	3,055	4,255	5,091	5,224	6,262	7,594	8,366
Retail	2,404	2,799	3,091	1,940	2,666	3,069	2,991	3,469	4,144	4,625
Institutional	1,023	1,274	1,496	1,116	1,589	2,022	2,233	2,793	3,450	3,741

contd...

contd...

	2005	*2006*	*2007*	*2008*	*2009*	*2010*	*2011*	*2012*	*2013*	*2014*
Variable annuities	1,039	1,225	1,346	854	1,130	1,291	1,250	1,396	1,614	1,649
"R" share classes[6]	85	132	186	140	226	296	290	339	451	478

1. Front-end load > 1 per cent. Primarily includes Class A shares; includes sales where front-end loads are waived.
2. Front-end load = 0 per cent and contingent deferred sales load (CDSL) > 2 per cent. Primarily includes Class B shares.
3. Front-end load d" 1 per cent, CDSL d" 2 per cent, and 12b-1 fee > 0.25 per cent. Primarily includes Class C shares; excludes institutional share classes.
4. All other load share classes not classified as front-end load, back-end load, or level load.
5. Front-end load = 0 per cent, CDSL = 0 per cent, and 12b-1 fee d" 0.25 per cent.
6. "R" shares include assets in any share class that ICI designates as a "retirement share class." These share classes are sold predominantly to employer-sponsored retirement plans. However, other share classes—including retail and institutional share classes—also contain investments made through 401(k) plans or IRAs.

Note: Components may not add to the totals because of rounding. Data exclude mutual funds that invest primarily in other mutual funds.

Source: Investment Company Institute and Lipper.

By contrast, no-load share classes have seen net inflows and rising assets over the past 10 years. No-load share classes have accumulated the bulk of the inflows to long-term funds in the past decade. In 2014, no-load share classes accounted for 64 per cent of long-term fund assets, up from 50 per cent in 2005.

Some of the shift toward no-load share classes can be attributed to do-it-yourself investors. However, a larger factor is the growth of sales through DC plans as well as sales of no-load share classes through sales channels that compensate financial professionals with asset-based fees outside of funds (for example, mutual fund supermarkets, discount brokers, fee-based advisers, full-service brokerage platforms).

Services and Expenses in 401(k) Plans

Employers are confronted with two competing economic pressures: the need to attract and retain quality workers with competitive compensation packages and the need to keep their products and services competitively priced. In deciding whether to offer 401(k) plans to their workers, employers must decide if the benefits of offering a plan (in attracting and retaining quality workers) outweigh the costs of providing the plan and plan services. These costs are both the contributions the employer makes to an employee's 401(k) account and the costs associated with setting up and administering the 401(k) plan on an ongoing basis.

To provide and maintain 401(k) plans, employers are required to obtain a variety of administrative, participant-focused, regulatory, and compliance services. Employers offering 401(k) plans typically hire service providers to operate these plans and these providers charge fees for their services.

As with any employee benefit, the employer generally determines how the costs of providing the benefit will be shared between the employer and employee. 401 (k) plan fees can be paid directly by the plan sponsor (the employer), directly by the plan participant (the employee), indirectly by the participant through fees or other reductions in returns paid to the investment provider, or by some combination of these methods.

One key driver of 401(k) plan fees is plan size. A Deloitte/ICI study of 361 DC plans in 2013 created and analysed a comprehensive plan fee measure, the "all-in fee." The study found that plans with more participants and larger average account balances tended to have lower all-in fees than plans with fewer participants and smaller average account balances. This observed effect likely results in part from fixed costs required to start up and run the plan, much of which are driven by legal and regulatory requirements. It appears that economies of scale are gained as a plan grows because these fixed costs can be spread across more participants, a larger asset base, or both. Plans with a higher percentage of their assets in equity investments tended to have higher all-in fees, reflecting the higher expense ratios associated with equity investing compared with fixed-income investing. The study also examined types of service providers, automatic enrollment, the number of investment options, and variables relating to plans' relationships with their service providers—but found little impact on fees.

More than 60 per cent of 401(k) assets at year-end 2014 were invested in mutual funds. Participants in 401(k) plans holding mutual funds tend to invest in lower-cost funds and funds with below-average portfolio turnover. Both characteristics help to keep down the costs of investing in mutual funds through 401(k) plans. For example, at year-end 2013, 38 per cent of 401(k) equity mutual fund assets were in funds that had total annual expense ratios of less than 50 basis points, and another 47 per cent had expense ratios between 50 basis points and 100 basis points. On an asset-weighted basis, the average total expense ratio incurred on 401(k) participants' holdings of equity mutual funds through their 401(k) plans was 58 basis points in 2013, less than the asset-weighted average total expense ratio of 74 basis points for equity mutual funds industry wide. Similarly, equity mutual funds held in 401(k) accounts tend to have lower turnover in their portfolios. The asset-weighted average turnover rate of equity funds held in 401(k) accounts was 35 per cent in 2013, less than the industry wide asset-weighted average of 41 per cent.

Types of Mutual Funds Used by Retirement Plan Investors

Retirement investors tend to hold equity investments. At year-end 2014, 58 per cent of the $7.3 trillion in mutual fund retirement assets held in DC plans and IRAs were invested in domestic or world equity funds. By comparison, about 52 per cent of overall fund industry assets—retirement and non-retirement accounts—were invested in domestic or world equity funds. Domestic equity funds alone constituted about $3.2 trillion, or 45 per cent, of mutual fund assets held in DC plans and IRAs.

Retirement investors also gain exposure to equities and fixed-income securities through balanced funds. At year-end 2014, 23 per cent of mutual fund assets held in DC plans and IRAs were held in balanced funds, which invest in a mix of equity, bond, and money market securities. At year-end 2014, the remaining 19 per cent of mutual fund assets held in DC plans and IRAs were invested in bond funds and money market funds. Bond funds held $1.0 trillion, or 14 per cent, of mutual fund assets held in DC plans and IRAs, and money market funds accounted for $364 billion, or five per cent.

Table 7.14: Majority of Mutual Fund Retirement Account Assets were Invested in Equities

Billions of dollars, year-end 2014						
	Equity Domestic	*Balanced*[1]	*Bond*	*Money market*	*Total*	*World*
IRAs[2]	$1,484	$465	$783	$593	$221	$3,546
DC plans	1,763	500	873	444	143	3,723
401(k) plans	1,312	406	730	321	99	2,868
403(b) plans	284	37	79	37	20	456
457 plans	62	16	19	14	2	112
Other private-sector DC plans[3]	105	41	46	72	23	287
Total	**3,248**	**965**	**1,656**	**1,037**	**364**	**7,269**

1. Balanced funds invest in a mix of equities and fixed-income securities. Most target date and lifestyle funds are counted in this category.
2. IRAs include traditional IRAs, Roth IRAs, and employer-sponsored IRAs (SEP IRAs, SAR-SEP IRAs, and SIMPLE IRAs).
3. *Other private-sector DC plans* include Keoghs and other private-sector DC plans without 401(k) features.

Note: Components may not add to the total because of rounding.

Source: Investment Company Institute, "The US Retirement Market, Fourth Quarter 2014".

Target Date and Lifestyle Mutual Funds

Target date and lifestyle mutual funds, generally included in the balanced fund category, have grown more popular among investors and retirement plan sponsors over the past decade. A target date fund follows a predetermined reallocation of assets over time based on a specified target retirement date. Typically the fund rebalances its portfolio to become less focused on growth and more focused on income as it approaches and passes the target date, which is usually indicated in the fund's name. A lifestyle fund maintains a predetermined risk level and generally uses words such as "conservative," "moderate," or "aggressive" in its name to indicate the fund's risk level.

Assets in target date and lifestyle mutual funds totalled $1.1 trillion at year-end 2014, up from $977 billion at year-end 2013. Target date mutual funds' assets were up 14 per cent in 2014, increasing from $618 billion to $703 billion. Assets in lifestyle mutual funds grew 10 per cent in 2014, rising from $359 billion to $394 billion. The bulk (89 per cent) of target date mutual fund assets was held in retirement accounts, compared with 43 per cent of lifestyle mutual fund assets.

THE ROLE OF MUTUAL FUNDS IN EDUCATION SAVINGS

Twenty-three per cent of households that owned mutual funds in 2014 cited education as a financial goal for their fund investments. Nevertheless, the demand for education savings vehicles has been historically modest since their introduction in the 1990s, partly because of their limited availability and investors' lack of familiarity with them. The Economic Growth and Tax Relief Reconciliation Act (EGTRRA), enacted in 2001, enhanced the attractiveness of Section 529 plans and Coverdell Education Savings Accounts (ESAs)—two education savings vehicles—by allowing greater contributions to them and making them more flexible. The Pension Protection Act (PPA), enacted in 2006, made the EGTRRA enhancements to Section 529 plans permanent. The Tax Relief, Unemployment Insurance Reauthorisation, and Job Creation Act of 2010 extended the EGTRRA enhancements to Coverdell ESAs for two years; the American Taxpayer Relief Act of 2012 made these enhancements permanent.

Assets in Section 529 savings plans increased 9.6 per cent in 2014, with $224.7 billion at year-end 2014, up from

$205.1 billion at year-end 2013. As of year-end 2014, there were 11.0 million 529 savings plan accounts, with an average account size of approximately $20,500.

Table 7.15: Characteristics of Households Saving for College

Percentage of US households saving for college,[1] mid-2014	
Age of head of household[2]	
Younger than 35	23
35 to 44	27
45 to 54	28
55 to 64	13
65 or older	9
Education level	
High school diploma or less	20
Associate's degree or some college	27
Completed college	22
Some graduate school or completed graduate school	31
Household income[3]	
Less than $25,000	5
$25,000 to $34,999	4
$35,000 to $49,999	11
$50,000 to $74,999	19
$75,000 to $99,999	16
$100,000 or more	45
Number of children in home[4]	
None	35
One	26
Two	25
Three or more	14

1. Households saving for college are households that own education savings plans (Coverdell ESAs or 529 plans) or that said paying for education was one of their financial goals for their mutual funds.
2. Age is based on the sole or co-decision maker for saving and investing.
3. Total reported is household income before taxes in 2013.
4. The number of children reported is children younger than 18 living in the home.

In mid-2014, as a group, households saving for college through 529 plans, Coverdell ESAs, or mutual funds held outside these accounts tended to be headed by younger individuals, with half younger than 45. Heads of households saving for college had a range of education attainment: 47 per cent had less than four years of college and 53 per cent had four years or more. These households also had a range of incomes: 39 per cent earned less than $75,000; 16 per cent earned between $75,000 and $99,999; and 45 per cent earned $100,000 or more. About two-thirds of these households had children (younger than 18) in the home, and 39 per cent had more than one child in the home.

Table 7.16: Total Net Assets, Number of Funds, and Number of Share Classes of the Mutual Fund Industry

	Year-end		
Year	*Total net assets Billions of dollars*	*Number of funds*	*Number of share classes*
1940	0.45	68	–
1945	1.28	73	–
1950	2.53	98	–
1955	7.84	125	–
1960	17.03	161	–
1965	35.22	170	–
1970	47.62	361	–
1975	45.87	426	–
1976	51.28	452	–
1977	48.94	477	–
1978	55.84	505	–
1979	94.51	526	–
1980	134.76	564	–
1981	241.37	665	–
1982	296.68	857	–
1983	292.99	1,026	–
1984	370.68	1,243	1,243
1985	495.39	1,528	1,528
1986	715.67	1,835	1,835
1987	769.17	2,312	2,312
1988	809.37	2,737	2,737

contd...

contd...

Year	*Total net assets Billions of dollars*	*Number of funds*	*Number of share classes*
1989	980.67	2,935	2,935
1990	1,065.19	3,079	3,177
1991	1,393.19	3,403	3,587
1992	1,642.54	3,824	4,208
1993	2,069.96	4,534	5,562
1994	2,155.32	5,325	7,697
1995	2,811.29	5,725	9,007
1996	3,525.80	6,248	10,352
1997	4,468.20	6,684	12,002
1998	5,525.21	7,314	13,720
1999	6,846.34	7,791	15,262
2000	6,964.63	8,155	16,738
2001	6,974.91	8,305	18,022
2002	6,383.48	8,243	18,983
2003	7,402.48	8,127	19,321
2004	8,095.80	8,045	20,041
2005	8,891.38	7,977	20,554
2006	10,398.16	8,123	21,264
2007	12,000.17	8,041	21,638
2008	9,602.89	8,039	22,262
2009	11,112.62	7,666	21,651
2010	11,832.99	7,554	21,910
2011	11,631.89	7,587	22,282
2012	13,052.23	7,588	22,635
2013	15,034.78	7,713	23,386
2014	15,852.34	7,923	24,222

Note: Data for funds that invest primarily in other mutual funds were excluded from the series.

Table 7.17: Total Sales, New Sales, Exchange Sales, Redemptions, and Exchange Redemptions of the Mutual Fund Industry

Billions of dollars, Annual					
Year	Total sales[1]	New sales	Exchange sales[2]	Rede- mptions	Exchange redeem- ptions[3]
1945	0.29	–	–	0.11	–
1950	0.52	–	–	0.28	–
1955	1.21	–	–	0.44	–
1960	2.10	–	–	0.84	–
1965	4.36	3.93	–	1.96	–
1970	4.63	3.84	–	2.99	–
1975	10.06	8.94	–	9.57	–
1976	13.72	11.92	1.52	16.41	1.44
1977	17.07	14.75	2.24	16.69	2.31
1978	37.16	35.40	3.97	31.53	3.94
1979	119.32	115.66	5.83	86.74	5.89
1980	247.42	238.96	10.10	216.08	9.94
1981	472.13	452.42	14.44	362.44	14.59
1982	626.94	604.09	28.25	588.35	27.86
1983	547.77	532.04	35.67	565.83	36.03
1984	680.12	661.74	36.66	607.02	37.11
1985	953.85	933.37	46.55	864.88	46.84
1986	1,204.90	1,179.40	107.75	1,015.64	107.96
1987	1,251.19	1,220.27	205.68	1,178.75	207.35
1988	1,176.81	1,143.62	134.28	1,166.67	134.24
1989	1,444.84	1,401.21	130.66	1,327.05	131.95
1990	1,564.81	1,517.41	138.79	1,470.83	140.98
1991	2,037.64	1,990.53	155.75	1,879.69	154.31
1992	2,749.68	2,704.69	197.43	2,548.28	198.15
1993	3,187.49	3,137.76	248.79	2,904.44	253.95
1994	3,075.63	3,019.76	317.55	2,928.62	325.00
1995	3,600.62	3,526.00	351.53	3,314.86	351.08

contd...

contd...

Billions of dollars, Annual					
Year	Total sales[1]	New sales	Exchange sales[2]	Rede-mptions	Exchange redem-ptions[3]
1996	4,671.44	4,586.71	504.73	4,266.20	503.94
1997	5,801.23	5,704.83	613.44	5,324.29	618.49
1998	7,230.40	7,126.92	742.97	6,649.27	743.37
1999	9,043.58	8,922.96	949.96	8,562.10	947.36
2000	11,109.54	10,970.50	1,149.75	10,586.59	1,145.42
2001	12,866.21	12,747.53	797.34	12,242.32	798.08
2002	13,168.76	13,084.32	747.34	13,011.36	745.65
2003	12,393.59	12,315.40	572.50	12,361.66	573.76
2004	12,191.21	12,101.07	409.00	12,038.96	417.95
2005	13,939.33	13,812.50	420.84	13,546.81	432.43
2006	17,409.26	17,228.70	487.72	16,751.98	492.20
2007	23,470.65	23,236.42	606.47	22,352.20	611.96
2008	26,346.73	26,132.96	733.84	25,725.70	728.84
2009	20,679.71	20,528.31	529.97	20,680.23	528.13
2010	18,209.76	18,052.99	420.18	18,319.72	434.88
2011	17,836.92	17,660.78	448.06	17,738.34	466.52
2012	17,022.02	16,830.75	422.03	16,620.55	434.12
2013	18,157.31	17,967.72	517.69	17,779.44	531.09
2014	18,715.54	18,499.61	425.48	18,389.31	433.36

1. Total sales are the dollar value of new sales plus sales made through reinvestment of income dividends from existing accounts, but exclude reinvestment of capital gains distributions.
2. Exchange sales are the dollar value of mutual fund shares switched into funds within the same fund group.
3. Exchange redemptions are the dollar value of mutual fund shares switched out of funds and into other funds within the same fund group.

Note: Data for funds that invest primarily in other mutual funds were excluded from the series.

Table 7.18: Total Net Assets of t he Mutual Fund Industry

Billions of dollars, year-end				
Year	Total	Equity	Long-term funds	Money market funds
1960	17.03	16.00	1.02	–
1965	35.22	32.76	2.46	–
1970	47.62	45.13	2.49	–
1975	45.87	37.49	4.68	$3.70
1976	51.28	39.19	8.39	3.69
1977	48.94	34.07	10.98	3.89
1978	55.84	32.67	12.31	10.86
1979	94.51	35.88	13.10	45.53
1980	134.76	44.42	13.98	76.36
1981	241.37	41.19	14.01	186.16
1982	296.68	53.63	23.21	219.84
1983	292.99	76.97	36.63	179.39

	Long-term funds				Money market funds			
	Equity $	Domestic $	World $	Hybrid $	Bond	Muni-cipal $	Taxable $	Tax-exempt $
1984	370.68	74.55	5.19	11.15	25.45	20.79	209.75	23.80
1985	495.39	103.39	7.94	17.61	83.20	39.44	207.55	36.25
1986	715.67	138.98	15.47	25.76	167.63	75.67	228.35	63.81
1987	769.17	158.02	17.43	29.25	171.40	76.97	254.68	61.42
1988	809.37	171.40	17.98	26.35	168.96	86.73	272.20	65.76
1989	980.67	221.45	23.59	35.64	166.25	105.66	358.62	69.47
1990	1,065.19	211.18	28.30	35.98	171.14	120.25	414.56	83.78
1991	1,393.19	365.21	39.52	52.04	239.77	154.20	452.46	89.98
1992	1,642.54	468.41	45.68	77.63	308.37	196.26	451.35	94.84
1993	2,069.96	626.54	114.13	142.33	367.05	254.60	461.88	103.44
1994	2,155.32	691.57	161.19	161.40	302.84	227.31	501.11	109.89
1995	2,811.29	1,052.57	196.51	206.70	349.21	253.29	631.32	121.69
1996	3,525.80	1,440.81	285.20	248.36	396.56	253.07	763.94	137.87
1997	4,468.20	2,021.66	346.37	311.90	457.50	271.89	901.23	157.66
1998	5,525.21	2,586.31	391.64	360.04	536.96	298.59	1,166.97	184.71
1999	6,846.34	3,456.64	585.25	374.64	545.18	271.48	1,413.25	199.90
2000	6,964.63	3,369.73	564.75	360.92	545.58	278.41	1,611.38	233.87
2001	6,974.91	2,947.93	444.47	358.03	642.96	296.22	2,026.23	259.08
2002	6,383.48	2,273.05	369.37	335.28	810.58	330.13	1,988.78	276.30
2003	7,402.48	3,118.32	535.05	447.57	925.21	336.31	1,749.73	290.29
2004	8,095.80	3,626.37	716.20	552.25	971.03	328.24	1,589.70	312.00

contd...

contd...

	Long-term funds				Money market funds			
	Equity $	Domestic $	World $	Hybrid $	Bond $	Muni-cipal $	Taxable $	Tax-exempt $
2005	8,891.38	3,929.72	955.73	621.48	1,018.68	338.95	1,690.45	336.37
2006	10,398.16	4,472.13	1,360.45	731.50	1,130.52	365.09	1,969.42	369.03
2007	12,000.17	4,694.65	1,718.57	821.52	1,305.51	374.15	2,617.67	468.09
2008	9,602.89	2,738.82	898.60	562.26	1,233.18	337.79	3,338.56	493.68
2009	11,112.62	3,564.56	1,307.98	717.58	1,748.11	458.50	2,916.96	398.94
2010	11,832.99	4,055.64	1,540.98	841.41	2,117.07	473.95	2,473.92	330.01
2011	11,631.89	3,856.91	1,356.08	883.06	2,346.90	497.53	2,399.72	291.70
2012	13,052.23	4,326.34	1,612.41	1,029.26	2,810.53	580.17	2,406.10	287.43
2013	15,034.78	5,728.52	2,034.20	1,267.33	2,787.10	499.29	2,447.72	270.61
2014	15,852.34	6,234.99	2,079.33	1,351.84	2,894.45	566.48	2,464.47	260.79

Note: Data for funds that invest primarily in other mutual funds were excluded from the series. The data contain a series break beginning in 1984. All funds were reclassified in 1984, and a separate category was created for hybrid funds. Components may not add to the total because of rounding.

Table 7.19: Number of Funds of the Mutual Fund Industry

Year-end				
Year	Total	Long-term funds		Money market funds
		Equity	Bond and income	
1970	361	323	38	–
1971	392	350	42	–
1972	410	364	46	–
1973	421	366	55	–
1974	431	343	73	15
1975	426	314	76	36
1976	452	302	102	48
1977	477	296	131	50
1978	505	294	150	61
1979	526	289	159	78
1980	564	288	170	106
1981	665	306	180	179
1982	857	340	199	318
1983	1,026	396	257	373

	Long-term funds				Money market funds			
	Equity		Hybrid		Taxable	Municipal	Taxable	Tax-exempt
	Domestic	***World***	***Domestic***	***World***				
1984	1,243	430	29	89	159	111	331	94
1985	1,528	519	43	103	229	174	350	110
1986	1,835	621	57	121	302	247	360	127
1987	2,312	743	81	164	415	366	389	154
1988	2,737	897	109	179	522	420	433	177
1989	2,935	941	128	189	561	443	470	203
1990	3,079	944	155	192	584	463	505	236
1991	3,403	985	206	211	658	523	552	268
1992	3,824	1,086	239	234	773	628	585	279
1993	4,534	1,280	306	281	951	796	627	293
1994	5,325	1,463	423	360	1,104	1,012	649	314
1995	5,725	1,611	528	411	1,167	1,011	676	321
1996	6,248	1,902	668	465	1,244	981	669	319
1997	6,684	2,183	768	500	1,287	933	685	328
1998	7,314	2,622	890	525	1,351	900	687	339
1999	7,791	3,004	949	531	1,375	887	704	341
2000	8,155	3,315	1,055	508	1,367	871	704	335
2001	8,305	3,610	1,085	473	1,308	814	690	325
2002	8,243	3,714	1,018	458	1,295	770	677	311
2003	8,127	3,659	929	474	1,313	779	660	313
2004	8,045	3,651	887	472	1,324	767	639	305
2005	7,977	3,659	912	481	1,315	740	593	277
2006	8,123	3,748	995	500	1,320	713	573	274
2007	8,041	3,678	1,060	496	1,326	676	545	260
2008	8,039	3,655	1,139	511	1,311	640	534	249
2009	7,666	3,419	1,172	481	1,291	599	476	228
2010	7,554	3,322	1,193	494	1,310	583	442	210
2011	7,587	3,260	1,265	519	1,348	563	431	201
2012	7,588	3,218	1,278	562	1,393	557	400	180
2013	7,713	3,194	1,345	602	1,457	560	382	173
2014	7,923	3,239	1,407	661	1,531	557	365	163

Note: Data for funds that invest primarily in other mutual funds were excluded from the series. The data contain a series break beginning in 1984. All funds were reclassified in 1984, and a separate category was created for hybrid funds.

Table 7.20: Liquid Assets and Liquidity Ratio of Long-term Mutual Funds

Year-end								
Year	*Liquid assets Millions of dollars*				*Liquidity ratio* Percent*			
	Total $	*Equity Funds $*	*Hybrid Funds $*	*Bond Funds $*	*Total percent*	*Equity Funds percent*	*Hybrid Funds percent*	*Bond Funds percent*
1984	12,181	7,295	878	4,007	8.9	9.1	7.9	8.7
1985	20,593	10,452	1,413	8,728	8.2	9.4	8.0	7.1
1986	30,611	14,612	2,514	13,485	7.2	9.5	9.8	5.5
1987	37,930	16,319	2,730	18,881	8.4	9.3	9.3	7.6
1988	44,980	17,742	2,986	24,252	9.5	9.4	11.3	9.5
1989	44,603	25,602	5,747	13,253	8.1	10.4	16.1	4.9
1990	48,440	27,344	4,198	16,899	8.5	11.4	11.7	5.8
1991	60,385	30,657	3,309	26,419	7.1	7.6	6.4	6.7
1992	73,984	42,417	6,560	25,007	6.7	8.3	8.5	5.0
1993	99,436	57,539	16,613	25,284	6.6	7.8	11.7	4.1
1994	120,430	70,885	19,929	29,616	7.8	8.3	12.3	5.6
1995	141,755	97,743	19,271	24,741	6.9	7.8	9.3	4.1
1996	151,988	107,667	17,954	26,367	5.8	6.2	7.2	4.1
1997	198,826	145,565	24,645	28,616	5.8	6.1	7.9	3.9
1998	191,393	143,516	25,289	22,588	4.6	4.8	7.0	2.7
1999	219,098	174,692	20,979	23,427	4.2	4.3	5.6	2.9
2000	277,164	225,023	26,798	25,343	5.4	5.7	7.4	3.1
2001	222,475	170,361	26,911	25,203	4.7	5.0	7.5	2.7
2002	208,939	120,500	25,423	63,016	5.1	4.6	7.6	5.5
2003	259,641	154,877	30,654	74,110	4.8	4.2	6.8	5.9
2004	307,111	184,140	36,419	86,552	5.0	4.2	6.6	6.7
2005	303,189	190,906	43,133	69,150	4.4	3.9	6.9	5.1
2006	346,768	218,670	57,461	70,637	4.3	3.7	7.9	4.7
2007	381,679	266,285	56,813	58,581	4.3	4.2	6.9	3.5
2008	296,540	185,536	52,712	58,291	5.1	5.1	9.4	3.7
2009	365,787	169,799	52,845	143,143	4.7	3.5	7.4	6.5
2010	330,295	192,757	61,013	76,525	3.7	3.4	7.3	3.0
2011	461,767	182,548	70,660	208,559	5.2	3.5	8.0	7.3
2012	515,396	200,436	99,570	215,390	5.0	3.4	9.7	6.4
2013	651,842	272,507	142,258	237,077	5.3	3.5	11.2	7.2
2014	725,615	291,691	148,623	285,301	5.5	3.5	11.0	8.2

* Liquidity ratio is the ratio of liquid assets divided by total net assets at year-end.

Note: Data for funds that invest primarily in other mutual funds were excluded from the series. Components may not add to the total because of rounding.

Table 7.21: Net New Cash Flow* of Long-Term Mutual Funds

Millions of dollars, annual				
Year	*Total*	*Equity funds*	*Hybrid funds*	*Bond funds*
1984	19,194	4,336	1,801	13,058
1985	73,490	6,643	3,720	63,127
1986	129,991	20,386	6,988	102,618
1987	29,776	19,231	3,748	6,797
1988	-23,119	-14,948	-3,684	-4,488
1989	8,731	6,774	3,183	-1,226
1990	21,211	12,915	1,463	6,833
1991	106,213	39,888	7,067	59,258
1992	171,696	78,983	21,725	70,989
1993	242,049	127,260	42,619	72,169
1994	75,160	114,525	21,998	-61,362
1995	122,208	124,392	3,738	-5,922
1996	231,874	216,937	11,795	3,141
1997	272,030	227,106	15,757	29,166
1998	241,796	156,875	10,265	74,656
1999	169,780	187,565	-13,018	-4,767
2000	228,874	315,711	-36,722	-50,115
2001	129,188	33,439	7,285	88,463
2002	120,583	-29,326	8,043	141,865
2003	215,884	144,055	39,079	32,750
2004	209,890	171,937	53,055	-15,102
2005	192,016	123,967	42,754	25,295
2006	227,078	147,773	19,857	59,448
2007	224,321	73,328	40,384	110,609
2008	-224,900	-229,407	-25,525	30,032
2009	389,078	-1,952	19,792	371,238
2010	243,222	-24,414	35,295	232,342
2011	27,953	-129,263	39,549	117,667
2012	198,441	-152,680	44,895	306,226
2013	159,674	159,553	71,293	-71,172
2014	96,090	25,216	27,346	43,528

* Net new cash flow is the dollar value of new sales minus redemptions combined with net exchanges.

Note: Data for funds that invest primarily in other mutual funds were excluded from the series.

Table 7.22: Sector Mutual Funds: Total Net Assets and Net New Cash Flow by Type of Fund

Millions of dollars									
Year	Total net assets Year-end								
	Consumer	Financial	Health	Natural resources	Precious metals	Real estate	Technology/ Telcom	Utilities	Other sectors
2000	1,042	16,087	45,921	2,955	1,108	11,675	103,853	22,908	3,917
2001	1,290	13,901	40,545	2,429	1,276	13,509	62,339	17,744	2,940
2002	1,096	10,885	30,087	2,230	2,431	17,745	31,308	11,275	2,082
2003	1,436	13,138	36,803	3,307	4,158	31,653	46,929	13,481	2,412
2004	1,631	12,917	40,147	5,844	4,215	49,927	42,403	19,201	2,974
2005	1,405	11,837	45,398	12,048	6,928	59,158	34,366	28,390	3,189
2006	1,928	12,269	44,744	14,723	9,741	81,329	32,891	34,589	3,950
2007	2,147	8,518	43,967	22,312	11,804	53,738	34,169	45,669	4,826
2008	1,776	4,857	31,337	9,967	7,776	33,503	16,331	23,240	1,766
2009	2,439	5,941	32,440	17,496	14,785	44,126	27,610	30,327	2,986
2010	3,113	6,286	32,507	22,853	22,926	56,830	30,738	33,332	4,597
2011	3,546	4,548	35,884	20,998	17,029	61,665	26,680	34,785	3,906
2012	4,675	5,901	44,105	22,041	15,293	77,033	28,570	35,400	5,001
2013	6,431	9,285	74,767	30,960	6,790	79,034	41,486	40,149	8,173
2014	7,017	9,415	103,447	36,904	6,005	106,106	45,358	41,556	8,969

Net new cash flow (Annual)									(Millions of dollars)
Year	Consumer	Financial	Health	Natural resources	Precious metals	Real estate	Technology/ Telcom	Utilities	Other sectors
2000	-122	-534	9,256	236	-203	339	43,837	1,015	-187
2001	254	-962	236	-182	-28	430	-4,458	-953	-198
2002	11	-1,603	-2,895	-70	480	3,612	-6,211	-2,076	-288
2003	9	-940	-767	327	456	5,177	73	-292	-145
2004	3	-1,535	-387	1,414	419	7,050	-6,165	1,571	148
2005	-209	-1,586	836	3,483	1,016	3,000	-8,541	3,311	121
2006	29	-1,017	-4,137	789	717	4,395	-4,456	556	-49
2007	94	-2,617	-3,378	1,724	-214	-15,282	-2,745	1,992	257
2008	209	96	-3,025	-268	832	1,791	-3,847	-3,397	-488
2009	82	-457	-3,163	1,767	2,249	492	1,768	254	386
2010	101	-626	-2,407	1,470	2,353	1,695	-1,391	-848	724
2011	262	-885	478	1,193	-1,336	916	-2,346	701	-286
2012	544	56	1,385	564	152	4,307	-1,515	-1,994	173
2013	794	859	8,582	5,411	-1,425	241	1,972	-1,409	977
2014	47	-256	7,645	5,823	-165	5,186	85	3,783	91

Note: Data for funds that invest primarily in other mutual funds were excluded from the series. Components may not add to the total because of rounding.

Table 7.23: Sector Mutual Funds: Number of Funds and Number of Share Classes by Type of Fund

	Year-end								
Year	*Number of funds*								
	Consumer	*Financial*	*Health*	*Natural resources*	*Precious metals*	*Real estate*	*Technology/ Telcom*	*Utilities*	*Other sectors*
2000	7	34	38	19	11	74	132	34	16
2001	9	41	57	18	10	75	155	40	17
2002	12	42	63	15	11	79	145	35	19
2003	11	38	58	16	11	91	124	33	19
2004	14	40	59	17	11	94	115	34	20
2005	14	41	53	18	11	93	103	32	19
2006	18	40	57	20	12	97	108	38	23
2007	19	40	52	20	11	96	98	39	25
2008	19	38	48	21	11	92	88	41	22
2009	19	36	41	20	11	90	79	37	23
2010	19	35	38	21	11	88	74	35	21
2011	19	32	34	26	10	84	69	33	21
2012	20	33	35	28	11	85	66	36	24
2013	19	32	35	32	11	88	68	41	24
2014	19	31	34	36	11	88	67	37	24

Year-end									
Number of share classes									
Year	Consumer	Financial	Health	Natural resources	Precious metals	Real estate	Technology/ Telcom	Utilities	Other sectors
2000	12	73	91	33	19	151	283	75	23
2001	17	88	145	32	21	156	350	89	25
2002	22	92	171	26	24	172	348	91	28
2003	19	85	155	33	26	214	290	88	28
2004	27	92	159	34	27	238	279	91	29
2005	26	95	137	38	27	240	260	94	27
2006	33	93	147	41	30	246	267	107	37
2007	41	95	133	47	34	252	249	113	42
2008	42	91	124	52	37	246	218	117	33
2009	42	80	101	50	37	246	199	105	41
2010	42	79	97	54	38	251	190	96	36
2011	43	72	80	75	33	243	184	89	36
2012	47	73	83	85	36	246	182	100	43
2013	41	72	83	97	34	261	188	109	44
2014	41	70	80	106	34	271	181	96	40

Note: Data for funds that invest primarily in other mutual funds were excluded from the series.

Table 7.24: Worldwide Total Net Assets of Mutual Funds

Millions of U.S. dollars, year-end								
	2007	*2008*	*2009*	*2010*	*2011*	*2012*	*2013*	*2014*
World	26,130,201	18,919,299	22,945,270	24,711,508	23,801,209	26,844,414	30,047,406	31,381,425
America	13,421,794	10,581,230	12,578,245	13,599,181	13,534,659	15,147,007	17,173,504	18,012,199
Argentina	6,789	3,867	4,470	5,179	6,808	9,185	11,179	15,630
Brazil	615,365	479,321	783,970	980,448	1,008,928	1,070,998	1,018,641	989,542
Canada	698,397	416,031	565,156	636,947	753,606	856,504	940,580	981,804
Chile	24,444	17,587	34,227	38,243	33,425	37,900	39,291	44,166
Costa Rica	1,203	1,098	1,309	1,470	1,266	1,484	1,933	2,092
Mexico	75,428	60,435	70,659	98,094	92,743	112,201	120,518	119,504
Trinidad and Tobago	N/A	N/A	5,832	5,812	5,989	6,505	6,586	7,121
United States	12,000,168	9,602,891	11,112,623	11,832,988	11,631,894	13,052,230	15,034,776	15,852,341
Europe	8,934,861	6,231,116	7,545,531	7,903,389	7,220,298	8,230,059	9,374,830	9,576,475
Austria	138,709	93,269	99,628	94,670	81,038	89,125	90,633	83,522
Belgium	149,842	105,057	106,721	96,288	81,505	81,651	91,528	90,211
Bulgaria	N/A	226	256	302	291	324	504	496
Croatia	N/A	N/A	N/A	N/A	N/A	N/A	N/A	2,058

	Millions of U.S. dollars, year-end							
	2007	2008	2009	2010	2011	2012	2013	2014
Czech Republic	7,595	5,260	5,436	5,508	4,445	5,001	5,131	5,563
Denmark	104,083	65,182	83,024	89,800	84,891	103,506	118,702	121,092
Finland	81,136	48,750	66,131	71,210	62,193	73,985	88,462	86,621
France	1,989,690	1,591,082	1,805,641	1,617,176	1,382,068	1,473,085	1,531,500	1,391,271
Germany	372,072	237,986	317,543	333,713	293,011	327,640	382,976	359,867
Greece	29,807	12,189	12,434	8,627	5,213	6,011	6,742	5,256
Hungary	12,573	9,188	11,052	11,532	7,193	8,570	12,158	11,375
Ireland	951,371	720,486	860,515	1,014,104	1,061,051	1,276,601	1,439,867	1,547,343
Italy	419,687	263,588	279,474	234,313	180,754	181,720	215,553	238,327
Liechtenstein	25,103	20,489	30,329	35,387	32,606	31,951	36,235	28,875
Luxembourg	2,685,065	1,860,763	2,293,973	2,512,874	2,277,465	2,641,964	3,030,665	3,208,264
Malta	N/A	N/A	N/A	N/A	2,132	3,033	3,160	3,522
Netherlands	113,759	77,379	95,512	85,924	69,156	76,145	85,304	75,751
Norway	74,709	41,157	71,170	84,505	79,999	98,723	109,325	112,223
Poland	45,542	17,782	23,025	25,595	18,463	25,883	27,858	26,098
Portugal	29,732	13,572	15,808	11,004	7,321	7,509	9,625	8,564

	Millions of U.S. dollars, year-end							
	2007	2008	2009	2010	2011	2012	2013	2014
Romania	390	326	1,134	1,713	2,388	2,613	4,000	4,932
Russia	7,175	2,026	3,182	3,917	3,072	N/A	N/A	N/A
Slovakia	4,762	3,841	4,222	4,349	3,191	2,951	3,292	4,183
Slovenia	4,219	2,067	2,610	2,663	2,279	2,370	2,506	2,553
Spain	396,534	270,983	269,611	216,915	195,220	191,284	248,234	274,049
Sweden	194,955	113,331	170,277	205,449	179,707	205,733	252,878	279,094
Switzerland	176,282	135,052	168,260	261,893	273,061	310,686	397,080	407,890
Turkey	22,609	15,404	19,426	19,545	14,048	16,478	14,078	15,292
United Kingdom	897,460	504,681	729,141	854,413	816,537	985,517	1,166,834	1,182,184
Asia and Pacific	3,678,325	2,037,536	2,715,233	3,067,323	2,921,276	3,322,198	3,356,204	3,646,276
Australia	1,192,988	841,133	1,198,838	1,455,850	1,440,128	1,667,128	1,624,081	1,601,132
China	434,063	276,303	381,207	364,985	339,037	437,449	460,332	708,884
Hong Kong	818,421	N/A	N/A	N/A	N/A	N/A	N/A	N/A
India	108,582	62,805	130,284	111,421	87,519	114,489	107,895	134,630
Japan	713,998	575,327	660,666	785,504	745,383	738,488	774,126	780,636

Millions of U.S. dollars, year-end								
	2007	2008	2009	2010	2011	2012	2013	2014
Korea, Rep.	329,979	221,992	264,573	266,495	226,716	267,582	285,173	312,150
New Zealand	14,925	10,612	17,657	19,562	23,709	31,145	34,185	41,560
Pakistan	4,956	1,985	2,224	2,290	2,984	3,159	3,464	4,156
Philippines	2,090	1,263	1,488	2,184	2,363	3,566	4,662	5,078
Taiwan	58,323	46,116	58,297	59,032	53,437	59,192	62,286	58,049
Africa	95,221	69,417	106,261	141,615	124,976	145,150	142,868	146,474
South Africa	95,221	69,417	106,261	141,615	124,976	145,150	142,868	146,474

N/A = not available

Note: Funds of funds are not included except for France, Italy, and Luxembourg. Data include home-domiciled funds, except for Hong Kong, the Republic of Korea, and New Zealand, which include home- and foreign-domiciled funds. Components may not add to the total because of rounding.

Source: International Investment Funds Association.

Table 7.25: Worldwide Number of Mutual Funds

	Year-end							
	2007	*2008*	*2009*	*2010*	*2011*	*2012*	*2013*	*2014*
World	66,362	69,049	67,533	69,492	72,607	73,235	76,206	79,669
America	15,474	16,476	16,935	17,992	19,749	21,095	22,026	22,962
Argentina	241	253	252	254	281	291	297	302
Brazil	3,381	4,169	4,744	5,618	6,513	7,468	8,072	8,560
Canada	2,038	2,015	2,075	2,117	2,655	2,866	2,963	3,164
Chile	1,260	1,484	1,691	1,912	2,150	2,286	2,385	2,418
Costa Rica	93	85	64	68	63	66	66	66
Mexico	420	431	407	434	464	488	487	486
Trinidad and Tobago	N/A	N/A	36	35	36	42	43	43
United States	8,041	8,039	7,666	7,554	7,587	7,588	7,713	7,923
Europe	35,210	36,780	34,899	35,292	35,713	34,470	34,743	35,163
Austria	1,070	1,065	1,016	1,016	1,003	995	981	938
Belgium	1,655	1,828	1,845	1,797	1,723	1,529	1,432	1,209
Bulgaria	N/A	81	85	90	92	95	98	103
Croatia	N/A	N/A	N/A	N/A	N/A	N/A	N/A	82
Czech Republic	66	76	78	80	80	80	85	106
Denmark	500	489	483	490	500	495	510	530

	Year-end							
	2007	2008	2009	2010	2011	2012	2013	2014
Finland	379	389	377	366	368	375	369	352
France	8,243	8,301	7,982	7,791	7,744	7,392	7,154	7,082
Germany	1,462	1,675	2,067	2,106	2,051	2,059	2,012	2,039
Greece	230	239	210	213	196	177	166	143
Hungary	212	270	264	276	152	167	182	189
Ireland	2,898	3,097	2,721	2,899	3,085	3,167	3,345	3,462
Italy	924	742	675	650	659	600	661	719
Liechtenstein	391	335	348	409	437	535	657	587
Luxembourg	8,782	9,351	9,017	9,353	9,462	9,435	9,500	9,839
Malta	N/A	N/A	N/A	N/A	59	54	69	63
Netherlands	450	458a	N/A	N/A	495	497	501	561
Norway	511	530	487	507	507	406	573	616
Poland	188	210	208	214	226	259	264	278
Portugal	180	184	171	171	173	157	153	137
Romania	41	52	51	56	105	62	64	72
Russia	533	528	480	462	472	N/A	N/A	N/A
Slovakia	54	56	54	58	63	58	54	67

	Year-end							
	2007	*2008*	*2009*	*2010*	*2011*	*2012*	*2013*	*2014*
Slovenia	106	125	125	130	137	131	114	111
Spain	2,940	2,944	2,588	2,486	2,474	2,349	2,267	2,238
Sweden	477	508	506	504	508	456	484	510
Switzerland	567	572	509	653	664	667	765	815
Turkey	294	304	286	311	337	351	373	395
United Kingdom	2,057	2,371	2,266	2,204	1,941	1,922	1,910	1,920
Asia and Pacific	14,847	14,909	14,795	15,265	16,198	16,703	18,375	20,373
Australia	N/A	N/A	N/A	N/A	N/A	N/A	N/A	N/A
China	341	429	547	660	831	1,065	1,415	1,763
Hong Kong	1,162	N/A	N/A	N/A	N/A	N/A	N/A	N/A
India	555	551	590	658	680	692	699	723
Japan	2,997	3,333	3,656	3,905	4,196	4,384	4,922	5,404
Korea, Rep. of	8,609	9,384	8,703	8,687	9,064	9,121	9,876	11,063
New Zealand	623	643	702	700	709	700	694	632
Pakistan	64	83	96	125	137	139	152	159
Philippines	40	43	41	43	47	48	47	52
Taiwan	456	443	460	487	534	554	570	577

	Year-end							
	2007	*2008*	*2009*	*2010*	*2011*	*2012*	*2013*	*2014*
Africa	831	884	904	943	947	967	1,062	1,171
South Africa	831	884	904	943	947	967	1,062	1,171

a Year-end data are not available. Data are as of September.

N/A = not available

Note: Funds of funds are not included except for France, Italy, and Luxembourg. Data include home-domiciled funds, except for Hong Kong, the Republic of Korea, and New Zealand, which include home- and foreign-domiciled funds.

Source: International Investment Funds Association.

3. MUTUAL FUNDS IN CANADA

The Growth of Canadian Mutual Funds

Four years later, in 1932, the first Canadian fund, Canadian Investment Fund Ltd. (CIF), was established and by 1951 had assets of $51 million. It changed its name to Spectrum United Canadian Investment Fund in November 1996 and to CI Canadian Investment Fund in August 2002.

The growth of mutual funds and their impact on investing in general was nothing short of revolutionary. For the first time, ordinary investors with minimal capital could pool their resources in a professionally managed, diversified basket of investments, rather than going the more expensive route of buying individual stocks of varying risks. This was considered a giant step in the democratisation of investments for the average person.

The first major sign of growth and popularity of mutual funds in Canada took place in the early 1960s when total assets doubled from $540 million in 1960 to more than $1 billion by the end of 1963. But the largest influx into mutual funds in Canada came during the 1990s when double-digit interest rates that had lured Canadian savers into GICs tumbled and investors moved into investments with the potential for higher returns.

Interest rates and mutual fund sales had a direct correlation in the 1990s. In May 1990, the Bank of Canada rate, on which financial institutions base their interest rates, stood at one of its highest levels ever – 14.05 per cent. From that point, the rate began a steady decline, hitting 6.81 per cent at the beginning of 1993 and 4.11 per cent at the end of the year.

As the bank rate fell, mutual fund sales surged, jumping 140 per cent from the end of 1992 to the end of 1993 as strong markets sent assets climbing to almost $114.6 billion. The Bank rate dropped to 3.25 per cent in January 1997 before slowly climbing to five per cent in January 2000.

Mutual funds clearly represented the fastest-growing segment of the Canadian financial services industry during the 1990s and through the turn of the century with the value of assets under management increasing by 1,700 per cent – from $25 billion in December 1990 to $426 billion by December 2001. These assets were managed in about 1,800 different mutual funds held in more than 50 million unit holder accounts.

In 2008, global markets were rocked by a financial crisis, triggered by an over-extended US housing market and marked by financial sector collapses and bailouts similar to the European crisis that spawned the original mutual fund.

Canada escaped largely unscathed compared to other countries, particularly the US, thanks to tighter mortgage rules and a regulated banking system. Canadian mutual funds survived, too, and after a brief downturn continue to thrive as a popular and valued savings device for Canadian investors.

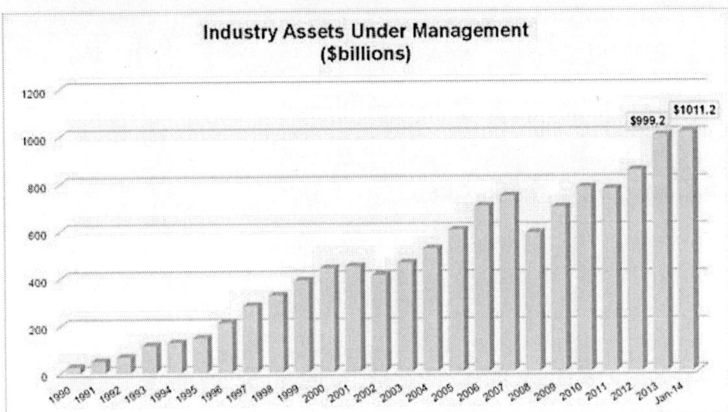

Fig. 7.1: Industry AUM.

The Mutual Fund Advantage

Mutual funds offer Canadians a superior means of accumulating wealth through access to a broad range of personalised investment solutions based on sound investing principles.

Mutual funds include:

- Professional portfolio management
- Streamlined and convenient administration
- Risk management through diversification
- Innovative solutions that meet a range of investment objectives and evolving investor needs
- Opportunities for foreign and domestic investment that may not otherwise be directly accessible to investors
- Liquidity, enabling investors to respond to changes in their personal circumstances
- Access to investing for all types of people, including those who prefer to invest small amounts at regular intervals
- Choice of purchase methods and fee structures, including full service, fee-for-service and do-it-yourself
- Accountability and fairness to investors through industry regulation and transparency

The Growth of the Industry and IFIC

To meet the growing regulatory and trade needs of the mutual fund industry, the Canadian Mutual Funds Association (CMFA) was established in 1962. Original members of the CMFA were individual mutual funds themselves, not fund management companies as is the case today.

In April 1963, the CMFA published a Code of Ethics and Regulation for its members. Ten years later, it formally incorporated with a mandate to engage in and support activities conducive to high ethical standards and efficiency of administration and operations within the Canadian mutual funds industry. In 1976, the CMFA changed its name to The Investment Funds Institute of Canada (IFIC).

Since then, IFIC has played an integral role in the regulatory development of the mutual funds industry in Canada, proactively influencing and advancing industry issues within the regulatory framework, while increasing members' efficiencies, knowledge and proficiency. IFIC provides a consistently high level of service to enable dealer and manager members to work together in a co-operative forum to enhance the integrity and growth of the industry and strengthen investor confidence.

4. MUTUAL FUNDS IN ASIA

By any basis of measurement, the growth of offshore mutual funds in Asia has been outstanding over the last 15 years or so. Statistics alone show that both the number of funds and the aggregate value of investment in them have increased massively since 1995. This article aims to provide some of the background behind this phenomenal growth, and also aims to give some pointers to what might happen in the future.

In 1995, the Asian mutual fund industry had not really extended much beyond Hong Kong, Taiwan and Singapore. While the Hong Kong and Taiwan markets had fully embraced use of offshore funds, Singapore, at the time, had restricted access only to locally incorporated products.

Fund distributors were mainly the financial advisers in these markets, along with a few private banks and US-owned broker/dealer securities companies. However, things were about to change. In Hong Kong, banks such as Citibank and Standard Chartered had already realised the need to offer a range of "third party" funds to their customer base, had set up investment services departments and were rapidly training front-line staff in the skills required to promote funds to their wealthier customers. They had developed analytical departments to select suitable funds and managers, acting as "gate-keepers". HSBC had not moved beyond selling own-label funds; however Hang Seng had begun to develop a third party fund distribution service. In Singapore, the local banks had already begun to realise that their own fund management companies were producing products their customers might want to buy, so they also set about the training of front-line staff to deliver sales on these.

Within five years, by 2000, all the major retail banks in Hong Kong and Singapore had got in on the act, and very shortly they came to dominate the distribution landscape for mutual funds. Volumes rose from a market share of less than 15 per cent to more than 85 per cent.

Meanwhile, in Taiwan, the securities companies there had set up mutual fund distribution teams, which were delivering big volume sales to the fund companies based in Hong Kong. Taiwan, which many observers have regarded as having "perfect demographics" for the mutual fund business, had easily the largest sales volume within the region, and with it had begun the phenomenon of "investor tours" to Hong Kong. Many retail investors would undertake two or three day trips, part of which was spent in the fund company offices, the other in the adjacent shopping malls. Billions of assets were raised as a result, boosting the Hong Kong economy at the same time.

In the mid-1980's, the Hong Kong Office of the Commissioner of Securities (the regulator at the time) issued guidelines allowing the approval of funds for public distribution in Hong Kong (this followed a number of public scandals where fraudulent activity occurred). Possibly under pressure from the leading companies of the time, and in the aftermath of the agreement between the UK and Chinese governments to handover rule of Hong Kong from July 1, 1997; funds that had a domicile overseas from Hong Kong were able to gain authorisation alongside those with

Hong Kong domicile. The presumption being that in the event that following the "handover" the economy collapsed and rule of law broke down, money invested via funds into securities could not be sequestered by the Chinese government as it was not actually in Hong Kong.

At the same time in Europe, the European Union (EU) had realised a need to formalise a patchwork of fund regulations and thus by 1985 they had developed UCITS (Undertaking for Collective Investment in Transferable Securities) as a set of guidelines to enable funds to be established, and for member states of the EU to approve their distribution. Luxembourg rapidly realised that by providing a central location with minimal local taxes, it was possible to create cross-border funds of interest to investors. These funds, known as "Societe d'Investment a Capital Variable" or SICAV, were an instant success. SICAVs were created as "umbrella" funds, whereby instead of single stand-alone funds such as unit trusts, multiple sub-funds each investing into a different market were able to be established, all under a single vehicle (or umbrella). These SICAVs were able to gain authorisation in Hong Kong, and fairly soon distributors in both Hong Kong and Taiwan realised they met the investment needs of many of their prospective clients.

Thus, the "offshore fund" boom commenced, although the irony was that as most "offshore funds" were located in Luxembourg, they were in fact "land-locked".

Singapore, observant of these developments to the north, was persuaded to change their restrictive approach to fund authorisation in 1997, as a result of which "feeder funds" feeding into SICAVs where management of assets was carried out in Singapore, initially, could be distributed. Shortly thereafter, this change was extended to enable a wider choice of funds, ultimately leading to a more general offering without the need to be a feeder fund.

Retail investors liked what they saw. They went to their banks for advice, and soon the whole bank fund distribution business mushroomed. Although many banks attempted to only sell proprietary funds, they soon realised that if they didn't offer those of a number of fund houses, their customers would take their business to the competitor bank along the street. Thus, it soon became necessary for banks to set up "gate-keeper" departments, to provide analysis and advice on selection of funds, and adopt approval lists of funds and fund companies. This also enabled the bigger bank distributors to gain leverage over the fund houses selected, to negotiate improved "terms of business". Generally, this meant that a bank distributor demanded, and received the whole of the front-end load for funds sold (five per cent usually) and a significant proportion of the annual management fee (often 50 bps to 75 bps) from sales made and assets under management. Fund distribution thus became an extremely profitable business for the banks, leading them to create ever larger "wealth management" departments. It has been estimated that many retail-focused banks in Asia were able to achieve more than 10 per cent of their revenues from wealth management by around 2005, from virtually zero ten years earlier.

While private banks had entered the mutual fund distribution market much earlier than their retail cousins, for many this became a bit of a roller-coaster ride. Not wishing to compete head-on with the retail banks, many of the private banks moved into hedge fund distribution, making the assumption, often not always as accurate as would be desirable, that their high net worth individuals (HNWI) were better equipped to understand the complexities of hedge funds as opposed to retail customers. This also led them to use structured products, where they were able to create more "attractive" investments for HNWI through use of leverage and other derivatives linked to hedge funds. These more "exotic" investment vehicles became more and more exotic over time, and the stock markets kept rising. Of course, as we all know, markets can fall as well as rise, and when in 2008 Lehman Bros collapsed, this, in effect, pulled the rug out from under many investor's aspirations for using mutual funds to accumulate their savings.

What has often perplexed fund management companies is why in Asia so few institutional investors have used funds to invest, despite their widespread use in Europe and North America. Essentially, the prime reason for this appears to have been a concern expressed by the trustees of many institutional and pension funds; that they don't wish to co-mingle assets with volatile retail investors, particularly where there is a prospect that rapid inflow or outflow of assets could occur. Many were also bothered by the relatively high charge structures mutual funds incur. Ease of access, high investment returns and immediate encashment didn't seem to be sufficiently attractive aspects of the mutual fund offering. This has also extended to the hedge fund arena, as few institutions in Asia have, to date, used hedge funds.

After the major crises of the last couple of years, most investors are very wary of where to put their money and from whom to receive advice. With the collapse of Lehman's in 2008, went the confidence that there were some organisations strong enough to survive. A contagion effect occurred where securities markets all took a big hit, none escaped.

This has led to greater efficiency in most securities markets, with increased regulation to prevent (or at least attempt to) any more serious collapses. With increased efficiency also comes less opportunity to find exceptionally priced stocks. As the US and European markets have found in the last ten years, fewer traditional mutual fund managers can consistently outperform their benchmarks. This led the U.S. to rapidly embrace the exchange traded fund (ETF) products on offer. From a low base, by 2010 this has become a multi-trillion dollar market. In the U.S., it has been the retail investor that has led the charge, proportionately taking around 60 per cent+ share. In Europe, it has been the institutional investor that has more readily accepted ETFs as the market there has rapidly increased in the last three years. For Asia, the ETF market is still in its early stages, and much of its success might depend on where and how they are distributed. Given the trading mentality of most Asian investors, it could be the opportunity that many securities companies have been looking for to enable them to enter the "wealth management" market aggressively.

Hedge funds in Asia have had a pretty rough time. Ignored by institutional investors, most Asian hedge funds have had to rely on raising money in the U.S.218

, Europe or Japan to grow. The regulators in Hong Kong and Singapore have provided regulations to enable hedge funds to be authorised and thus promoted to the wider (retail) investing public, but incorporated requirements that even the biggest and best have difficulty in complying with. This has not been without its difficulties. Hedge funds will need a sustained period of excess returns to provide the confidence necessary to encourage investors to use their products.

For mutual funds, quite clearly, the range and choice of funds now available covers just about every possibility. QDII regulation in China, whereby a number of domestic asset managers were allowed to set up funds locally that could invest internationally, have provided a fillip in the last couple of years. The performance of most QDII funds has been very disappointing and thus the demand for more of these has fallen rapidly.

As with all investment products, the demand is very often determined by the end-investor wanting to buy-in. Experience shows, despite the extent of investor education that has been carried out, that most investors, whether retail or institutional, tend to buy at or near the top, and sell when times are negative. At the time of this writing, the returns from most markets, after their initial recovery from the collapse in 2008, has tailed off. Observers look to a sustained period of high, positive, market performance before they expect to see sales volumes for all types of funds rising to or exceeding previous high points of the 2006-07 period.

WHAT TO EXPECT FROM YOUR MUTUAL FUNDS IN 2015?

Table 7.26: Performance of equity indices

Returns (absolute %)					
Indices	*Year 2010*	*Year 2011*	*Year 2012*	*Year 2013*	*Year 2014 **
S&P BSE Sensex	17.4	-24.8	25.2	8.1	29.6
S&P BSE 200	16.2	-27.3	30.8	3.4	34.4
S&P BSE Mid-Cap	16.1	-34.8	38.6	-6.8	51.5

Calendar Year returns considered

*returns up to December 29, 2014

Source: ACE MF, Personal FN Research.

Year 2014, proved to be the best year for Indian equity markets when performance of last five calendar years is considered. Markets didn't only witnessed strong rallies but also reached to new highs. Clear mandate to NDA Government was the biggest catalyst to ferocious rallies. There have been huge expectations from the Modi-led NDA Government. The new Government is expected to put Indian economy on fast track. The pre-election rally that began in September 2013 got stronger by January 2014 and markets just kept rising thereafter. Betting big on India, foreign institutional investors (FIIs) pumped in close to Rs 97,000 crore in India during the year gone by. Mutual Funds invested nearly Rs 23,200 crore during the year on net basis. However, it is noteworthy that until the NDA Government was formed in May, mutual funds were net sellers as they offloaded stocks roughly worth Rs 113 crore. This suggests that, many investors may have expected a hung parliament situation and therefore, might have exited in pre-election rallies. Having said this, retail interest revived after the stable government was formed with majority. Those who speculated about market movement may have missed the greater part of the on-going rally. If investors expected the market to fall post-election and waited for right buying opportunities at lower levels, investors may not have got any such opportunity as markets just kept rising without any significant correction.

How Mutual Funds performed?

Mutual funds have not only generated superior returns as compared to those generated by some prominent indices, but have outperformed them with a good margin. Equity diversified funds have recorded stellar performance in 2014; irrespective of their market cap focus or investment style they outperformed broader markets.

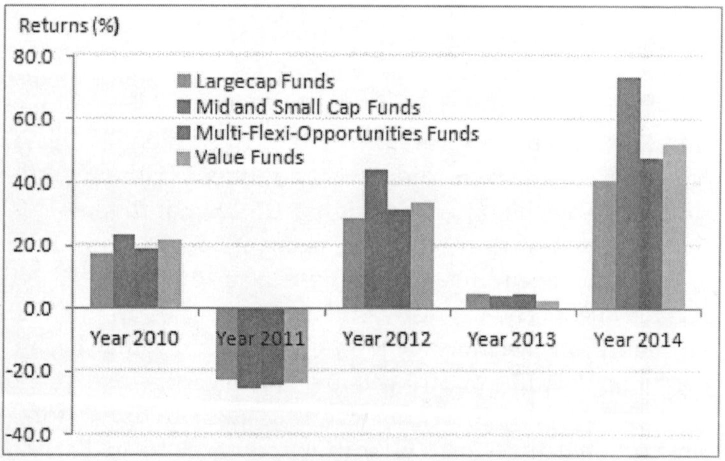

Fig. 7.2: Mutual Funds-Shinning again.

Category average returns have been considered for the each calendar year. For the year 2014, returns up to December 29, 2014 have been considered. For the purpose of calculating average returns, a sample of 48 large cap funds, 34 midcap funds 61 multi-flexi and opportunities funds and 19 value funds has been considered *(Source:* ACE MF, Personal FN Research).

Midcap oriented funds are the clear winners as they generated 73.4 per cent returns on an average in 2014. This was followed by the 52.3 per cent returns generated by the category of value funds. While large cap funds yielded close to 41.0 per cent returns, category of multicap-flexi cap and opportunity funds generated 48.1 per cent average returns during the passing year.

What supports the on-going rally?

Nothing has changed significantly on the ground except for the fact that inflation has cooled off considerably, albeit due to higher base effect. Industrial growth remains anemic and GDP growth still hovers at around five per cent mark. However, it is expected that, NDA Government would take all steps necessary for staving off economic lull and rebuilt business confidence that was lost due to so called poor performance of the previous Government pertaining to policy decision-making. The new Government has introduced a whole host of changes in the bureaucratic system and has cleared hundreds of infrastructure projects stuck for approval; however, none has translated into improved economic indicators. So speaking about the current market situation, what we have been witnessing it just a "hope rally". It started on a lower valuation base and now appears to be tiring as nothing has significantly improved on the ground and valuations have become expensive too.

Would rally continue in 2015?

The finance minister has hinted at second generation reforms which are expected to be introduced in the first full budget of the NDA Government, scheduled to be presented in February 2015. If much awaited reforms fall short of expectations, there is a possibility that markets might correct considerably. Besides this, inflation, interest rate movement, industrial growth and the performance of India Inc. would affect the market movement in 2015. International factors such as monetary policy stance of developed economies, commodity prices and geo-political conditions may also impact the market movement in India.

What should the investors do with diversified equity funds?

Investors shouldn't speculate on any particular event and stay invested in mutual funds for long-term. One should invest in diversified equity funds that have a proven track record of consistent performance. Sector specific funds may generate good returns for you in one year but there is always a possibility that they might incur heavy losses in another. On the contrary, diversified equity funds not only give a chance to generate superior returns but they also expose the investors to lower risk as they invest across sectors.

The investors should consider the investors personal financial goals, the investors risk appetite and current financial circumstances as important factors before deciding upon how much to invest in diversified equity funds. The investors personalised asset allocation created keeping in mind the investors financial goals, may help the investors invest wisely.

Under current market scenario, the investors would be better off if the investors opt for the Systematic Investment Plans (SIPs) offered by mutual funds. Given that, market valuations are rich at present and future of the on-going rally is contingent upon significant improvement in the fundamentals, there is a possibility that, markets may experience a bumpy ride ahead. By opting for SIP route, the investors may ensure that, the investors get benefits of rupee-cost averaging, as the investors buy more units of mutual funds when the Net Asset Value (NAV) falls due to fall in the markets. So let's welcome 2015 but with caution.

8

Can Mutual Funds be Considered as a Tool for Financial Inclusion?

Mutual Funds as a Tool for Financial Inclusion

The role of Mutual Funds in promoting savings continues to be insignificant in India. Despite a long history, assets of mutual funds in India constitute less than 10 per cent of GDP. A cross-country comparison suggests that mutual funds are very popular all over the world. However, assets under them in India are relatively low as compared with other emerging market economies. One of the major reasons for relatively low activity of mutual funds in India is that penetration, especially in the rural areas remains small. This is an important issue from the perspective of financial inclusion of low-income households in the formal financial system. It is generally perceived that mutual funds are popular mainly with the middle and high-income groups and have not been found to be an attractive investment avenue for the low-income groups. Thus, if the sector has to grow fast, it needs to devise appropriate schemes to attract the saving of low-income groups, especially in rural areas. This is the only way to ensure participation of all categories of investors in the financial markets, which is crucial for sustained development, both of the financial sector and the economy as a whole.

Financial Inclusion Through Mutual Funds

Financial inclusion helps in the process of ensuring access to appropriate financial products and services needed by vulnerable groups such as weaker sections and low-income groups at an affordable cost in a fair and transparent manner by mainstream institutional players. It has become one of the most critical aspects in the context of inclusive growth and development. India has, for a long time, recognised the social and economic imperatives for broader financial inclusion and has made an enormous contribution to economic development by finding innovative ways to empower the poor. Starting with the nationalisation of banks, priority sector lending requirements for banks, lead bank scheme, establishment of regional rural banks (RRBs), service area approach, self-help group-bank linkage programme, etc., multiple steps have been taken by the Reserve Bank of India (RBI) over the years to increase access to the poorer segments of society.

In 2008, the Rangarajan Committee Report extended the scope of financial inclusion from the traditional definition of opening bank accounts among the unbanked population, to providing access to financial services at an affordable cost to the vast sections of disadvantaged and low income groups. Commercial banks have been at the vanguard of the financial inclusion crusade by opening no-frills bank accounts for low income group customers. There is a latent need for innovative products that can address the financial needs of this segment. The Indian mutual fund industry is poised to play a significant role by harnessing the emerging technological innovations and regulatory measures.

While the composition of mutual funds, shares and debentures is less than 10 per cent of the gross household savings in India, the increase of its proportion in the household savings basket over the past few years is an encouraging trend. As per the available reports from AMFI, equity and balanced funds (with 351 schemes among the total number of 918 schemes) constitute 34 per cent of Assets Under Management as on 30th September 2010. The participation of retail investors is highest in these categories and account for almost 67 per cent of total investment in equity oriented schemes. Statistics reveal that non-metros are steadily increasing their share in the new collections by mutual funds, thereby increasing the reach of mutual funds to hitherto unserved markets. The 3,000 investor awareness programmes conducted by the fund houses covering about 280 cities and 2,50,000 participants is expected to further facilitate the penetration of mutual fund products across India.

The increasing awareness amongst investors about mutual fund products and the change in the commission structure for mutual fund distributors is leading to a discernible shift in the product mix being sold to customers today. There has been a significant increase in the inflows in Systematic Investment Plans (SIP), and the introduction of daily and weekly SIP by fund houses has helped attract smaller-ticket size customers. Now many financial advisors have started advising retail investors of investing in Fixed Maturity Plans as compared to bank fixed deposits.

Regulatory guidelines, especially the Know Your Customer (KYC) norms, being made mandatory from January 2011, have at times stood in the way of financial inclusion as low-income earners and migrants rarely have acceptable identity papers. The notification by the Ministry of Finance in December 2010 that the Aadhaar number being issued by the Unique Identification Authority of India (UIDAI) will be an officially valid document to satisfy KYC norms is expected to promote the cause of financial inclusion significantly. UIDAI is expected to complete 600 million enrollments by 2014 and thus usage of the Aadhaar number by the mutual fund industry would help it to increase its reach.

Table 8.1: Category-wise Assets Under Management Held by Retail Investors (Rs Crore)

Category	*Investor*	*2009*		*2010*		*2011*	
AUM		*% to Total*	*AUM*	*% to Total*	*AUM*	*% to Total*	*AUM*
Liquid Funds	Total	90058.84	100.00	75752.81	100.00	74699.86	100.00
Retail Investors	672.65	0.75	1348.18	1.78	689.61	0.92	
Gilt Funds	Total	5966.92	100.00	3461.02	100.00	3507.28	100.00
Retail	233.15	3.91	146.93	4.25	150.23	4.28	
Debt Funds	Total	197452.67	100.00	314329.93	100.00	294217.44	100.00
Retail	8070.63	4.09	18146.67	5.77	17836.04	6.06	
Equity Funds	Total	109512.59	100.00	199810.78	100.00	197562.81	100.00
Retail	71012.71	64.84	133298.38	66.71	132318.51	66.98	
Balanced Funds	Total	11649.82	100.00	15783.06	100.00	17552.40	100.00
Retail	7946.83	68.21	8969.41	56.83	8886.48	50.63	
Gold ETFs	Total	743.14	100.00	1590.63	100.00	4400.20	100.00
Retail	174.15	23.43	482.49	30.33	1220.68	27.74	
ETFs other than Gold	Total	659.91	100.00	956.59	100.00	2516.43	100.00
Retail	59.04	8.95	117.9	12.33	272.01	10.81	
Fund of Funds investing overseas	Total	2720.89	100.00	2861.16	100.00	2520.41	100.00
Retail	901.08	33.12	945.91	33.06	851.92	33.8	

The participation of retail investors is highest in these categories and account for almost 67 per cent of total investment in equity oriented schemes. Statistics reveal that non-metros are steadily increasing their share in the new collections by mutual funds, thereby increasing the reach of mutual funds to hitherto un-served markets. The 3,000 investor awareness programmes conducted by the fund houses covering about 280 cities and 2,50,000 participants is expected to further facilitate the penetration of mutual fund products across India. The increasing awareness amongst investors about mutual fund products and the change in the commission structure for mutual fund distributors is leading to a discernible shift in the product mix being sold to customers today. There has been a significant increase in the inflows in Systematic Investment Plans (SIP), and the introduction of daily and weekly SIP by fund houses has helped attract smaller-ticket size customers, now many financial advisors have started advising retail investors of investing in Fixed Maturity Plans as compared to bank fixed deposits. Slew of launches by the capital protection funds, are appealing the first-time investor unwilling to take exposure to equity oriented instruments. The new investor protection measures put in place by Securities and Exchange Board of India (SEBI) regarding exposure of these products to real estate paper as well as in Information Technology sector is expected to make these more popular. Similarly, many fund houses have launched micro-SIP plans with very low threshold limits to attract both the urban and rural economically challenged customers to start investing in mutual funds. It is vital to have a technologically efficient platform with low transaction costs and regulatory norms that are synchronised with the socio-economic traits displayed by this customer segment, for these plans to be successful. Regulatory guidelines, especially the Know Your Customer (KYC) norms, being made mandatory from January 2011, have at times stood in the way of financial inclusion as low-income earners and migrants rarely have acceptable identity papers. The notification by the Ministry of Finance in December 2010 that the Aadhaar number being issued by the Unique Identification Authority of India

(UIDAI) will be an officially valid document to satisfy KYC norms is expected to promote the cause of financial inclusion significantly. UIDAI is expected to complete 600 million enrolments by 2014 and thus usage of the Aadhaar number by the mutual fund industry would help it to increase its reach. According to Telecom Regulatory Authority of India (TRAI), of the 700 million mobile subscribers in India, about 225 million cell phone users reside in rural India. A survey conducted in 2007 showed that of the 321 million earning population aged between 18 to 59 years, only about 120 million Indians from rural India had bank accounts. Extensive use of technology is the only way to deliver financial services in a secure environment at an affordable cost to the vast multitude of Indians that do not have access to formal financial services.

2011 has thus ushered in innovations and improvements on multiple fronts, which when leveraged in a holistic manner will enable financial inclusion on a scale that was not possible earlier. Mutual funds with its array of products designed around affordable ticket size, lower time horizon (compared to insurance), various risk-return options (depending on nature of product), increasing reach as well as a distribution structure aligned to promote stay-invested behaviour can use innovative technological delivery systems to provide access to greater level of financial services to segments that are currently deprived of the same.

The following paragraphs further explain and indicate the progress of financial inclusiveness in the mutual fund industry through the analysis of unit holding pattern.

Unit Holding Pattern in 2001-02

As on March 31, 2002 there are a total number of 3.08 crore investors accounts (it is likely that there may be more than one folio of an investor which might have been counted more than once and actual number of investors would be less) holding units of Rs 1,00,594 crore. Out of this total number of investors accounts, 3.02 crore are individual investors accounts, accounting for 98.04 of the total number of investors accounts and contribute Rs 55,487 crore which is 55.16 of the total net assets. Corporate and institutions which form only 1.46 per cent of the total number of investor's accounts in the mutual funds industry, contribute a sizeable amount of Rs 43,403 crore which is 43.15 per cent of the total net assets in the mutual funds industry. The NRIs and OCBs constitute a very small percentage of investors accounts and contribute Rs 306 crore (0.30 per cent) of net assets.

Table 8.2: Unit Holding Pattern of Mutual Funds Industry. as on 31st March, 2002

Category	Number Of Investors Accounts	% To Total Investors Accounts	Net Assets (Rs.Crore)	% To Total Net Assets
Individuals	30238065	98.04	55487	55.16
NRIs[21]	154622	0.50	1398	1.39
FIIs	1123	0.00	306	0.30
Corporates/ Institutions/ Others	450132	1.46	43403	43.15
TOTAL	30843942	100.	100594	100.

FI: Financial Institutions, FII: Foreign Institutional Investors.
Source: SEBI, 2002.

Unit Holding Pattern in 2008-09

As on March 31, 2009 there are a total number of 4.76 crore investors accounts (it is likely that there may be more than one folio of an investor which might have been counted more than once and actual number of investors would be less) holding units of Rs 419,321.66 crore. Out of this total number of investors accounts, 4.61 crore are individual investors accounts, accounting for 96.75 per cent of the total number of investors accounts and contribute Rs 1,55,283.21crore which is 37.03 per cent of the total net assets. Corporate and institutions who form only 1.21 per cent of the total number of investors accounts in the mutual funds industry, contribute a sizeable amount of Rs 2,36,233.35 crore which is 56.34 per cent of the total net assets in the mutual funds industry. The NRIs and FIIs constitute a very small percentage of investors accounts (2.04 per cent) and contribute Rs 27,805.10 crore (6.63 per cent) of net assets. The details of unit holding pattern are given in the following.

Table 8.3: Unit Holding Pattern Of Mutual Funds Industry. as on 31st March, 2009

Category	Number Of Investors Accounts	% To Total Investors Accounts	Net Assets (Rs.Crore)	% To Total Net Assets
Individuals	4,60,75,763	96.75	1,55,283.21	37.03
NRIs	9,71,430	2.04	22,821.28	5.44
FIIs	146	0.00	4,983.82	1.19
Corporates/ Institutions/ Others	5,75,938	1.21	2,36,233.35	56.34
TOTAL	4,76,23,277	100	4,19,321.66	100

FI: Financial Institutions, FII: Foreign Institutional Investors.

Source: Association of Mutual Funds in India (AMFI), 2009.

Role of Public Vs Private Sector

The following paragraph depicts the performance of public and private sector in financial inclusion programme by the year 2002.

Private Sector

Out of a total of 41.61 lakhs investors accounts in the private sector, 40 lakhs are individual investors accounts i.e. 96.11 per cent of the total investor's accounts are in private sector mutual funds. However, the private sector mutual funds manage 41459 crores of the net assets contributes nearly 42 per cent of the total net assets.

Public Sector (other than UTI)

Out of a total of 2.67 lakhs investor's accounts, 22.22 lakhs are individual investor's accounts i.e. 97.95 per cent of the total investors. Hence, the contribution made by this sector is, net asset value Rs 7,701 cores and it is only 8 per cent of aggregate net assets.

Unit Trust of India

The major contributor for financial inclusion in mutual fund industry is Unit Trust of India. Out of a total of 24.41 lakhs investor's accounts, 24.01 lakhs are individual investor's accounts i.e. 98.375 per cent of the total investors. The total contribution by UTI is net asset value Rs 51433 crores and it is nearly 51 per cent of aggregate net assets. Details of unit holding pattern of private sector and public sector mutual funds (other than UTI), and Unit Trust of India, are given in the following tables:

Table 8.4: Unit Holding Pattern Of Private Sector MFS. As on 31st March, 2002

Category	Number Of Investors Accounts	% To Total Investors Accounts	Net Assets (Rs.Crore)	% To Total Net Assets
Individuals	4000117	96.11	15024.71	36.24
NRIs	32267	0.78	523.47	1.26
FIIs	35	0.00	288.61	0.70
Corporates/ Institutions /Others	129423	3.11	25622.19	61.80

Table 8.5: Unit Holding Pattern Of Unit Trust Of India MF. As on 31st March, 2002

Category	Number Of Investors Accounts	% To Total Investors Accounts	Net Assets (Rs.Crore)	% To Total Net Assets
Individuals	24016586	98.37	37345.74	72.61
NRIs	113869	0.47	729.88	1.42
FIIs	132	0.00	11.06	0.02
Corporates/ Institutions/ Others	283689	1.16	13346.93	25.95
TOTAL	24414276	100.	51433.61	100.

FI: Financial Institutions, FII: Foreign Institutional Investors.

Source: SEBI, 2000.

The growth data indicates that there is overwhelming response by investors in mutual funds. This is a clear outcome for the economic development through financial inclusion strategies of mutual fund organisation. Out of a total of 4.76 crore investors accounts in the mutual funds industry, (it is likely that there may be more than one folio of an investor which might have been counted more than once and therefore actual number of investors may be less) 3.16 crore investors accounts i.e. 66.27 per cent of the total investors accounts are in private sector mutual funds whereas the 1.61 crore investors accounts i.e. 33.73 per cent are with the public sector mutual funds which includes UTI Mutual Fund. However, the private sector mutual funds manage 80.46 per cent of the net assets whereas the public sector mutual funds own only 19.54 per cent of the assets. Details of unit holding pattern of private sector and public sector mutual funds are given in the following table:

Table 8.6: Unit Holding Pattern of Private Sector MFS.
As on 31st March, 2009

Category	Number Of Investors Accounts	% To Total Investors Accounts	Net Assets (Rs.Crore)	% To Total Net Assets
Individuals	3,03,62,538	96.21	1,21,676.51	36.06
NRIs	8,13,062	2.58	21,093.62	6.25
FIIs	128	0.00	4,888.98	1.45
Corporates/ Institutions/ Others	3,83,783	1.22	1,89,723.52	56.23
TOTAL	3,15,59,511	100.	3,37,382.63	100

FI: Financial Institutions, FII: Foreign Institutional Investors.

Public Sector

The Table indicates the growth of Unit Trust of India Mutual Fund and Public Sector (other than UTI) during the period 2003-2009. It is observed that there is a continuous growth in assets under management by UTI MF up to the April, 2008 followed by a marginal decrease in the year 2009. It is apparent that there was a four-fold increase of assets in case of UTI and seven times increase in case of other public sector mutual funds during 2003-2009.

Table 8.7: Trends in AUM of Public Sector Mutual Fund

Year	UTI Rs. Crores	Simple Index	Public Sector (other than UTI)	Simple Index
April 2003	13,532	100	7897	100
April 2004	19,848	147	12001	152
April 2005	20,478	151	11924	150
April 2006	30,109	223	23967	303
April 2007	33,517	248	29747	376
April 2008	52,549	388	50251	636
February, 2009	49,225	364	56822	719

Note: Simple Index calculated based on the year April 2003.

Private Sector

It is necessary to study the role of private sector in the economic development through accumulation of investment by the people. Thus, the Table 8.7 indicates the growth of private sector mutual funds during the period 2003-2009. It is observed that there is a continuous growth up to April, 2008 and a marginal decrease in the year 2009. During 2003-08, there were nine-fold growths in the assets under management see.

Comparative Analysis

Here, a comparative analysis indicates the role of private sector and public sector during 2003-2009. The Table 8.8 shows average annual growth rate in the AUM of the UTI, Public Sector (other than UTI) and the private sector mutual funds during 2003-2009. It is interesting to note that the highest percentage of overall growth is observed during the year 2005-06, followed by the year 2007-2008. Hence, we can conclude that in these two years there was positive influence of fluctuations in portfolio management. Only in the years 2004-05 and 2008-2009 there were overall negative growth rates recorded.

Table 8.8: Average Annual Growth Rate in AUM during April, 2003-February, 2009

Year	UTI % Growth	Public Sector (other than UTI)	Private % Growth	Overall % Growth
2003-2004	52.36	52	38.87	47.74
2004-2005	4.49	-2	-1.42	0.35
2005-2006	44.15	100	29.23	57.39
2006-2007	17.87	24.12	20.91	2.96
2007-2008	37.91	68.27	32.59	46.25
2008-2009*	-6.33	13.08	-13.67	-2.30

*Up to February, 2009

Economic development through the retail sector can also be examined to study the impact of financial inclusion. The following table focuses on the role of retail sector in India's mutual fund industry as on Sept. 30, 2012.

Table 8.9: Increasing Role of Retail Sector - Asset Under Management and Folios - Category-wise - Aggregate - As on September 30, 2012

Types of Schemes	Investor Classification	AUM (Rs. Cr)	% to Total
Liquid/Money Market	Corporates	119889.43	81.78
	Banks/FIs	20021.25	13.66
	FIIs	929.51	0.63
	High Networth Individuals*	4758.34	3.25
	Retail	1003.03	0.68
	Total	**146601.57**	**100.00**
Gilt	Corporates	2157.19	64.27
	Banks/FIs	9.95	0.30
	FIIs	1.25	0.04
	High Networth Individuals*	969.84	28.89
	Retail	218.32	6.50
	Total	**3356.51**	**100.00**
Debt Oriented	Corporates	189955.49	53.87
	Banks/FIs	5233.96	1.48
	FIIs	2273.02	0.64
	High Networth Individuals*	129990.37	36.86
	Retail	25173.09	7.14
	Total	**352625.92**	**100.00**
Equity Oriented	Corporates	17606.93	9.40

contd...

	Banks/FIs	2058.96	1.10
	FIIs	1324.19	0.71
	High Networth Individuals*	36158.07	19.30
	Retail	130153.47	69.49
	Total	**187301.63**	**100.00**
Balanced	Corporates	2003.30	11.62
	Banks/FIs	34.17	0.20
	FIIs	10.59	0.06
	High Networth Individuals*	6100.95	35.39
	Retail	9090.42	52.73
	Total	**17239.42**	**100.00**
Gold ETF	Corporates	5943.59	53.07
	Banks/FIs	9.80	0.09
	FIIs	1.80	0.02
	High Networth Individuals*	2143.80	19.14
	Retail	3099.87	27.68
	Total	**11198.85**	**100.00**
ETFs(other than Gold)	Corporates	500.12	27.69
	Banks/FIs	53.74	2.98
	FIIs	174.83	9.68
	High Networth Individuals*	715.57	39.61
	Retail	362.13	20.05
	Total	**1806.39**	**100.00**
Fund of Funds investing Overseas	Corporates	344.51	14.38
	Banks/FIs	5.33	0.22
	FIIs	0.00	0.00
	High Networth Individuals*	1137.21	47.47
	Retail	908.73	37.93
	Total	**2395.79**	**100.00**
	Grand Total	**722526.08**	

Suggestions to Improve Mutual Funds to Aid Financial Inclusion

- **Introduce micro denomination SIP schemes:** The mutual funds industry should have micro denomination SIP schemes for values such as Rs 20 per month or Rs 50 per month to ensure that the lowest segment of society is able to enter the mutual fund market.

- **Make post offices centre for mutual fund distribution:** Post offices, which are located in almost all villages and in remote areas, can be used to distribute mutual funds. This will ensure financial inclusion in the real sense as it will enable reach to the poorest and farthest segments of the country.
- **Provide incentive schemes:** The government should work out some incentive schemes for those mutual funds which achieve the targets for specified amount of SIPs from villages and towns beyond the top 15 cities. This will ensure that more business comes from small towns and that financial inclusion reaches the desired target market.
- **Postal agents to be compulsorily made independent financial advisors:** Mutual funds should make postal agents their independent financial advisors which will ensure that the products reach the grassroots. The funds can be provided targets regarding the number of postal agents who must become independent financial advisors.

As nearly three-fourths of India still lives in villages, investment potential of savings lies in rural areas. In developed economies, household investment in the equity market is 35 per cent while in India it is four per cent (which includes direct investment in shares and through mutual funds). This shows there is huge untapped potential for productive deployment of savings and mutual funds, which are low risk instruments offering steady returns, are a good way through which first time investors can enter the capital market and get financially included.

A study by Microsave clearly highlights the problems

1. 37 per cent of BCs are dormant and 25 per cent of BCs are unable to process transactions. Above all, there is a very high level of attrition rate among BCs, principally on account of the insufficient attention that

is paid to their BCs and general lack of trust. Banks view financial inclusion as a "mandatory requirement" rather than a future business option. The current discourse on the subject has been largely on ensuring viability of BC outlets and the lack of client-centricity continues.

2. Reports also highlight how the poor are victims of mis-selling when the local elite become BCs. Thus, BCs/BC agents should come from a socially acceptable and trusted community. NABARD's experiences in piloting the use of women SHG members as BCs in banks have shown encouraging results. Women SHGs can effectively function as a rallying point for creating a "pull" for financial services. Added to this is the "neighbourhood" factor and trust, which can work to the advantage of an effective financial inclusion outreach in a limited area like a village.

3. The poor are a heterogeneous lot, and their needs are better addressed through the right kind of local intermediaries rather than the formal banking system. Trusted peer support from, say, "Bank *Sakhis*" can also help spread financial literacy. These BCs also serve a community cause with minimal services charges and earning. They derive greater value in recognition and dignity in the work they do for their peers and hardly crave for compensation. Similarly, well-functioning federations of SHGs can serve as the anchor institutions and effectively function as BCs and enablers of financial services.

4. But all this demands key investments in human capital in these people's institutions, so that these BCs understand the nuances of digital inclusion, banking products and features, Know Your Customer norms and so on to make financial inclusion a reality.

5. The current approach for financial inclusion has been overtly focused on technology-enabled banks.

Core banking solutions and their linkage with payment systems has largely been the yardstick for participation of banks in the financial inclusion drive. While this is a necessity, it has resulted in deliberately leaving co-operative banks out of the financial inclusion drive even though many fulfil technological requirements. Being localised institutions, these banks have a long affinity with their clients. It is, therefore, critical to leverage these institutional linkages to achieve the national goal of financial inclusion.

6. Current RBI instructions on financial inclusion plans don't cover group-based lending models such as joint liability groups (JLGs) and SHGs; although these approaches have helped the unbanked connect with banks. Why is a client segment that avails of two or three basic services from the bank out of the ambit of financial inclusion?

7. Finally, the banker's attitude needs to change from sheer target-chasing to facilitating the poor's entry into the formal financial system. Banks, RBI and the government need to send the right message and remove barriers to enable greater participation of the poor in the formal banking system for their economic good. The understanding gained through banking with SHGs and community groups needs to be effectively leveraged for widening the depth and range of financial inclusion.

8. Though all the approaches are intended to enable economic inclusion, the actions don't reflect a commonality of purpose. As a result, these institution- and programme-specific approaches actually leave a large segment of this populace clueless and unaware that these efforts are being made for their good. The fact that a majority of the basic savings bank account opened are dormant or have minimal or zero deposit balances is a testimony to this fact.

CONCLUSION

Financial inclusion in a large scale is possible only if the banks join hands with like minded partners in their initiative. While business correspondent model introduced by RBI enables such partnerships to evolve, the major concerns would be as under:

- As there is no proven/tested model, the initial take off may be slow till sufficient experience is gathered.
- It is essential that the programme is viable for all the partners. However, payment of fee/commission, etc. to the business correspondent, has no precedence and will evolve over time.
- Risk management, operations, registration, credit, etc. are major issues.
- Cash management by the business correspondents is also an issue which can affect the reputation of the bank.

Financial inclusion is not a onetime effort; it is an ongoing process. It is a huge project which requires concerted and team efforts from all the stake holders – the Government, financial institutions, the regulators, the private sector and the community at large. From the sporadic attempts of today dispersed across the nation, it should gather momentum and grow in geometric proportions and develop into a focused and effective movement. If this is to be achieved, it requires the passionate involvement, dedication and commitment of all stake holders. It requires a major mindset change in the minds of every individual involved – banker, bureaucrat, regulator *et al*, and, therefore, creating awareness at all levels.

At the same time, the role of technology in the whole scenario cannot be undermined either. It has to be admitted that today, more than even before, technology plays a vital role in bringing about integration in society of all social and economic classes. Accessibility, affordability, appropriateness and benefits determine how deep financial inclusion penetrates the social fabric of the village. Financial inclusion can empower even the poorest person and bring about a dramatic change in his fate.

As observed by Dr Yunus, ".......basic ingredient of overcoming poverty is packed inside each poor person. All we need to do is to help this person to unleash this energy and creativity.... Only place in the world where poverty will exist will be in the museums and no longer in human society." With combined efforts of all the stake holders, viz., policy-makers, regulators, banks, NGOs, MFIs and other similar entities, this can be made possible.

Does the financial inclusion helps Mutual Funds in India?

Not completely as there are plenty of challenges ahead for the fund houses. Still the concept of Mutual Funds is not known to many of the investors in India. Since its inception in 1964 to till date, the mutual funds are confined to the boundaries of tier-1 cities. Low investor awareness levels and financial literacy pose the biggest challenge to channelise the household savings into Mutual Funds. Majority of the investors lack an understanding of risk-return, asset allocation and portfolio diversification concepts. Moreover, the Indian Mutual Fund industry is governed by the strict enforcement of SEBI (mutual fund) Regulations 1993. The approach of the fund houses to reach the rural investors is a hundred million questions as their profitability will be affected. The employees of the companies may not show interest to work in rural areas. The infrastructure facilities also pose a problem.

Mutual funds clearly have a significant role to play in financial development. Their mode of aggregating pools of saving from a large number of retail investors and deploying these resources in a variety of financial markets, based on different risk-return preferences simultaneously enhances efficiency, stability and inclusion. It is also relatively easy for them to be transparent about both their strategies and outcomes. There are clearly barriers to achieving these objectives. Some of these have to do with penetration, others with the preferences of investors, particularly with respect to duration, some more with legitimate regulatory concerns about systemic risk and yet others with gaps or imbalances in the broader regulatory framework. However, if there is broad agreement that appropriately regulated mutual fund activity can play a large part in financial development in all its dimensions, these barriers can surely be addressed in a collaborative way between the three stakeholders – the investors, the fund managers and the regulators.

Mutual funds have a huge scope to penetrate the rural India and thereby can develop a symbiotic process with financial inclusion strategies for better and longer lasting results.

9

Comparative Analysis of Systematic Investment, Withdrawal and Transfer Plans

Understanding Systematic Investment Plans

Systematic investment plan as the name suggest allows a user to build an investment portfolio with a small systematic investment at regular intervals. The investor can choose his or her preferred mode of investment as monthly, quarterly or annually and invest the funds according to his or her convenience. Users of systematic investment plans can choose from various investment vehicles to invest their money including stocks, mutual funds, ETFs and even gold funds. Amount can be invested in any investment vehicle. e.g. Fixed Deposit, debt fund, stocks, mutual fund, real estate, ETF(gold, oil), commodities ETF. People do SIP, if they are confident of long-term prospects of underlying and don't want to lose from short-term fluctuations.

What kind of people do SIP?

- Most Salaried people don't have any lump sum amount of money to begin with.

- People who feel they can't time the market. Rather than putting effort on buying at the lowest possible price, they are okay with buying at average price.

Advantages of investing using a systematic investment approach

1. Investment discipline

The one basic rules of investing is to always maintain a focused and dedicated approach towards investment. A large number of people enter the investment markets with a lot of enthusiasm but fail to maintain a monthly investment towards building a regular investment corpus. Investing in a systematic investment plan allows users to maintain a monthly investment scheme which is far easier to maintain in the long run rather than investing a lump-sum amount each year. Investing in systematic investment plans must be considered by all investors who are yet to attain an investment discipline allowing them the convenience to invest a pre determined short sum every month towards their future.

2. *Rupee cost averaging*

Rupee cost averaging, also commonly known as RCA is one of the very significant reasons why investing in a systematic investment plan must be considered by almost every investor. Investors investing a fixed amount of money every month towards any investment vehicle allow them to purchase more units or stocks when the price of the investment is lower. This reduces the average cost of purchasing of the financial asset over time. Considering a long-term investment approach, rupee cost averaging can even out any market ups and downs in the long-term, allowing the investor to gain maximum benefits ion his or her investments over time.

In simplistic terms, let us consider an investor is investing a monthly fixed amount in a mutual fund investment plan.

Considering the fact that the investor invests the same amount each month irrespective of the market cycle, be it a bull phase or a bear phase, the average cost of investment is eventually maintained at a lower level allowing maximum gains in the long term.

3. *Power of compounding*

One of the basic rules of being a successful investor is to start early. Since all investment and returns are based on the power of compounding, an investor starting out early can earn much higher returns than a one starting out late even with a slightly higher corpus. Since a systematic investment plan do not seek a large amount of investment and users can start investing with a low sum each month depending on their financial condition, it allows them to start investing much early in life.

Let us consider Mr A and Mr B and understand how the power of compounding helps the investor using a systematic approach.

Mr A started investing in a systematic investment plan investing a sum of Rs 1000 when he was 30 years old. By the time Mr A reaches 50 years of age, he would have invested Rs 24 Lakhs if the money grew on an average rate of 7 per cent per annum.

Now let us consider Mr B who starts out earlier than Mr A and started investing the same amount of Rs 1000 from the time he was 20 years old or ten years earlier than Mr A. Mr B's investment growing at the same rate of 7 per cent per annum would end up as high as Rs 36 Lakhs by the time he is 50 years old.

So while both Mr A and Mr B invested same amount each month, the one starting out early has made a substantial gain compared to the one starting out late.

4. Investment convenience

A systematic investment plan as the name suggests is systematic in nature allowing the investor the advantage of investing small amount of money each month without any hassles. The investor can send a onetime instruction to his or her bank to allow auto debit of the investment amount each month from his or her savings bank account allowing systematic investments without worrying about missing out on any monthly investment.

5. Other benefits

A systematic investment plan offers a number of miscellaneous benefits that make investment quite comfortable and an enjoyable experience. One can start investing in a systematic investment plan with a very low amount of Rs 500 or Rs 1000 per month. This allows users of all financial backgrounds to invest in capital markets without feeling the pinch of a lump-sum investment. A large number of fund houses waive off entry or exit load on mutual funds in case the investment is done through a systematic investment plan. SIPs also offer a taxation benefit as SIPs are taxed for capital gains on first in first out basis.

6. Stress-free way of investing

Investor doesn't have to worry about timing the market. It's stress-free. Once the mechanism is set-up, fixed amount will be deducted from the investors account.

7. Short-term fluctuation doesn't harm as much:

If the price goes down by 10 per cent in the next month the investors have a consolation that they are buying at reduced price too. If the market recovers to previous level, the investor actually make money overall.

Table 9.1: Comparison of Sip and One Time Lump Sum Investment

Month	NAV	Mr. SIP investor		Mr. One Time Investor	
		Amount Invested	Units Accumulated	Amount Invested	Units Accumulated
1	10	5000	500.00	30000	3000
2	11	5000	454.55	0	0
3	9	5000	555.56	0	0
4	8	5000	625.00	0	0
5	8	5000	625.00	0	0
6	11	5000	454.55	0	0
Total units accumulated		3214.65		3000	
Value of investment (Rs.)		35361.11		33000	
Avg. price / unit		9.332		10	

Source: www.moneycontrol.com

8. It encourages saving habit in the investor

A little every month by month can make to huge amount at the end of 40 years. If the investor invests 20,000 Rupees every month for 40 years in a mutual fund, and assumes that mutual fund give annual returns of 20 per cent over a period of 40 years then at the end of 40 years, the investor will have 340 crores.

9. Flexibility

While it is advisable to continue SIP investments with a long-term perspective, there is no compulsion. Investors can discontinue the plan at any time. One can also increase/ decrease the amount being invested.

10. Removes emotion from the decision to invest

When an investor must decide when to invest, they always look for reasons not to invest. "Now" is always the hardest time to invest. If the market was up yesterday the investor may think its high and defer the investment until the market goes down (which may never happen). If the market was down yesterday the investor may defer the investment until the market stops dropping (and miss an upswing or invest in at higher prices). A systematic investment plan effectively removes the emotion from the decision on when to invest because to be "systematic" a regular recurrent date must be set for investment, and that date must be adhered too.

Disadvantages of Systematic Investment Plans

1. If price of underlying (investment vehicle) doubles in first month and don't move much after that, then the investor won't have handsome returns.
2. If the investor have significant amount of cash to begin with, then it doesn't make much sense to do SIP and keep the rest of amount as cash in initial period.
3. SIP averages out short-term fluctuation and gives returns similar to long-term growth of underlying. Bad part is, the investor invest the same amount at market highs and lows. It would be better, if the investor could invest more at lows and less at highs.

Precautions to be Taken While Investing Through Sips

However, the past five years of lackluster performance have led to a spate of SIP cancellations. Perhaps it is time to refresh the investor knowledge about SIP fundamentals.

1. An SIP is not a product or a fund. It is simply an investment process. Instead of basing investment decisions on expectations of how the market will behave, SIPs facilitate a disciplined participation in the market through ups and downs. Since a fixed amount is invested across time, SIPs enable a reduction in average cost. Therefore, the returns from an SIP are not likely to be different from those of the mutual fund in which the investment is made.

   Many investors believe that if they invest through SIPs, they will earn better returns. That is not true. The returns will depend on how the fund has performed at all times.

2. The benefit of this option has to be measured across cycles. If the investors invest via an SIP as the NAVs are moving up, then while computing the investors' return, the investor will value all the investors' SIPs at the current NAV, which would be higher than the investors' cost of acquisition.

   However, in a falling market, all the investors' SIPs will be valued at the lower NAV, and hence, will look bad. The returns are measured on the basis of where the investors stand today, and that will bias the investors' gain or loss. If the investor persist across cycles, the investors' investment in both the equity and SIPs will look good.

3. There is no point in comparing lump-sum investments and SIPs. They are two completely different ideas, and the latter will typically beat SIPs. When the investor invests a lump sum amount, a larger chunk of the investor's money works for a longer period of time.

   On the other hand, a SIP is a slow model, where the investors build the investors' wealth with each installment. Had the investor invested Rs 10,000 per month in the Sensex since its inception in 1979—406 months in all— the investor would have about Rs 1.6 crore today.

   A lump-sum investment of the same amount, Rs 4.06 lakh at that time would be worth over Rs 8 crore today. If the investor have a lump sum handy, the investor are better off not trying to go for an SIP unless the investor think the market is falling and the investors want to invest at lower levels.

4. SIPs are not about smart market timing; they simply allow the investor to invest regularly. If the investors are a salaried person with a regular income and monthly saving, SIPs are just the thing for the investor.

5. When the investor cancel the investors' SIP, the investor need to find a way to deploy the money the investor are saving. Even if the investors keep it idle in the bank, seeking a safe investment option, the investors have made a significant asset allocation decision.

   The investor have reduced the investors' exposure to equity and increased it to cash. The investors have to ask if this helps the long-term goals and wealth. Cancelling a SIP in a down market amounts to under weighing equity in a bear market. If the investor choose to come back when the market moves up again, the investor are invariably coming in at a higher NAV, and lose the benefit of having invested at the bottom.

   The investors' money moves with the market in a SIP, and when the investor leave and join at will, the investor indulge in trying to time the market. When this attempt converts into buying at peaks and selling at the bottom, there is no money to be made.

6. An SIP in a debt fund is not a great idea, especially when the investor wants to invest a lump-sum. A debt fund earns steady and regular interest income. The lesser the investor participate, the lesser the investor earn. In equity, the market cycles may modify the investors' benefits in the short term, but with a debt fund, holding a lump sum to invest, and then choosing a SIP is clearly inefficient. If the investor has the money, put it to work.

A SIP in equity will be subject to market volatility but will do well in the long run, just like any other equity investment. To cancel a SIP in a falling market is to take the timing call that the investor will not participate in a falling market.

Understanding Systematic Withdrawal Plans

The world of financial markets is constantly evolving with new financial products entering the markets and some older products getting phased out. A relatively newer financial scheme known as a Systematic Withdrawal Plan or SWP is slowly becoming popular with many investors, especially those requiring a steady monthly income from their investments. Systematic Withdrawal Plans offer individual investor the advantage of withdrawing a fixed amount of money from his or her investment at the same date on every month for a designated tenure period.

The working mechanism of systematic withdrawal plans makes them the exact reverse of a systematic investment plan or SIP. While SIPs have become very popular with a large number of retail investors, not many people are aware of the option of a systematic withdrawal plan or SWP.

Systematic Withdrawal Plan as the name suggests offers investors a choice of withdrawing a fixed sum of money systematically each month on a fixed date from his or her investment corpus. Financially a systematic withdrawal plan is the exact opposite to a systematic investment plan where the investor invests a fixed amount of money each month in his or her investment corpus. The amount of money to be withdrawn and the frequency of the withdrawal are fixed by the investor depending on his or her preferred choice. The investor can seek withdrawal of money monthly, quarterly or annually depending on his or her individual financial need. An SWP (Systematic Withdrawal Plan) allows an investor to withdraw designated sum of money and units from the fund account at pre-defined regular intervals. It allows the investor a certain level of independence from market instability and helps in avoiding market timing. The investor can reinvest the redeemed cash in another portfolio or use it as a source of regular income. It is suitable for retirees who are looking for a fixed flow of income. SWP help investors who require liquidity as it permits them to access their money precisely when they need it to meet their objectives.

Opting for a systematic withdrawal plan (SWP) reduces the risk of irregular cash flow. Even when the scheme is making losses, it will pay the amount opted for by the investor by digging into the principal, if needed. With a systematic withdrawal plan, an investor's money will continue to grow as long as the investment is performing at a rate that is higher than the rate of withdrawal. For this reason, it is wise to diversify your investments. However, diversification makes sense for quite a few types of investments besides mutual funds. Things get better in case of SWP from equity funds. As the long-term capital gains from equity mutual funds are exempt in case of holding beyond a year, you end up paying no tax on the withdrawals. Inflation Protection: Most of the fixed income instruments do not offer inflation beating returns. So, though the principal may be secure, the income might fall short of needs in future. Here again SWP scores in terms of generating returns to keep up with inflation especially if you opt for an equity fund. The only drawback in the SWP is that it will at some point eat into your capital. But judicious mix of investment instruments will ensure that your primary goal of income generation will be met without you running out of money in times of need. So the conclusion is that SWP is a noteworthy strategy to use for generation of regular income in various scenarios.

To activate an SWP, one needs to simply fill out an instruction slip with the AMC stating the folio number, the withdrawal frequency, and date for the first withdrawal and the bank account to credit the proceeds.

Let us try and understand the working mechanism of a systematic withdrawal plan using a simple illustration.

Let us assume Mr A has 10,000 mutual fund units as part of his investment portfolio. Let us assume that the net asset value of the each mutual fund unit is Rs 20. This makes the total investment of Mr A to be Rs two Lakhs.

Now let us assume Mr A wants a monthly income of Rs 5000 each month and adopts a systematic withdrawal plant to that effect. For the first month Mr A withdraws Rs 5000 his investment would get depleted by 250 units (since 5000/20 NAV is 250). Now with each subsequent month while Mr A would withdraw a fixed amount of Rs 5000, the NAV of the mutual fund units would also increase as per market dynamics. Let us assume that NAV of the units held by Mr A now increase in value to reach Rs 20.15 per unit. The number of units required for a Rs 5000 withdrawal would hence reduce to 248.14 units.

Now effectively Mr A withdrew Rs 10,000 in total from his overall investment corpus of Rs two Lakhs. His balance should be Rs 1, 90,000 but is effectively Rs 191462.4 making for effectively better earning with a systematic withdrawal scheme in place.

Advantages of Systematic Withdrawal Plans

Systematic withdrawal plans have a number of intrinsic benefits including tax benefits, fixed income and a customised cash flow each month.

- **Tax Advantage:** In case of investing in debt mutual funds, a systematic withdrawal plan scheme would effective reduce the overall tax liability of the individual investor compared to a dividend scheme. While dividends paid out by mutual funds are not liable for any tax, mutual fund companies pass on the dividend distribution tax they are charged to the investor. The DDT rate charged by mutual fund houses to the investors ranges from 12.5 per cent in case of balanced and debt funds to 25 per cent in case of liquid or money market funds. In case the investor opts for a systematic withdrawal plan, the profit earned from ale of units at each withdrawal is taxable but treated as long term capital gain taxed at a flat rate of 10 per cent without indexation or at 20 per cent with indexation benefits. Thus systematic withdrawal plans are more cost effective when it comes to tax liability compared to a divided pay out scheme.

- **Fixed Income:** Systematic withdrawal plans are an effective financial tool for those investors seeking a fixed monthly income from their investment corpus. This can be an effective tool for elderly or senior citizens allowing them the comfort of getting a fixed amount each month from their investment rather than relying on dividends which can vary each month as per market dynamics and functioning of the fund in question.

Dividend Option

- Quantum, frequency of payout decided by fund houses
- Payouts made only from the capital appreciation portion
- Principal remains untouched as dividends are paid from capital appreciation portion
- A 12.5 per cent dividend distribution tax is deducted from the payouts

SWP Option

- Investors decide both quantum and frequency of payouts
- Payouts can be made from capital appreciation and principal
- Principal amount may erode if capital appreciation is less than each payout installment
- Investors are liable to pay capital gains tax - short/ long-term

Disadvantages

1. One cannot run an SIP and SWP in the same fund.

2. Inflation is likely to increase the monthly withdrawal amount each year to meet expenses.

3. There will be fluctuations in the inflation rate as well as the portfolio return which can considerably impact the portfolio.

4. Since an SWP is nothing but redemption of units from the scheme, the tax treatment of each withdrawal will be the same as in the case of full withdrawal of equity and debt funds. Hence, for units where the period of holding has not crossed 12 months for equity funds, there might be a short-term capital gains tax. For debt funds, there will be a tax liability (short-term capital gains on holding for less than 36 months and long-term capital gains on longer holding periods) which need to be factored in. You also need to be mindful of the exit load of the scheme before activating the SWP on that folio.

Understanding Systematic Transfer Plan

Investors who want to invest lump-sum money in schemes with stable returns and ensure small exposure to equity schemes in order to avail of the potential for higher growth through equities opt for STP.

Investors can use Systematic Transfer Plan (STP) as a defense mechanism in volatile market. This plan is used to transfer investment from one asset or asset type into another asset or asset type. Read this space to know all about STP and how does it work?

STP refers to Systematic Transfer Plan where in an investor invests a lump-sum amount in one scheme and regularly transfers (i.e. switches) a pre-defined amount into another scheme. Every month on a specified date an amount you choose is transfered from one mutual fund scheme to another of your choice.

STP is a variant of SIP. STP is essentially transferring investment from one asset or asset type into another asset or asset type. The transfer happens gradually over a period.

Systematic Transfer Plan is of two types; fixed STP, and capital appreciation STP. A fixed STP is where investors take out a fixed sum from one investment to another. A capital appreciation STP is where investors take the profit part out of one investment and invest in the other.

Example of STP

Suppose an investor has invested 5 lakhs in debt funds because he thought market is trading at close to peak. The PE ratio of the market is 25 and hence he thinks that fall is imminent. The market indeed fell to a level where he can make entry to equities. However, there are overall weak sentiments which may push market further down. What is the best strategy in this case?

He can take out five lakhs out of debt fund and invest in equity oriented mutual fund. The risk is that if the market goes further down, fund value will also fall. This is a risky strategy. Moreover, if the weak sentiments prolong for some time, the investor will lose on the opportunity cost because the money is stuck with an investment which has gone down in value. In an STP, the investor can withdraw a fixed amount from his debt fund investment and invest in equity oriented fund. This can go on for several months depending upon choice. It essentially acts as a defense against any adverse movement of the market.

Even when the market is losing value at the rate of one per cent per month, the STP plan has worked as a defense against the fall. Even after 12 successive falls, the return after 12 months is 9.56 per cent which is quite good. Had this been done in a lump-sum amount of 5 lakhs, here is the payoff. The investor has actually lost 11.36 per cent over the same period. This is the advantage of STP.

The fundamental idea remains the same. The only difference in capital appreciation STP is that only the profit part of the investment is transferred in the other asset. For example, the investor has invested five lakhs in debt fund. In a month, suppose the return is one per cent. This means that his investment has grown by Rs 5000. Investor will take out this money and invest in equity fund. This strategy is good for conservative investors who want to protect their principal and take risk with the returns.

Disadvantages

1. STP is a possibly the second best investment strategy after SIP. It is one of the best risk mitigation strategies of the market. All risk mitigation strategies cap the loss but also reduce returns when market is bullish.
2. Investors need to follow it with discipline. STP, just like SIP, benefits only when followed properly. Breaking STP because of short=term market movement or interest rate movement will only harm the investment in long-term.
3. The investor needs to understand the assets and the stages they are in. For example, it would be unwise to transfer money from debt to equity when the market is closer to peak value. Similarly, it would be counter-productive to transfer money from equity to debt when the market is close to bottom.

Triggers allow you to keep track of the timing of the transfer of funds. You can specify the event, the amount or the number of units to be redeemed and help ensure that you book some profits and maintain the desired asset allocation in the portfolio.

Triggers could be based on actual occurrence of one or more of the below events:

- Value of the investment reaching a specified value
- NAV of the scheme reaching a specified value

- Level of capital appreciation
- Level of the market indices or
- A specified date

Depending upon the investors risk appetite and objectives, he should carefully consider the above discussed methods of investing. If the investor monitors his investment a little he can easily gain a lot by deciding when to buy and sell the funds. To ease the burden of constant monitoring, the investor can choose any of the above mentioned plans.

Bibliography and References

Books

Baid (2007), *IIBF Mutual Funds Products and Services*, Taxman Publications (P) Ltd, New Delhi.

Bansal (1997), *Mutual Funds Management and Working*, Deep and Deep Publications, New Delhi.

Baumol, Goldfeld, Gordon, and Koeh (1990), *The Economics of Mutual Fund Markets: Competition versus Regulation.* Boston, MA: Kluwer Academic Publishers.

Bhalla (2001), *Management of Financial Services*, Anmol, New Delhi.

Bogle (1999), *Common Sense on Mutual Funds: New Imperatives for the Intelligent Investor.* New York: John Wiley & Sons, Inc.

Datta Chaudhuri and Seal (2008), *Mutual Fund Industry: Issues and Experiences*, ICFAI University Press, Hyderabad.

Dave (1996), *Mutual Funds in India: Challenges, Opportunities and Strategic Perspectives*, UTI Institute of Capital Markets, Mumbai.

Financial Inclusion - RBI Circular No. RBI/ 2005-06/233 RPCD.RF.BC.54/ 07.38.01/2005-06 dated 13.12.2005.

Friend, Blume and Crockett (1970), *Mutual Funds and Other Institutional Investors: A New Perspective*, McGraw Hill Book Company, New York.

Friend, Brown, Herman and Vickers (1962), *A Study of Mutual Funds*, US Securities and Exchange Commission, USA, Government Printing Office, Washington.

Gordan and Natrajan (1997), *Emerging Scenario of Financial Services*, Himalaya Publishing House, Mumbai.

Gupta (1992), *Mutual Funds and Asset Preference*, Society for Capital Market Research and Development, New Delhi.

Gupta (2002), *Mutual Funds in India: A Study of Investment Management*, Anmol Publications Pvt. Ltd, New Delhi.

Investment Company Institute (ICI). 2002, "US Household Ownership of Mutual Funds in 2002: Fundamentals." Investment Company Institute Research in Brief, 11(5), October.

Investment Company Institute (ICI). 2002. "Mutual Fund Factbook." June.

Investment Company Institute fact book 2013.

Jain and Sondhi (2004), *Financial Performance of Equity Mutual Funds in India*, ICFAI University Press, Hyderabad.

Krishnamurthi (1997), *Genesis of Mutual Funds in India*, Vision Books, New Delhi.

Mohanarao (1998), *Working of Mutual Funds Organisation in India*, Kanishka Publishers and Distributors, New Delhi.

Mukherjee (2005), *Profile of Indian Financial System and Financial Market Operations*, Kundu Grandsons, Kolkata.

Pasricha (1996), *Mutual Funds in India: Performance and Prospects*, (in Bhatia B S and Batra, GS edited "Management of Financial Services), Deep and Deep Publications, New Delhi.

Pathak (2013), *The Indian Financial System: Markets, Institutions and Services*, Pearson, New Delhi.

Rajan (2009), "A Hundred Small Steps - Report of the Committee on Financial Sector Reforms".

Rangarajan (2008), "Report of the Committee on Financial Inclusion".

Reserve Bank of India - "Annual Reports and 'Report on Trend and Progress of Banking in India", various issues.

Sadhak (2003), *Mutual Funds in India*, Response Books, New Delhi.

Sadhak (2003), *Mutual Funds in India: Marketing Strategies and Investment Practices*, Response Books, New Delhi.

Sahadevan and Thiripalraju (1997), *Mutual Funds: Data Interpretation and Analysis*, PHI, New Delhi.

Sato and Ramachandran, eds., *Japan, Europe, and International Financial Markets: Analytical and Empirical Perspectives*. New York: Cambridge University Press.

SEBI, Handbook of statistics in Indian Securities Market, 2013.

Sen (1996), *Mutual Funds in India: Challenges, Opportunities and Strategic Perspectives*, UTI Institute of Capital Markets, Mumbai.

Shitole and Thyagarajan (2012), *Performance Evaluation of Mutual Funds in India*, Adhyayan Publishers and Distributors, New Delhi.

Singh (2001), *Mutual Funds and the Indian Capital Market-Performance and Profitability*, Kanishka Publishers and Distributors, New Delhi.

Singh (2003), *Mutual Funds in India*, Rajat Publications, New Delhi.

Sirri and Tufano (1993), "Competition and Change in the Mutual Fund Industry." In Samuel B. Hayes III (ed) *Financial Services: Perspectives and Challenges*. Boston, MA: Harvard Business School Press.

Status of Microfinance in India: 2010-11, NABARD.

Swaminathan (2011), *Performance of Mutual Funds in India: A Comparative Study of Public and Private Sector Mutual Funds*, Gyan Publishing House, New Delhi.

Turan and Bodla (2001), *Performance Appraisal of Mutual Funds*, Excel Books, New Delhi.

Valueresearch Mutual Fund Year Book (2008 to 2013), New Delhi.

Walter (1999). "The Asset Management Industry in Europe: Competitive Structure and Performance under EMU." in Dermine J. and Hillion P. (eds) *European Capital Markets and a Single Currency*. Oxford University Press.

World Bank Global Findex 2012.

Journals and Magazines

Anagol (1992), "Role of Self Regulatory Organisation in Mutual Fund Industry in India", *Chartered Financial Analyst*, IUP Publications, Vol. 7 (1), p. 11.

Ansari (1993), "Mutual Funds in India: Emerging Trends", *The Chartered Accountant, The Institute of Chartered Accountants of India,* Vol. 42 (2), pp. 88-93.

Arditti (1971), "Another Look at Mutual Fund Performance", *The Journal of Financial and Quantitative Analysis, School of Business Administration, University of Washington,* Vol. 6 (3), pp. 909-912.

Badrinath (2008), "Contra Fund in India: A Quick Look", *Portfolio Organiser,* IUP Publications, January, pp. 31-34.

Bansal (1991), "Challenges For Mutual Funds In India", *Chartered Secretary, The Institute of Company Secretaries of India,* Vol. 21 (10), pp. 825-26.

Bansal (2003), "Mutual Funds: Eight Steps to nirvana", *Chartered Financial Analyst, IUP Publications,* Vol. 9 (12), pp. 34-40.

Baur, Sundaram and Smith (1995), "Mutual Funds: The US Experience", *Finance India, Indian Institute of Finance,* Vol. 9 (4), pp. 945-957.

Bekaert, Campbell and Robin (2002). "The Dynamics of Emerging Market Equity Flows." *Journal of International Money and Finance,* June.

Bodla and Garg (2007), "Performance Appraisal of Mutual Funds in India: A Case Study of Growth Schemes", *GITAM Journal of Management,* Vol. 5 (4), pp. 29-43.

Cai and Yamada (1997), "The Performance of Japanese Mutual Funds", *The Review of Financial Studies, Society for Financial Studies,* Vol. 10 (2), pp. 237-273.

Carhart, (1997), "On Persistence in Mutual Fund Performance." *Journal of Finance,* Vol. 53, 57-82.

Carlson (1970), "Aggregate Performance Of Mutual Funds, 1948-1967", *Journal of Financial and Quantitative Analysis,* School of Business Administration, University of Washington, Vol. 5 (1), pp. 1-32.

Chakraborty, Jain and Kallianpur (2008), "Mutual Fund Performance An Evaluation of Select Growth Funds in India", *South Asian Journal of Management,* Association of Management Development Institutions in South Asia, Vol. 15 (4), pp. 79-92.

Chander (2000), "Performance Appraisal of Mutual Funds in India", *Finance India,* Indian Institute of Finance, Vol. XIV (4), pp. 1256-1261.

Chander (2006), "Informational Efficiency, Parameter Stationary and Bench Mark Consistency of Investment Performance, *The ICFAI Journal of Applied Finance,* March.

Chang and Lewellen (1984), "Market Timing and Mutual Fund Investment Performance", *The Journal of Business,* University of Chicago Press, Vol. 57 (1), pp. 57-72.

Chen and Stockum (1986), "Selectivity, Market Timing and Random Beta Behaviour of Mutual Funds: A generalised Model", *Journal of Financial Research,* Southern Finance Association and the South Western Finance Association, Vol. 9 (1), pp. 87-96.

Chordia (1996), "The Structure of Mutual Fund Charges." *Journal of Financial Economics*, Vol. 41, 3-39.

Collins and Philip (1997), "The Optimal Amount of Assets under Management in the Mutual Fund Industry." *Financial Analyst Journal*, September/October, 67-73.

Christopherson, Ferson and Turner (1999), "Performance Evaluation Using Conditional Alphas and Betas", *Journal of Portfolio Management, Institutional Investors Journals*, Vol. 26 (1), pp. 59-72.

Ciccotello and Grant (1996), "Information Pricing: The Evidence from Equity Mutual Funds", *The Financial Review*, Eastern Finance Association, Vol. 31 (2), pp. 365-380.

Coggin, Fabozzi and Rahman (1993), "The Investment Performance of US Equity Pension Fund Managers: An Empirical Investigation", *The Journal of Business*, University of Chicago Press, Vol. 48 (3), pp. 1039-1055.

Comer (2006), 'Hybrid Mutual Funds and Market Timing Performance, *Journal of Business*, Vol. 79, No.2, pp 771- 797.

Cortez and Silva (2002), "Conditioning Information on Portfolio Performance Evaluation: A Re-examination of Performance Persistence in the Portuguese Mutual Fund Market", *Finance India, Indian Institute of Finance*, Vol. XVI (4), pp. 1393-1408.

Cumby and Glen (1990), "Evaluating the Performance of International Mutual Funds", *The Journal of Finance*, American Finance Association, Vol. 45 (2) pp. 496-526.

Dahlquist, Engstrom and Soderlind (2000), "Performance and Characteristics of Swedish Mutual Funds", *Journal of Financial and Quantitative Analysis*, School of Business Administration, University of Washington, Vol. 35 (3), pp. 409-423.

Dellva and Olson (1998), "The Relationship between Mutual Fund Fees and Expenses and their Effects on Performance", *The Financial Review, Eastern Finance Association*, Vol. 33 (1), pp. 85-104.

Dixit and Ghosh (2013), "Financial Inclusion For Inclusive Growth of India – A Study", *International Journal of Business Management & Research*, Vol. 3, Issue 1, pp. 147-156.

Dollar (1992), "Outward-Oriented Developing Economies Really Do Grow More Rapidly: Evidence from 95 LDC, 1976-1985." *Economic Development and Cultural Change*, 40(3).

Elango (2004), "Which Funds Yield More Returns?" *The Management Accountant*, The Institute of Cost Accountants of India, Vol. 39 (4), pp. 283-290.

Elton, Gruber, and Christopher (1996), "The Persistence of Risk-Adjusted Mutual Fund Performance." *Journal of Business*, 69(2), 133-157.

Fama, (1972), "Components of Investment Performance", *The Journal of Finance, American Finance Association*, Vol. 27 (3), pp. 551-567.

Ferson and Schadt (1996), "Measuring Fund Strategy and Performance in changing Economic Conditions", *The Journal of Finance*, American Finance Association, Vol. 51 (2), pp. 425-61.

Ferson and Warther (1996), "Evaluating Fund Performance in a Dynamic Market", *Financial Analysts Journal*, CFA Institute, Vol. 52 (6), pp. 20-28.

Friend and Vickers (1970), "Portfolio Selection and Investment Preference", *The Journal of Finance*, American Finance Association, Vol. XX (3), pp. 391-415.

Gangadhar (1992), "The Changing Pattern of Mutual Funds in India", *The Management Accountant*, The Institute of Cost Accountants of India, Vol. 27 (12), pp. 924-28.

Gottesman and Morey (2006), "Manager Education and Mutual Fund Performance", *The Journal of Empirical Finance, Elsevier*, Vol. 13 (2), pp. 145-182.

Guhadeb and Banerjee, (2009), "Downside Risk Analysis of Indian Equity Mutual Funds: A Value at Risk Approach", *The International Research Journal of Finance and Economics, Eurojournals*, Issue 23, January, pp. 216-230.

Gupta (1974), "The Mutual Fund Industry and Its Comparative Performance", *Journal of Financial and Quantitative Analysis*, School of Business Administration, University of Washington, Vol. 9 (5), p. 891.

Gupta (1989), "Mutual Funds", *The Management Accountant*, The Institute of Cost Accountants of India, Vol. 24 (5), pp. 320-322.

Gupta (2001), "Mutual Funds in India: A Study of Investment Management", *Finance India*, Indian Institute of Finance, Vol. XV (2), pp. 631-637.

Gupta (2011), "Indian Mutual Fund Industry: Current State and Future Outlook", *Indian Journal of Finance*, Vol. 5 (4), pp. 38-48.

Gupta and Gupta (2004), "Performance Evaluation of Selected Indian Mutual Fund Schemes: An Empirical Study", *The ICFAI Journal of Applied Finance*, Vol. 10 (12), pp. 81-98.

Gruber (1996), "Another Puzzle: The Growth in Actively Managed Mutual Funds", *The Journal of Finance*, American Finance Association, Vol. 51 (3), pp. 783–810.

Henriksson (1984), "Market Timing and Mutual Funds Performance: An Empirical Investigation", *The Journal of Business, University of Chicago Press*, Vol. 57 (1), pp. 73-96.

Ippollito (1989), "Efficiency with Costly Information: A Study of Mutual Fund Performance, 1965-1984", *The Quarterly Journal of Economics*, MIT Press, Vol. 104 (1), pp. 1-23.

Jayadev (1996), "Mutual Fund Performance: An Analysis of Monthly Returns", *Finance India, Indian Institute of Finance*, Vol. X (1), pp. 73-84.

Jayam (2002), "Debt Be Not Proud, Equity's Back", *Business Today*, April, pp. 42-45.

Jensen (1968), "The Performance of Mutual Funds in the Period 1945-1964", *The Journal of Finance*, American Finance Association, Vol. 23 (2), pp. 389-416.

Kajshmi, Deo and Murugesan (2008), "Performance of the Indian Mutual Funds; A Study with special reference to growth schemes', *Asia-Pacific Business Review*, Vol. IV, No. 3, July-September, pp 75-81.

Khorana and Nelling (1998), "The Determinants and Predictive Ability of Mutual Fund Ratings", *Journal of Investing*, Institutional Investors Journals, Vol. 7 (3), pp. 61-66.

Khorana, Servaes and Wedge (2007), "Portfolio Manager Ownership and Fund performance", *The Journal of Financial Economics, Elsevier*, Vol. 85 (1), pp. 179–204.

Klemosky (1973), "The Bias in Composite Performance Measures", Journal *of Financial and Quantitative Analysis*, School of Business Administration, University of Washington, Vol. 8 (3), pp. 505-514.

Klemosky (1977), "How Consistently Do Managers Manage", *Journal of Portfolio Management*, Institutional Investors Journals, Vol. 3 (2), pp. 11-15.

Kon (1983), "The Market Timing Performance of Mutual Fund Managers", *The Journal of Business*, University of Chicago Press, Vol. 56 (3), pp. 323-347.

Kumar (1999), "In Search of Turnaround Strategies For Mutual Fund Industry", *The Management Accountant*, The Institute of Cost Accountants of India, Vol. 34 (5), pp. 337-343.

Lal and Sharma (1992), "Mutual Fund-A Buoyant Financial Instrument", Finance India, Indian Institute of Finance, Vol. VI (4), pp. 811-18.

Levine and David (1992), "A Sensitivity Analysis of Cross-Country Growth Regressions." *American Economic Review*, 82(4), 942-963.

Levine and Sara (1998), "Stock Markets, Banks and Economic Growth." *American Economic Review*, 88(3), 537-58.

McDonald (1974), "Objectives and Performance of Mutual Funds, 1960-69", *Journal of Financial and Quantitative Analysis*, School of Business Administration, University of Washington, Vol. 9 (3), pp. 311-333.

Malhotra. and Robert McLeod. (1997), "An Empirical Analysis of Mutual Fund Expenses." *Journal of Financial Research*, 20(2), 175-190.

Malkiel (1995), "Returns from Investing in Equity Mutual Funds 1971 to 1991." *Journal of Finance*, 50(2), 549-572.

Mehru (2004), "Problems of Mutual Funds in India", *Finance India*, Vol. XVIII (1), pp. 220-224.

Mendoza (2009), "Addressing Financial Exclusion through Microfinance: Lessons from the State of Madhya Pradesh, India", *The journal of International Policy Solutions*, Vol. 11, pp. 25-35.

Muthappan and Damodharan (2006), "Risk Adjusted Performance Evaluation of Indian Mutual Fund Schemes", *Finance India, Indian Institute of Finance*, Vol. XX (3), pp. 965-983.

Narasimhan and Vijayalakshmi (2001), "Performance Analysis of Mutual Funds in India", *Finance India, Indian Institute of Finance*, Vol. XV (1), pp. 155-174.

Panigrahi (1996), "Mutual Funds: Growth, Performance and Prospects", *Economic and Political Weekly*, Vol. XXXI (12), pp. 765-775.

Ramamurthy and Reddy (2005), "Recent Trends in Mutual Fund Industry", *SCMS Journal of Indian Management*, July 2005.

Ramasamy and Yeung (2003), 'Evaluating Mutual Funds in an emerging market: factors that matter to financial advisors', *International Journal of Bank Marketing*, Vol. 21, No. 3, pp. 122-136.

Reid (2000). "The 1990s: A Decade of Expansion and Change in the US Mutual Fund Industry." *Investment Company Institute Perspective*, 6(3), July.

Saha (2003), "Indian Mutual Fund Management, *The Management Accountant, The Institute of Cost Accountants of India*, Vol. 38 (10), pp. 765-771.

Saha and Rama Murthy (1993-94), "Managing Mutual Funds: Some Critical Issues", *Prajnan, Journal of Social and Management Sciences*, National Institute of Bank Management, Pune, Vol. XXII (1), pp. 25-35.

Sahu (1992), "A Critical Review of the Mutual Fund Regulations", *Chartered Secretary*, The Institute of Company Secretaries of India, Vol. 22 (12), pp. 1076-1078.

Sahu and Panda (1993), "The Role and Future of Mutual Funds In India", The *Management Accountant*, The Institute of Cost Accountants of India, Vol. 28 (2), pp. 91-93.

Sarkar (1991), "Mutual Funds in India: Emerging Trends", *The Management Accountant*, The Institute of Cost Accountants of India, Vol. 26 (3), pp. 171-174.

Sarkar (2013), "Financial Inclusion: Fostering Sustainable Economic Growth in India", *The Banker*, Vol. VIII, No. 4, pp. 44-53.

Sarkar (2013), "Financial Inclusion Part-II: Fostering Sustainable Economic Growth in India", *The Banker*, Vol. VIII, No. 5, pp. 32-40.

Sarkar and Majumdar (1994), "Performance Evaluation of Mutual Funds in India", *NMIS Management Review*, Vol. VI (2), pp. 64-78.

Sathis (2004), "Investors Perceptions: A Survey by MARCH Marketing Consultancy and Research", *Chartered Financial Analyst*, IUP Publications, Vol. 10 (7), pp. 35-36.

Sekhar (2013), Role of Indian Mutual Funds in Financial Inclusion: Public Vs Private Sector. *Journal of Business and Management Sciences,* 1(1), 4-9.

Shankar (2008), 'Lessons from recent events in the mutual fund debt markets', Dec 1st, *The Hindu.*

Sharath (2004), "Evaluating Indian Mutual Funds", *Chartered Financial Analyst, IUP Publications,* Vol. 10 (7), p. 83.

Sharpe (1966), "Mutual Fund Performance", *The Journal of Business,* University of Chicago Press, Vol. 39 (1), pp. 119-138.

Shashikant (1993), "Accounting Policy and Practices of Mutual Funds: The Need for Standardisation", *Prajnan, Journal of Social and Management Sciences,* National Institute of Bank Management, Pune, Vol. XXIV (2), pp. 91-102.

Shleifer and Wolfenzon (2002), Investor Protection and Equity Markets, *Journalof Financial Economics,* October.

Singh and Chander (2000), "Appraisal of Mutual Funds in India", *The Indian Journal of Commerce,* July-September, pp. 39-52.

Singh and Chander (2003), "What Drives the Investors towards Mutual Funds: An Empirical Analysis", *The ICFAI Journal of Applied Finance,* Vol. 9 (8), pp.38-46.

Sondhi and Jain (2005), "Financial Management of Private and Public Equity Mutual Funds in India: An Analysis of Profitability", *The ICFAI Journal of Applied Finance,* Vol. 2 (6), pp. 14-27.

Subha and Bharati (2007), "An Empirical study on the performance of select mutual fund schemes in India", *Journal of Contemporary Research in Management,* Vol. I, No.1, 2 Jan-June.

Sudhakar and Sasi Kumar (2005), 'Performance Evaluation of Mutual Funds: A Case Study', *Southern Economist,* November, pp. 19-23.

Treynor (1965), "How to Rate Management of Investment Funds", *Harvard Business Review,* Vol. 43 (1), pp. 63-75.

Treynor and Mazuy (1966), "Can Mutual Funds Outguess the Market?", *Harvard Business Review,* Vol. 44 (4), pp. 131-136.

Tripathy (1996), "Mutual Fund In India: A Financial Service in Capital Market", *Finance India,* Indian Institute of Finance, Vol. X (1), pp. 85-91.

Tripathy (2006), "Market Timing Abilities and Mutual Fund Performance: An Empirical Investigation into Equity Linked Savings Schemes", *Vilakshan,* XIMB Journal of Management, August, pp. 127-138.

Tufano and Sevick (1997), "Board Structure and Fee-Setting in the US Mutual Fund Industry." *Journal of Financial Economics,* 46, pp. 321-55.

Vidhyashankar (1990), "Mutual Funds: Emerging Trends in India", *Chartered Secretary, The Institute of Company Secretaries of India,* Vol. 20 (8), pp. 639-640.

Viramgami (2009), "Resource Mobilisation by Indian Mutual Fund Industry", *Indian Journal of Finance,* Vol. III (3), pp. 33-38.

Volkman and Wohar (1995), "Determinants of persistence in relative performance of Mutual Funds." *The Journal of Financial Research,* Southern Finance Association and the South Western Finance Association, Vol. 18 (4), pp. 415–430.

Wermers (1999), "Mutual Fund Herding and the Impact on Stock Prices", *The Journal of Finance,* The American Finance Association. Vol. 54 (2), pp. 581–622.

Williamson (1972), "Measurement and Forecasting of Mutual Fund Performance: Choosing an Investment Strategy", *Financial Analysts Journal,* CFA Institute, Vol. 28 (6), pp. 78-84.

Yadav and Mishra (1996), "Performance Evaluation of Mutual Funds: An Empirical Analysis", *MDI Management Journal,* Vol. 9 (2), pp. 117-125.

Yoon K Choi (2006), Relative Portfolio Performance Evaluation and Incentive Structure, *Journal of Business,* Vol. 79, No. 2, pp. 903-921.

Zekri (2005), "Socially Responsible Investing and Portfolio Diversification", *The Journal of Financial Research,* Southern Finance Association and the South western Finance Association, Vol. 28 (1), pp. 41-57.

Websites

Agrawal (2011), "Measuring Performance of Indian Mutual Funds" Finance India, available at http://ssrn.com/abstract=1311761.

Barras, Laurent, Scaillet, and Wermers (2008), "False Discoveries in Mutual Fund Performance: Measuring Luck in Estimated Alphas", September, available at http://ssrn.com/abstract = 869748.

Beck, Thorsten, Asli Demirgüç-Kunt, and Ross Levine. 2000. "A New Database on Financial. Development and Structure." World Bank working paper.

Beck, Thorsten, Asli Demirgüç-Kunt, and Ross Levine. 2001. "Law, Politics, and Finance." World Bank Policy Research Paper 2585.

Caprio, Gerard and Daniela Klingebiel. 1999. "Episodes of Systematic and Borderline Financial Crises." World Bank working paper.

Davis, E Philip. 2001. "The European Pension Management Industry." Brunel University working paper.

Demirguc-Kunt, Asli and Ross Levine. 1999. "Bank-Based and Market-Based Financial Systems: Cross-Country Comparisons." World Bank working paper.

Demers, Elizabeth and Baruch Lev. 2000. "A Rude Awakening: Internet Shakeout in 2000." New York University working paper.

Engen, Eric M. and Andreas Lehnert. 2000. "Mutual Funds and the US Equity Market." Federal Reserve Bulletin, December.

James, Estelle, Gary Ferrier, James Smalhout, and Dimitri Vittas. 1999. "Mutual Funds and Institutional Investments: What is the Most Efficient Way to Set Up Individual Accounts in a Social Security System?" World Bank Policy Research Paper 2099.

Kaminsky, Graciela, Richard Lyons, and Sergio Schmuckler. 2000. "Mutual Fund Investment in Emerging Markets: An Overview." World Bank working paper.

Kaufmann, Dani, Art Kraay, and Peter Zoido-Lobaton. 1999. "Aggregating Governance Indicators." World Bank Policy Research Paper 2195.

Otten, Roger and Mark Schweitzer. 1998. "A Comparison Between the European and the US Mutual Fund Industry." Limburg Institute of Financial Economics, Maastricht University, working paper.

Rao and Ravindran (2003), "Performance Evaluation of Indian Mutual Funds", Working paper www.papers.ssrn.com/sol3/papers.cfm?abstract_id=433100.

Roy and Deb (2003), "The Conditional Performance of Indian Mutual Funds: An Empirical Study" available at http://ssrn.com/abstract=593723.

Vamvakidis, Athanasios. 1998. "Regional Trade Agreements Versus Broad Liberalisation: Which Path Leads to Faster Growth? Time Series Evidence." IMF Working Paper 98/40.

www.amfiindia.com,

www.bloomberg.com,

www.bseindia.com,

www.equitymaster.com,

www.fundsupermart.com,

www.investopedia.com,

www.moneycontrol.com,

www.morningstar.com,

www.mutualfundsindia.com,

www.nabard.com,

www.nse.com,

www.personalfn.com,

www.rbi.org.in,

www.sbi.co.in,

www.sebi.gov.in,

www.ssrn.com,

www.valueresearchonline.com.

Papers Presented/Prepared/Thesis

Anand Sinha (2012), "Financial Inclusion and Urban Cooperative Banks", edited transcript at the launch of the financial inclusion program of COSMOS Bank at Pune.

Chakrabarty (2011), "Financial Inclusion and Banks: Issues and Perspectives", RBI Bulletin, November, 2011.

Chakrabarty (2011), "Financial Inclusion: A Road India Needs to Travel", RBI Bulletin, November, 2011.

Chakrabarty (2012), "Empowering MSMEs for Financial Inclusion and Growth – Role of Banks and Industry Associations", address at SME Banking Conclave 2012.

Chakrabarty (2013), "Financial Inclusion in India: Journey So Far And the Way Forward", Key note address at Finance Inclusion Conclave Organised by CNBC TV 18 at New Delhi.

Chakrabarty (2013), "Revving up the Growth Engine through Financial Inclusion", address at the 32th SKOCH Summit held at Mumbai.

Chattopadhyay (2011), "Financial Inclusion in India: A Case-study of West Bengal". RBI Working Paper Series, WPS (DEPR): 8/2011.

Batra and Bhatia (1992), "Indian Mutual Funds: A study of Public sector", *paper presented, UTI Institute of Capital Market, Mumbai.*

Dash, Sindhu, Deepa and Kavitha (2008), "A Study on Granger Causality in the CAPM," paper presented at the ICQMOIT 2008 Conference at IBS, Hyderabad.

Gupta and Sehgal (1998), "Investment Performance of Mutual Funds: The Indian Experience", paper presented at UTI-ICM Second Capital Market Conference, Mumbai.

Ghosh (2014), "Performance Analysis of Indian Mutual Funds in Fluctuating Economic Conditions: A study in reference to the financial crisis of the year 2008." thesis, Calcutta University.

Leeladhar (2005), "Taking Banking Services to the Common Man – Financial Inclusion", Commemorative Lecture at the FedbankHormis Memorial Foundation at Ernakulam.

Narayan Chandra Pradhan (2013), "Persistence of Informal Credit in Rural India: Evidence from All-India Debt and Investment Survey and Beyond", RBI Working Paper Series, WPS (DEPR): 5/2013.

Shah and Thomas (1994), "Performance Evaluation of Professional portfolio Management in India", *paper prepared by CMIE.*

Shome (1994), "A Study of Performance of Indian Mutual Funds", unpublished thesis, Jhansi University.

Syama Sundar (1998), "Growth Prospects of Mutual Funds and Investor perception with special reference to Kothari Pioneer Mutual Fund", Project Report, Sri Srinivas Vidya Parishad, Andhra University, Visakhapatnam.

Turner (2008), 'Financial Globalisation and Emerging Market Capital Flows', BIS papers No.44, Bank for International Settlements.

Magazines

- Capital Market
- Dalal Street Investment Journal
- Money Life
- Mutual Fund Insight
- Outlook Money
- The Management Accountant
- Wealth Insight

(all the magazines were subscribed and referred from January 2009 to January 2015).

HAPPY INVESTING!

Index